# THE TWO FORGERS

# THE TWO FORGERS

*a biography of*

## HARRY BUXTON FORMAN & THOMAS JAMES WISE

*by*

## JOHN COLLINS

OAK KNOLL BOOKS

© John Collins 1992

Published by
OAK KNOLL BOOKS
414 Delaware Street,
New Castle, DE 19720, U.S.A.

Library of Congress Cataloging-in-Publication Data

Collins, John (John F. R.)
The two forgers : a biography of Harry Buxton Forman &
Thomas James Wise  by John Collins.
p. cm.
Includes bibliographical references and index.
ISBN 0–938768–29–8
1. Wise, Thomas James, 1859–1937. 2. Forman, H. Buxton (Harry
Buxton), 1842–1917. 3. Literary forgeries and mystifications—
History. 4. Book collectors—Great Britain—Biography.
5. Bibliographers — Great Britain—Biography. 6. Forgers—Great
Britain—Biography. 7. Pamphlets—Forgeries—History. I. Title.
Z989.W8C64 1992
0002'.074'0922—dc20
[B]      91–24086

Designed by David Chambers

Printed in Great Britain

# CONTENTS

# LIST OF ILLUSTRATIONS

I should like to express my thanks to the Board of the British Library for permission to reproduce material from the Ashley Library and I am particularly grateful to the British Library photographer Laurence Pordes for his skill and patience. I must also thank all the other individuals and libraries who were kind enough to give me permission to publish material in their collections. A number of the illustrations are reduced, some of them substantially.

# ACKNOWLEDGEMENTS

An account of the genesis of this book and detailed acknowledge-
ments will be found in the Notes at the end. I must thank, in
particular, my friends and colleagues at Maggs Bros who put up
with my absences without complaint; also my children, Daniel,
Elizabeth, Martha and Sam, for their forbearance. Nicolas
Barker amiably allowed me to plagiarize our joint work and that
of Carter and Pollard, and read the manuscript to great effect.
David Chambers rescued the book at a point when it might have
ground to a halt, took over the negotiations and designed it.
Finally, without the help of my wife Alison, who typed the
whole thing at least twice and spent months wrestling with the
forgers, I owe more than I can say. Without her help, the book
would never have appeared.

John Collins

1.  Thomas James Wise, an etching *c.* 1920

# PROLOGUE

Crewe House in Mayfair is almost the last of the old metropolitan country houses. Before the war it was still occupied by Lord Crewe, a dignified elder statesman and a pillar of the Liberal Party. In 1931 he was over 70, not long retired as ambassador in Paris, and could look back on a career in which he had occupied many of the great offices of state. He entertained in an ample old fashioned way with a retinue of servants and a table laden with gold plate. On 26 June, for instance, after a long investiture, the King and Queen dined at Crewe House. About a fortnight earlier, on 10 June, the Roxburghe Club held their anniversary dinner with Lord Crewe as the host. The party comprised the president, Lord Aldenham, the Duke of Alba and Berwick, the Marquess of Lansdowne, the Earl of Crawford & Balcarres, the Earl Spencer, the Earl of Powis, Viscount Mersey, le Comte Alexandre De Laborde, Lord Hillingdon, the Hon. Sir John Fortescue, Sir Frederic Kenyon, A. Chester Beatty, Sydney Cockerell, Charles St John Hornby, Owen Morshead, Lt Commander John Murray and Thomas James Wise. The guests in top hats and tail coats entered the front door to be ushered in by the footman and announced by the butler.

The Roxburghe Club was and is the oldest and the most exclusive bibliophile club in the world. It was founded in 1812 to celebrate the sale of the library of the Duke of Roxburghe ('sold in His Grace's late residence in St. James's Square') and in particular of the Valdarfar Bocaccio, which made the unprecedented price of £2,260 (lot 6292: 17 June).

Seating at the anniversary dinner was in order of precedence and most of the guests could be placed in Burke's peerage or the Almanach de Gotha. At the bottom of the table were A. Chester Beatty (a mining millionaire and the greatest collector of illustrated manuscripts in his generation), Sydney Cockerell (Director of the Ashmolean Museum), C. St J. Hornby (owner of the firm of W.H. Smith and erstwhile proprietor of the Ashendene Press), Owen Morshead (Royal Librarian at Windsor), John

1

2.   Harry Buxton Forman *c*. 1905

Murray (the third of that name to run the famous publishing house) and Thomas J. Wise.

It is with this last gentleman that the present book is much concerned. A retired commodity broker, he was the owner and collector of what was said to be the finest private library in the kingdom. He had come from humble origins in the streets of Islington to this extraordinary eminence in a different world. Three years later, his life was falling to ruins about him. On 30 June 1934, news-vendors were posting placards 'Famous books denounced as forgeries' and the press headlines read 'Faked first editions sensation' or 'First Edition Forgeries'. The articles were based on a book by two young booksellers with the mild and scholarly title, *An Enquiry into the nature of certain nineteenth century pamphlets*. Mr Wise was directly accused of stocking, selling and authenticating a large number of forgeries: he was indirectly accused of actually manufacturing them. It was rather as if the Archbishop of Westminster had been shown by two junior sacristans, to be the brains behind an organization selling London tapwater as a Holy relic of Lourdes.

The *Daily Herald* sent a reporter down to the Queen's Hotel, Hastings to see Mr Wise and ask for an explanation. His rambling defence was generally unconvincing. He spent much time blaming a colleague and friend of his – one Buxton Forman – who had been dead for nearly twenty years. This attempt to pass the buck was widely disbelieved and Wise made no more convincing explanation in the three years of life that were left to him. In fact, in a twisted and incomplete way, there was some truth in the Hastings story. There were two forgers, and their story begins with the senior of them, Harry Buxton Forman.

3. Naval surgeons, a lithograph *c.* 1835

# 1

# FORMAN'S CHILDHOOD

George Ellery Forman was a West Country man, born in Plymouth in 1800 and probably from a seafaring family. He trained as a naval surgeon, which meant (or should have meant) six months in a pharmacy and eighteen in a hospital, besides several courses of lectures. He was appointed assistant surgeon in 1822, and surgeon – an important step – in 1828. He married soon after: his bride was Maria Courthope whose family came from Whilligh in Sussex, though she was born in Rotherhithe. His first ship as full surgeon was the sloop *Ferret* with 10 guns and 75 men. She joined the Mediterranean fleet in 1830 and remained on station until 1832.

The first two children, George (1833) and Anne (1836), were both born in Portsmouth and it was there that George Ellery returned to be appointed surgeon to HMS *Excellent*, an old three decker commissioned as the first school for naval gunnery (which HMS *Excellent* still is).

Surgeons (but not assistant surgeons) had been given a distinguishing uniform in 1805 and were formally admitted to wardroom rank: they were accepted as officers and gentlemen. The work somewhat belied the splendid lithograph by Martin which we reproduce on p. 4. Conditions were rough and unsettled. Sailors were signed on for a particular commission in a particular ship: continuous service was not introduced until 1856 and their uniform not until 1857. The form reproduced on p. 6 shows what a sick man had to exist on in 1827. Grog consisted of 1 part overproof rum to 2 parts water and up till 1825, half a pint a day was supplied. The *Regulations and Instructions for the Medical Officers of H. M. Fleet*, first published in 1825, directed the surgeons in detail. They could bind up limbs and supply trusses for ruptures (which were very frequent); they could dose venereal disease with mercury; they could enforce lemon juice; but for many emergencies – for example outbreaks of cholera – they were helpless and could only exercise humanity and listen with patience as their instructions enjoined.

The Napoleonic navy was much too large for peace time: it

# No. 2, APPENDIX TO SURGEONS' INSTRUCTIONS.

PROPORTIONS in which BEDDING, LEMON JUICE, and NECESSARIES, are to be supplied for the USE of the SICK on Board His Majesty's Ships and Vessels.

| | ANNUAL PROPORTION. | | | | | | | | | Rupture Trusses | | | | | | Cast Iron Saucepans | | | SIX MONTHS' PROPORTION. | | | | | | Lemon Juice | | PACKAGES. | | | | | | |
|---|---|---|---|---|---|---|---|---|---|---|---|---|---|---|---|---|---|---|---|---|---|---|---|---|---|---|---|---|---|---|---|---|---|
| | Sheets | Pillows | Night-caps | Hair Beds | Lemon Juice | Calico | Welch Flannel | Lint | Tourniquets | Right side | Left side | Double | Bed Pans | Urinals | Spitting Pots | 2 Quarts | 3 Pints | 1 Pint | Tea | Soft Sugar | Sago | Rice | Pearl Barley | Soap | Cases | Bottles | Calico | Grocery | Tea | Sago | Rice | Pearl Barley | Trusses |
| | Pairs | No. | No. | No. | Gall. | Yds. | Yds. | lbs. | No. | No. | No. | No. | No. | No. | No. | No. | No. | No. | lbs. | lbs. | lbs. | lbs. | lbs. | lbs. | No. | No. | No. | No. | No. | No. | No. | No. | No. |
| First Rate | 20 | 20 | 20 | 20 | 45 | 100 | 64 | 10 | 16 | 12 | 6 | 4 | 2 | 2 | 8 | 1 | 1 | 2 | 36 | 206 | 30 | 56 | 56 | 26 | 5 | 90 | 1 | 1 | 1 | 1 | 1 | 1 | 1 |
| Second Rate | 16 | 16 | 16 | 16 | 36 | 80 | 54 | 9 | 12 | 12 | 6 | 3 | 2 | 2 | 7 | 1 | 1 | 2 | 32 | 174 | 26 | 48 | 48 | 21 | 4 | 72 | 1 | 1 | 1 | 1 | 1 | 1 | 1 |
| Third Rate | 12 | 12 | 12 | 12 | 27 | 65 | 44 | 6 | 10 | 9 | 6 | 3 | 2 | 2 | 6 | 1 | | 2 | 27 | 142 | 20 | 40 | 40 | 15 | 3 | 54 | 1 | 1 | 1 | 1 | 1 | 1 | 1 |
| Fourth Rate | 9 | 9 | 9 | 9 | 18 | 40 | 24 | 4 | 8 | 6 | 6 | 3 | 2 | 2 | 3 | 1 | 1 | 2 | 14 | 96 | 12 | 22 | 22 | 10 | 2 | 36 | 1 | 1 | 1 | 1 | 1 | 1 | 1 |
| Fifth Rate | 7 | 7 | 9 | 7 | 18 | 30 | 15 | 4 | 6 | 6 | 3 | 3 | 2 | 2 | 3 | 0 | 1 | 2 | 10 | 80 | 10 | 20 | 20 | 8 | 2 | 36 | 1 | 1 | 1 | 1 | 1 | 1 | 1 |
| Sixth Rate | 4 | 4 | 4 | 4 | 9 | 24 | 10 | 4 | 4 | 3 | 3 | 3 | 2 | 1 | 2 | 0 | 1 | 1 | 6 | 48 | 6 | 10 | 10 | 6 | 1 | 18 | 1 | 1 | 1 | 1 | 1 | 1 | 1 |
| Sloop | 3 | 3 | 3 | 3 | 4½ | 15 | 10 | 2 | 4 | 3 | 3 | 3 | 1 | 1 | 1 | 1 | | 1 | 4 | 32 | 4 | 8 | 8 | 4 | 1 | 9 | 1 | 1 | 1 | 1 | 1 | 1 | 1 |
| Cutter, &c. | None allowed. | | | | 4½ | 10 | 4 | 2 | 4 | 3 | 3 | 3 | 1 | 1 | 1 | 0 | 1 | 1 | 2 | 16 | 3 | 4 | 4 | 2 | 1 | 9 | 1 | 1 | 1 | 1 | 1 | 1 | 1 |

In War, the above stated Quantities of Calico, Flannel, Sago, Rice, and Pearl Barley, to be encreased One Half.

N.B. The Articles of Tea, Sugar, and Soap, being in the Purser's charge as General Ship Stores, are in future to be demanded of that Officer, from time to time as wanted, care being taken that the whole quantities obtained do not exceed the allowance specified in the above Scale, and regular Receipts are to be granted for the same by the Surgeon, who will, of course, take care to exclude such Articles in the Demand, (Form, No. 7,) which they may make on the Board's Officers.—Lemon Juice also, being supplied as Ship's Stores on Foreign Stations, is, in the like manner, to be obtained from the Purser when abroad.

4. Admiralty instructions for treating the sick, 1827

dropped rapidly from 145,000 men to 19,000. Surgeons were no exception and when his *Excellent* commission came to an end in 1835, George Forman signed up as surgeon-superintendent in the convict ship *Lady McNaughton* and set sail for New South Wales. By this time, the early disasters had been left behind and convict ships were generally healthier than emigrant ships: the surgeon-superintendents had considerable powers to keep them so.

The family soon moved to Camberwell in Surrey, still a small village but rapidly being developed as part of London. They lived in Camden Place, near the Rosemary Branch archery ground and on the edge of the green fields, mostly of fruit and vegetables grown for the metropolis. Between voyages three more children were born: Mary (1838), Alfred (1840) and Henry (1842). The family paid rent on a pew in the new church of St George's, Well Walk, where the children were christened, and had two or three servants to help with the five children. Their father's fifth and final voyage in a convict ship was to Tasmania. The *John Brewer* set sail in November 1841 from Sheerness, with 200 male convicts (one died) and a crew of 40 under a Scottish captain (the cook was a Spaniard and one of the ABs a Corfiot).

On 11 July 1842, a new baby was born and on 10 August he was christened Henry Buxton. In later life he came to dislike Henry and firmly called himself Harry Buxton Forman, by which name we shall know him. In November, his father returned and recorded in his diary, 'I find an addition to my family . . . now a fine fellow of 4 months'.

On the advice of his boss, that formidable bureaucrat Sir William Burnett, Inspector-General of Naval Hospitals and Fleets, G. E. Forman decided to retire on half pay and go into private practice, a common option among his confrères. After the strong meat of the navy, they felt quite able to cope with anything a quiet English village might produce. The family migrated to Teignmouth in South Devon, between the hills, the sea and the Teign estuary. There was clearly a family connection since at least one other family of Formans was established in the town and of course George Ellery was a Devonian.

In the early nineteenth century, Teignmouth was both an important Devon port and a fashionable seaside resort. It had a long connection with the Newfoundland trade and many Teign-

5. Teignmouth from across the river, a lithograph, c. 1845–50

mouth families had relations there. Many Teignmouth boats went out with salt and general goods and returned with fish. Clay and granite were worked locally and exported. The granite came from Haytor, high on the edge of Dartmoor and was brought down by stone tramway and the Stover canal: it was used for London Bridge (now in Arizona), the British Museum and the General Post Office – a building in which Harry Buxton Forman was to work for many years.

Sir Edward Pellew started a naval migration to Teignmouth. He was appointed Commander in Chief Mediterranean – perhaps the most evocative post in the whole British navy – in 1811 and in 1812 he and his wife bought West Cliff House, sited a little outside the town. He was followed by other naval officers, including two other admirals. John Sweetland was a Devon man who was appointed a deputy Commissary General in 1802 and from 1804 to 1807 he served in Gibraltar as Principal Commissary of Stores and Provisions (he had a higher salary than anyone except the Governor). Soon after this he returned to Teignmouth and drew many years' substantial half pay, dying in 1844. He founded the town's mechanics institute in 1834 and lived in a large house – 'Hermosa' in Landscore Road – which was much admired for its spreading lawns, trees and an orangery (Sir Edward had one too: it survives). He was an old friend of the Forman family – the connection dating at least from Gibraltar when George Ellery served in the Mediterranean, and perhaps earlier. When the family came to Teignmouth in 1843, they stayed at first at 'Hermosa'. They soon moved to a house in Northumberland Place (alias Strand) an attractive street winding out of the west end of 'The Den', the grassy open space along the seafront. Northumberland Place runs beside the estuary and there are several picturesque alleys with views of boats on The Salty, and the red rocks and green fields of Shaldon beyond.

John Keats, who Harry Buxton Forman was years later to spend many months editing, stayed in Teignmouth for two months in 1818. It was chosen for his brother Tom's health and his probable West Country and nautical origins – a William Keats Sweetland (relationships unknown) owned property there. Keats didn't like it much, denouncing the weather and the Devon men and turning a piece of bitcherell on the Devon girls.

6. Teignmouth, the Den looking north, a lithograph *c.* 1845–50

Where be ye going, you Devon Maid?
And what have ye got there in the Basket?
Ye tight little fairy just fresh from the dairy,
Will ye give me some cream if I ask it?

I love your Meads, and I love your flowers,
And I love your junket mainly,
But 'hind the door I love kissing more,
O look not so disdainly.

I love your hills, and I love your dales,
And I love your flocks a-bleating –
But O, on the heather to lie together,
With both our heads a-beating!

I'll put your Basket all safe in a nook,
Your shawl I hang up on the willow,
And we will sigh in the daisy's eye
And kiss on a grass green pillow.

He also wrote that he was very 'peedisposed' to Devon, printed
by Forman in one of his rare lapses from editorial virtue, as
predisposed. Keats took lodgings for two months in a house
which may have been in Northumberland Place and may have
been that now known as Keats Cottage or any other of a
hundred or so houses. The odds must be strongly against Keats's
occupancy of Keats Cottage.

In 1849 the Formans were at 16 Northumberland Place: from
December 1849 to January 1850 at No. 10 and from 2 January
onwards at No. 11. At the 1851 census they were still at 11 but
later in the year, they knocked two houses into one and called it
15 Northumberland Place. The 1861 census springs a surprise by
remarking that Northumberland Place and Strand 'are entered
as Strand by which name it is commonly known': none of the
houses is numbered. In 1871 we are back to Northumberland
Place and numbers, but they have changed again.

To cut a long story short, Northumberland Place alias Strand,
would need a full-scale thesis to elucidate its architectural
history and renumbering. We cannot identify any of the houses
in which the Forman family lived for some eighteen years: and as
the attempt to identify Keats's two months was not made
until some eighty years afterwards and depends on the muddled
recollections of an old man, it is doomed.

Harry had a happy childhood and, as people do, he cherished
the memories. When he came to write his last book, he put one

of them on paper, dedicating it to his brother.

> My dear Alfred – my earliest recollections are of digging on the sands
> at Teignmouth, between the sea and those red cliffs now bastioned
> by Brunel's long sea-wall, and of gathering wild convolvuluses at the
> foot of the cliffs before the railway was there. I was little more than a
> year and a half old then; and my guide, philosopher and friend was my
> elder brother, you some three years and a half old.

This was in the year of their arrival – London children escaping
into clean air and sparkling water. The medical practice
flourished as the town became more prosperous, helped by the
arrival of the railway in 1846. This was originally Brunel's glorious failure of an atmospheric railway. It was soon replaced by
conventional engines but his route remains and is still one of the
most beautiful stretches of line in the British Isles.

The family continued to increase – Jessie Hester arriving in
1844, to be followed by Sidney Wells in 1845 and finally William
Courthope Gardiner in 1848 (Maria Forman – née Courthope we
may remember – was then 43). The family went to their parish
church of St Michael the Archangel in East Teignmouth; this
was the fashionable church and much irritation was caused by
people cross parishing from West Teignmouth. All three children were baptised there, though the fine fifteenth century font
they used was given away in 1911; doubtless it did not suit the
church. This dates from 1823 (chancel added in 1877, tower in
1887). 'An almost unbelievable effort in neo-Norman' according
to Pevsner: it is less charitably known as the ugliest in all Devon.
Its design (especially the doorway) seems to be an apology for
pulling down the original Norman church in 1822.

The census enumeration of 1851 reminds us of the state of the
family, which comprised George Ellery Forman 51, his wife Maria
46, Anne 15, Mary 13, Alfred 10, Henry 8, Jessie 7, Sidney 5 and
William 2. They had three servants, a cook of 26 and two nurse-
maids of 24 and 20: all three were local girls. Northumberland
Place had a very nautical flavour: among their neighbours were a
lieutenant RN, a ship owner, several fishermen, a sailor, a mar-
iner, a rope maker and a beach pilot.

Alfred, the eldest boy, was the only scholar not 'at home': he
was probably taught by Thomas Edgelow who kept a Gentlemen's Seminary at Hillford House in Bitton Street. Alfred left
this establishment in 1854 to join the Royal Naval School in

New Cross – an obvious choice for the eldest son of a surgeon RN. Harry went to the same local school, by then christened Thorn Park School and left in 1860: he stayed longer which may suggest greater academic ability than his brother. In 1861, the headmaster Thomas Edgelow described himself as Principal Proprietor of a boarding school employing four Teachers and seven Servants with twenty-four Scholars. As Mr Edgelow had twelve children of his own, one can see why he started a school – and indeed six of his were listed as attending it. By 1862, the school had moved to Coombe Vale Road and the name had inflated to Thorn Park Classical and Mathematical School. We can learn a little of what the school was actually like, because from 1863 to 1866, Edmund Gosse was a pupil there. His father sent him to share in the odour of sanctity which was supposed to envelop the school. In his famous *Father and Son*, Edmund recorded,

> sometimes I was more unhappy than I had ever been before. No one, however, bullied me, I was dimly and indefinably witness to acts of uncleanliness and cruelty, I was the victim of no such acts and the recipient of no dangerous confidences. I suppose my queer reputation for sanctity, half dreadful, half ridiculous, surrounded me with a non-conducting atmosphere .... I was extremely nearsighted and in consequence was placed at a gross disadvantage, by being unable to see the slate or the blackboard on which our tasks were explained. This fact was never commented upon or taken into account by a single person until the Polish lady who taught us the elements of German and French, drew someone's attention to it in my sixteenth year. I was not quick, but I passed for being denser than I was because of the myopic haze that enveloped me.

Sir Edmund Gosse rose to become a major literary mandarin, to write the one masterpiece, *Father and Son*, quoted above and a lot of other books, mostly popular literary history. His life and that of Harry Buxton Forman occasionally intersected in London but there was no warmth in their relationship. If they knew that they shared a school and missed each other by only a year or so, there is little sign of it.

Forman may well have been taught the same elements of German and French as Gosse and like him became a most competent linguist in later life. Many years later, the former cast his mind back and gave a tantalizing glimpse of his Devon and his Teignmouth long ago.

My Nell & William & good Ned Bray
Seemed ever dimmer & more away;
Right little of livelihead I found
In the Sire & Maid of The Outward Bound;
And the woman asleep in her Widdicombe grave
– The poor dead Hannah whose tress I save –
And the Witch of the Copse with her dark romance,
And George Gale's slayers & dear Mad Nance,
All strange on my sense their talk would fall
If they ever came to talk at all.

Moving to London in 1860 was a severe dislocation. He joined his two brothers at 22 Lansdowne Place, South Lambeth, which borders on their old territory of Camberwell. The 1861 census shows that they shared No. 22 with Sarah Ellis, a china dealer who was perhaps their landlady. Among the occupations in the Place were an ornamental basket-maker, grocer, shoemaker, bricklayer and one William Worman, a surgical instrument maker. In what was clearly a modest household, the three brothers were listed thus:

| George Forman | 28 | Clerk in Russian trade |
| Alfred Forman | 20 | Clerk in Colonial Broker |
| Henry Forman | 18 | Clerk in Post Office |

Harry Buxton Forman was to serve the Post Office for nearly fifty years and his work there requires a new chapter.

# FORMAN AT THE POST OFFICE

Forman joined the Post Office 'a raw lad out of the West Country' to use his own words, as a supplementary class clerk in the Secretary's Office on 18 April 1860. To be employed as an established worker in the P.O. was a coveted job, not easy to get. One had to be recommended by a person of influence and then (at least in theory) pass an exam. But as Trollope, the P.O.'s most famous literary figure recounts, this was often a dead letter.

> I was asked to copy some lines from *The Times* newspaper with an old quill pen, and at once made a series of blots and false spellings. "That won't do, you know" said Henry Freeling to his brother Clayton. Clayton, who was my friend, urged that I was nervous, and asked that I might be allowed to do a bit of writing at home and bring it as a sample on the next day. I was then asked whether I was a proficient in arithmetic. What could I say? I had never learned the multiplication table, and had no more idea of the rule of three than of conic sections. "I know a little of it" I said humbly, whereupon I was sternly assured that on the morrow, should I succeed in showing that my handwriting was all that it ought to be, I should be examined as to that little of arithmetic. If that little should not be found to comprise a thorough knowledge of all the ordinary rules, together with practised and quick skill, my career in life could not be made at the Post Office. Going down the main stairs of the building – stairs which have, I believe, now been pulled down to make room for sorters and stampers, – Clayton Freeling told me not to be too downhearted. I myself, was inclined to think that I had better go back to the school in Brussels. But nevertheless I went to work, and under the surveillance of my elder brother, made a beautiful transcript of four to five pages of Gibbon. With a faltering heart I took these on the next day to the office. With my calligraphy I was contented, but was certain that I should come to the ground among the figures. But when I got to 'The Grand', as we used to call our office in those days, from its site in St Martin's le Grand, I was seated at a desk without any further reference to my competency. No one condescended even to look at my beautiful penmanship.

Trollope joined in 1834, but much was still similar in 1860. In particular, the magnificent building of Devon granite by Sir Robert Smirke; finished in 1829, was still the headquarters. St Martin's le Grand served both as the Post Office headquarters

7. The GPO at one minute to six, an oil painting by Hicks

and the main London Post Office, with a public right of way right through the lofty central hall. A commanding building on a site just beside St Paul's, and with departing mail coaches to watch, it rapidly became one of the sights of London.

> At night, as the big hall clock drew on to the hour of six, and especially on Friday when the American mail was despatched, the central hall wore an animated aspect. Onlookers who came to post their letters, but stopped to see the sight, thickened into a crowd: public excitement grew apace. Vociferous cries of "Stand back!" and "Clear the way!" from the hall constables resounded. At the first stroke of six, expectation was at fever-heat. Belated messengers rushed up with sacks of newspapers and merchants' clerks with letters by the score, until the sixth great shock of sound a universal shout, followed by a glorious bang of all letter-boxes and windows announced the closing of the post.

Hicks's painting gives a graphic picture of the same event, painted in the year Forman joined. The shy Devon boy must have found it a great change from tiny Teignmouth.

The 'Secretary's Office' sounds rather nondescript, but the Secretary was the professional head of the P.O.: the Post Master General himself being a political appointment. So the Secretary's office was the headquarters' staff and remarkably small it was for such a large enterprise. At first the salary was not very great; but compared with many other employments, it had great advantages. There were regular automatic increments; there was security of employment; a chance of promotion; paid medical attention and a pension (at the end of forty years' service). Few other employees in Victorian England were so lucky. Forman grumbled at first about the salary – 'not very grand for those obliged to live and breed in London' he said – but gradually improved himself. A supplementary clerk got £80 p.a. which rose by £5 increments to a maximum of £150 p.a., a respectable if not grand salary. Forman never reached that £150, for in 1867 he was promoted Senior Clerk Second Class (£260 p.a. by £15 increments to £380), in 1872 Principal Clerk First Class (£420) in 1881 Principal Clerk Lower Section (£500), and in 1885 Principal Clerk Upper Section (£625 by £25 to £800). In addition to this last, he received £80 p.a. as Clerk in Waiting with 10s per waiting for table money (i.e. expenses). As Clerk in Waiting he was on night duty and was left in sole charge of the postal departments. This is described by F. E. Baines, a fellow employee

8.   London letter carriers, a wood engraving, 1861

(though not, I think, a friend of H.B.F.'s) in his reminiscences published in 1895.

> a solitary taper may tremble in the room of the Clerk-in-Waiting. Perchance, for tranquility of thought, he has turned out the electric lamp and is smoking the cigarette of contentment, or the tranquil pipe; is meditating the evening meal, or reviewing that problem of which his branch has yet to find the solution. Gone to the House is the Chief of all postmen; to their lorries, the lesser lights; the stealthy watchmen pervade the corridors; the fire brigade unwind the hose. Northward, the moonlight plays fantastic tricks with the new buildings, fast ripening into completion.

In 1893, H.B.F. had abandoned the night duty rota and reached £800 (the scales had been revised upwards) + £75 acting allowance as Assistant Secretary + £100 as Controller of Packet Services. In 1894 he was appointed Assistant Secretary: in 1899 he was on £1,200 (he was one of six assistant secretaries) and finally in 1905 (just before retirement) he was joint second secretary on £1,300. He retired in 1907 at 65, having served forty-seven years and secured a C.B. and a comfortable pension of two-thirds of his final pay. He had risen higher in the P.O. than any other literary man of his time – what had he done and how had he done it?

**Instructions to H. Buxton Forman, Esq., deputed by the Postmaster General to make Enquiries on the Continent and furnish a Report.**

---

Mr. Forman,                    General Post Office, December 14, 1881.
      You will be good enough to proceed to—
          Brussels,
          Berlin,
          Vienna,
          Berne, and
          Paris,*
and ascertain in each case :
      I.—Whether the railways are to any, and, if so, to what extent the property of the State.
      II.—Whether the railways which are not the property of the State receive any subsidy from the State, or are exempt from any taxes, or obtain any privileges in

9.    Part of Forman's official instructions
for his report on European parcel post, 1882

He had become an acknowledged specialist in overseas posts, their details and organization. His clear and penetrating intelligence – and ability in French and German – was harnessed to a job calling for mastery of a mass of trees without losing sight of the wood. He seems first to have gone abroad on post office business in 1880 when he attended the Parcel Post Conference. His first major independent assignment was his *Report on the Parcel Post in Belgium, Holland, Germany, Austria, Switzerland and France* 1882. He did proceed and his analysis of the different posts is clear and even brutal. Of Holland,

> The parcel delivery companies in town and country are pretty numerous; and it is thought not unlikely that many of them will be ruined by the parcel post. Petitions and the usual agitators have been resorted to: but the law has passed: and the Government does not propose to concern itself with restricted 'class interests'

or

> There are delivery companies and carriers in France; but the parcels post, as now preferred by the railways, is not such as to have inter-fered very largely with such undertakings; and complaint is not at present rife. The special parcel post within Paris is performed by the only company which was in the habit of doing a house-to-house delivery in that city. Another company has complained of the advan-tage conferred on the Paris company, in the shape of the parcel post business; but it was considered sufficient to tell the complainant he was free to compete by doing a similar service cheaper on his own account.

The descriptions are sometimes enlivened by literary touches as in the description of German parcels offices,

> I saw in some of the offices, besides the numerous inscrutable parcels, hares, turkeys, fish well-packed in frails and baskets, meat sewn up in cloths, kegs of brandy and caviare and every imaginable kind of 'dry goods' parcel. The 'plant' is all substantial, the vans handsome, the horses good, the men spruce and presentable.

The report was urgently needed, as Great Britain had agreed at the International Postal Congress in November 1880 (in Paris: Forman attended) to introduce an international parcel post without having an inland service. This latter had then to be cobbled together in rather a hurry and the consequence was that the Post Office lost money. As Forman wistfully observed, 'gra-tuitous traction clauses in British Railway Acts may perhaps be safely dismissed as Utopian'. He notes that in Belgium (which offered the best comparison with the putative English parcel service) the Railway Companies took about 40 per cent of the tariff, while the proposed stake of the railways in England was 'an unknown quantity, somewhere beyond ½'. In fact the Post Office (Parcels) Act 1882 gave the railway companies 55 per cent of the postage on parcels and they were still, on the more profitable parts, able to run their own services in competition: and the act was to run for twenty-one years!

There was often a conflict in the P.O. between service and profit. Was the P.O. a commercial organization or should it provide the best service irrespective of cost? The dialectic was never fully resolved. Forman seems to have been a cautious proponent of service, but with considerable ability to trim away unnecessary losses. Inland Parcel Post was introduced in 1883. It needed a vast new plant, bigger post offices and sorting offices, more staff, more transport and more money: and it saw the final demise of the 'letter carrier'; he was now called a 'postman'.

In the same year, Forman was appointed acting surveyor of the British Post Offices in the Mediterranean (1883), a fascinating post, the allure of which one catches tantalizing glimpses in the archives. There was, for example, a British Post Master in Constantinople from 1857 onwards but, 'There is nothing in the records of the Department to show that the Sublime Porte was informed of the intention to open the Office.' Forman's brief tenure as surveyor allowed him to sort out the problems involved in the transhipment of Eastern mail across the isthmus of Suez. He was following in Trollope's footsteps. The great novelist was sent out to Alexandria in 1858 to produce a report: he also finished *Doctor Thorne*. Forman certainly produced a report: perhaps he also got on with his edition of Keats which was published in 1883. Despite the canal (opened in 1869) mails were carried by train across Egypt until 1888, as the canal passage was for a long time very slow. Forman seems to have picked his way with great skill between the opposing parties of London, the Postmaster General of Bombay, and the staff at Alexandria who were made redundant on his advice. He got on well with the Post Office Janissary

> I took Ali Amir Agha with me to Cairo, where he was of the greatest service in smoothing the way in situations where a European alone would have found himself awkwardly placed. I gathered a most favourable impression of Ali's intelligence, integrity and readiness in all situations; and I should be loth to recommend a measure which would throw him on his resources after 22 years of faithful service.

He was transferred to Suez and kept on.

Forman naturally attended the Lisbon International Post Congress in 1885. He went with the boss – Sir Stevenson Arthur Blackwood, Secretary of the Post Office from 1880 until his death in 1893. Sir Arthur's strong evangelical piety cannot have been to Forman's taste, but as Post Office officials they saw eye to eye, and under his patronage, he became clearly recognized as the European expert in St Martin's le Grand. In 1887 he described to a close friend another European mission.

> I had to go to Paris & Rome to make a fresh arrangement for the special conveyance of the Eastern Mails across France and Italy. It was a most difficult and anxious business because the charges, which I have long considered iniquitously high, had the sanction of many years, and moreover the two countries combined as it were against us to keep them up. What I had to do was not only to obtain a reduction of about one third in the charges, but to get a proper logical principle for the future settlement accepted and admitted openly in the face of all the Post Offices of the World and also to break up the Franco–Italian coalition, so as to play one country against the other. It was by far the most difficult and delicate piece of work I ever had to do for the Post Office: but I had the good luck to succeed on all the points, the mere saving to the tax-payer being £22,000 a year. I should not care to have such missions often, because this one involved the absolute exclusion of everything else from one's mind and life for nearly a month; and this sort of hard hammering at one set of considerations for so long a time is liable to turn a man into a mere piece of diplomatic machinery.

In 1891 there was another international congress, in Vienna this time. The delegates tangled with a mass of regulations, many contradictory, and all in French: their final printed proceedings run to nearly 1,000 pages. H.B.F. was able to make a number of contributions, particularly in pointing out where the congress was contradicting itself *vis à vis* the previous deliberations in Lisbon. In the midst of a wearisome consideration of *surtaxe maritime* he suddenly produced an inspiring peroration on world government.

'Messieurs, vous êtes le premier parlement humain: l'Union postale universelle constitue la première fédération du Monde entier. Inspirez-vous de cet auguste fait, et, si vous savez, ne statuez que selon le droit et la justice!' It must have given the other delegates rather a shock, to judge by the grey speeches that surround it. Forman was full of beans and he even ran off a couple of poems, from one of which we can bear to quote a few verses:

> Congress
> (Vienna 20 May – 4 July 1891)
> The world's first parliament again
> Decoys me from my quiet neighbours,
> To quit my house and toil amain
> In 'universal postal' labours,
>
> To prate in French from morn to night
> Of postage rates and dues of transit,
> And what is wrong and what is right
> And whether we shall fix or chance it.

(18 more stanzas follow)

Sir Arthur Blackwood died in 1893 and in the same year Forman was promoted to his major post – Controller of Packet Services. Algernon Blackwood, Sir Arthur's son, was later to write excellent ghost stories and an autobiography in which he describes his father's house.

> Ordinary people, "worldly" as he called them, left us alone. A house where no wine was served at dinner, where morning and evening prayers were de rigeur, a guest even being asked to "lead in prayer" perhaps, and where at any suitable moment you might be drawn aside and asked "Have you given your soul to Jesus?" was not an attractive house to stay in.

Forman contributed a detailed and deeply felt obituary of Sir Arthur to *St. Martin's-le-Grand; the Post Office Magazine,*

> It is when you travel with a man, especially if you pass weeks in the same rooms with him in a foreign country, that you learn infallibly what he is made of; and before I had been many days at Meurice's Hotel (in Paris) that I knew he was a man indeed, and reckoned him as a friend. There were reasons best forgotten why I was disposed to resist any inclination to come into other than strictly official relations with the Chief: but within a week I was a helpless captive to the charm of his companionship, the broad sunshine of his beautiful cheerful disposition, and the genuine unselfishness of his character. To the best of my belief, there were few men old or young at the Conference who were not similarly captured; and while I found myself devoting my whole energies to mastering the technical and diplomatic work we had in hand with the added zest of the feeling that I was doing all I could to help a Chief whom I liked and respected, I contemplated with the pride of a common nationality the easy and princely manner in which he made the work go smoothly by the personal regard which he inspired.

He deals with his decisive action in the serious strike in 1890 (Blackwood helped the blacklegs) and then comments on Sir Arthur at the Vienna Congress when his health was failing.

> Still he had the humour, the raciness and the *aplomb* to stand with a glass of Apollinaris water in his hand for ten or fifteen minutes at one of the banquets, and, in proposing the health of the ladies, deliver an admirably appropriate and amusing speech in that bright fluent French of his, picturesque with British idiom. . . still when occasion required his serious intervention at the Congress, he could tower up in the might of his six feet three and sixteen stone, in all the dignity and command of his personality, and indignantly beat down factious opposition and injustice to the interests which he represented. . . I never met a man who had a gigantic physique and keen tastes under more absolute control. It is easy to preach temperance and practise it too if you do not like alcohol. It is easy for those who have feeble passion and are unimpressionable to lead moral lives. If you cannot sit on a horse or handle a gun it is no privation to refrain from sport. It is not difficult to do without good cigars if the smell of tobacco offends you. To be economical in your expenditure on dress is no privation if you do not know the difference between a good tailor and a bad one. . . to keep your temper among all the frets and provocations of life is no hard task if your temper is that of an average cauliflower. . . . As to his habitual early rising for purposes of study and work, I recall a conversation of many years ago which comes home to me across his grave with a sad significance. We were comparing notes on the subject of early rising, and he turned round, in bright convincing manner and said, "Do you know, Forman, I once calculated how many years I had added to my working life by getting up at six o'clock in the morning": he stated the number of years; but it has escaped me. "Do you like getting up early?" I asked. "Well I can't say I particularly like it," he said. Pushed as to whether it was an effort to him, he admitted that it was not altogether without effort. "Then" said I, somewhat grimly, "have you calculated how many years you have cut off at the other end?" The answer was very characteristic. "Ah! that is in other hands than mine. No, I have not."

All this and much more is uncharacteristically wholehearted for Forman. He does work in a few ambivalent touches: he quotes, for example, the fashionable *mot* when Sir Arthur was appointed: 'the Lords Commissioners, having tried everything at the Post Office and found it incorrigible, had determined to test the efficacy of prayer.' The rational Positivist and the evangelical Christian were arm in arm, and indeed, it seems a distinct possibility that Sir Arthur went some way towards returning Harry to his childhood piety. Another absolutely characteristic Forman touch was that he also printed his tribute to Sir Arthur separately for private circulation, fifty copies only in violet ink.

In 1893, the term 'packet services' referred not to packets or parcels, but to the ships (or packets) that carried the post overseas. The name of the office harks back to the time in the early nineteenth century when the Post Office, a pioneer in the use of steamships, ran its own packet services. In 1893, this had long ceased and the P.O. used commercial companies, the most important being Cunard to North America and the Peninsular and Orient Steam Navigation Company (the P.&O.) to India and beyond. The Post Office paid regular subsidies to the companies which were not directly related to the amount of mail carried. The return on postage did not by any means cover the subsidies: in 1895 the subsidies were about £730,000 while the postage (and subventions from colonial post offices) brought in some £300,000. Many people thought the Post Office could have secured better terms, but it was difficult to get real competition. As the century advanced, the deficit was reduced (Forman played a part in this) but on the India run there was really no alternative to the P.&O. The investment (ships, men, coaling stations, etc.) necessary to start a new service, was too large to contemplate and the alternative of splitting the route into smaller stations for individual tenders had its own obvious defects in a fractured service. On the North Atlantic, where there was much more possibility of competition, the Post Office was thwarted by the 'Liverpool ring' and Cunard kept the contract until 1927. The Controller of Packet Services did demand and get strict timetables (with severe penalty clauses) and fast, frequent ships. From the St Martin's le Grand point of view, a further complication was the hue and cry after ocean penny postage and particularly imperial penny post. This was eventually conceded in 1898, but the decision was a political one taken in the interests of cementing the Empire together and as the P.O. predicted, they lost money on it.

One can observe Forman at work among these and other cross currents by consulting the surviving volumes of official correspondence in the Post Office archives. Leafing through the thick volumes, one feels somewhat like Kipling's Mrs Hauksbee who saw the naked machinery of the Great Indian Government, stripped of its casings and lacquer, and paint and guard rails. She was a little afraid at first, and felt as if she had taken hold of a

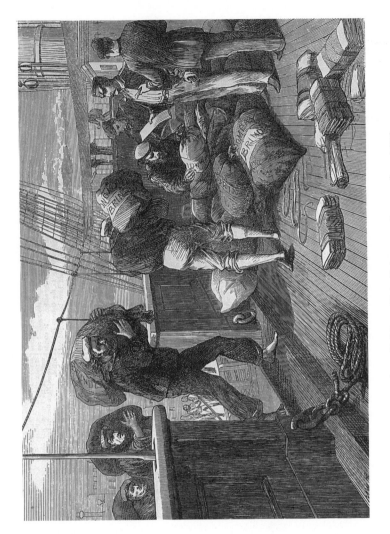

10.   A mail ship at Brindisi, a wood engraving, 1872

lightning flash by the tail, and did not quite know what to do with it.

I have the honour to acknowledge the receipt of your letter of the 29th of last month (No. 470 colis postaux), stating the conditions in which parcel mails from the Seychelles can be conveyed from Zanzibar to Mauritius and the French possessions in the Indian Ocean. A letter has been written to the Postmaster General at Zanzibar. [to the Director General of Posts, Buenos Aires].

With reference to your letter of the 18th December last, reporting that the contract packet 'Ormuz' timed to leave Adelaide for this country on the 13th of that month, had been in collision in Australian waters and would be detained for 5 or 6 weeks, I am directed to acquaint you, for the information of the Directors of the Orient Steam Navigation Company, that the Postmaster General has under consideration the amount of the absolute penalty incurred under Clause 25(2) of the Contract. The Company has clearly incurred a deduction from the subsidy to the extent of £250 for failure to provide a mail ship at Adelaide ready to put to sea at the appointed time, and a further sum of £350, that is to say £50 a day for the succeeding seven days which elapsed before the mails were conveyed by the next Peninsular and Oriental Packet. The Postmaster General regrets... [to The Secretary, Orient Steam Navigation Company 4 March 1901].

At this period the Post Office did not delegate responsibility easily. In the course of his work Forman wrote a letter containing a warrant for £66,250; considered the effects of quarantine being declared in Japan against ships from Shanghai; and dealt with the speedy delivery of ammunition to British Guiana. But he also wrote about the contamination of tea samples with fruit; the despatch of chrysalids of butterflies from France ('this Department... will not object to receive by Parcel Post the objects in question'); a parcel containing wedding cake sent from India to Italy and redirected to Ealing and then refused by the addressee; a parcel despatched from Liverpool to Valparaiso and the contents – a frock, hose, ties, lace and a fruit loaf – gnawed by rats or mice; the despatch of 5 tons of saluting cartridges to Australia by the Admiralty on a Mail packet; and the Mail bag dropped overboard off Kinsale, washed ashore at Court Macsherry and despatched to London from Cork. It is an impressive display of mastery of a mass of detail together with a firm grasp of general principles. He was, of course, also much involved in committee work, the most important being the Committee on

11. Demolishing the GPO, an etching, 1911

Eastern and Australian Mail Services which reported in 1895–96 (Forman was the sole P.O. representative) and the *Conference on Postage within the British Empire* 1898. It was in this latter that Penny postage for the Empire was established. In Queen Victoria's Diamond Jubilee honours in 1897, he was promoted to the Most Honourable Order of the Bath, 'to be an additional member of the Civil Division of the said most Honourable Order' or in other words he was given a C.B., a natural reward for a civil servant of his seniority.

Meanwhile in 1895, he had moved across the road to G.P.O. North, a building in Portland Stone designed by Henry Tanner and started in 1889: it is now a sad shell awaiting demolition or a new interior. In 1905 he took part in the ceremony of laying the foundation stone of the King Edward Building, a most elaborate ceremony, with addresses and processions. He described to an American acquaintance how

> The coat that you admired so much came into requisition with the new collar and cuffs last Monday the 16th of October when, as I dare say you saw in the papers, I was duly trotted out to make my antique bow to H.M. King Edward VII.

This presaged the tearing down in 1910–11 of what had become known as G.P.O. East. Forman's career, like that of Smirke's great building was drawing to a close. In 1906 he had a serious operation (probably for prostate) and in 1907 he retired. There is no doubt that Forman was a devoted servant of the Post Office and much of his retirement speech rings true.

> The right sort of obedience is loyal obedience – the kind of obedience which I have had from those who served under me, and the kind which I have endeavoured to give to all under whom I have served – twenty Postmasters General and six Secretaries. The obedience I mean is a thinking and reasonable obedience. . . the way to treat your chief is to say to him "I understand that the policy of the moment is so and so, and that we are to do so and so; I am here not to carry out your will blindly, but to tell you first as clearly as I can what are the objections, and when you have made up your mind that the objections do not hold, then I am here to carry our your will literally and loyally" . . . loyal obedience is to carry out your instruction, not in the sense that "I have got to do something I don't want to do and by Jove I'll do it", but in such a way that you will not put the Postmaster General in any difficulty which you can possibly foresee for him, either in his own person or in those of his successors.

Admirable ethics for a civil servant! His leaving present showed much generosity and insight. Forman had a complete collection of Kelmscott Press – all but the grandest and most expensive book, the Chaucer: and it was a Kelmscott Chaucer he was given.

I first read Chaucer in the earliest years of my service in the Post Office, now I will read him again from your copy; and as I read him I shall see faces between the lines and stanzas – I see there is plenty of room – and perhaps I may draw faces in the margin, if I develop artistic proclivities in my last years. The faces will be those I see around me today. . . . I part from you with extreme regret, for I have formed many affections here – I am not ashamed to say so or to confess myself to be an emotional person. The friendships and affections I shall carry away with me; but I hope I shall often see you all again; and I shall perhaps come back among you thinking that I am playing my old daily part in the fairy-tale of the Post Office which has lasted me over 47 years. I will say only one thing more. . . . the fairy-tale of the Post Office being over for me, I have but to 'turn the page and choose another tale'.

# 3

## FORMAN IN LONDON

We left Forman in lodgings with his brothers; we must retrace our steps and consider his life outside the office. In 1865 the three brothers moved to 3 Grove Hill Terrace, Grove Hill, a leafy part of Camberwell, even now having some shadow of the magnificent gardens of John Lettsom the eighteenth century doctor. In 1866, they had to move to a larger house nearby, to accommodate their mother and father. He was evicted from his quiet retirement in the little Devon village of Kingsteighton by the loss of all his savings in a financial crash. However, Dr Forman died in 1867 and the brothers and their two sisters moved back to Camberwell at 68 The Grove. Harry and Alfred were particularly close friends and the intellectual excitement of their early London years is particularly evident and particularly well documented in their friendship with Richard Maurice Bucke.

Bucke was born in England in 1837, and the following year the family emigrated to Ontario. By 1854, he was an orphan, and he set off to see the world. He worked all over the American West in a variety of jobs. In 1857 he was lost in the Sierra Nevada for five days without food or fire: his companion died and he lost a foot from frostbite. He returned to Canada and in 1862 graduated in medicine from McGill. He then spent two years in post graduate study at University College London, when he met the Formans. Forman and Bucke remained correspondents almost until Bucke died in 1902 (he went outside to have a last look at the stars, but fell down and hit his head). Quite often in their long correspondence they hark back to the magic early days in London. It was on a second visit in 1872, that Bucke had a 'classic example of mystical illumination' (William James) after an evening with the Forman brothers. Bucke described it in the third person

> He and two friends had spent the evening reading Wordsworth, Shelley, Keats, Browning and especially Whitman. They parted at midnight and he had a long drive in a hansom (it was in an English city). His mind, deeply under the influence of the ideas, images and emotions called up by the reading and talk of the evening, was calm

12. Bucke in his library, 1899

and peaceful. He was in a state of quiet, almost passive enjoyment. All at once, without warning of any kind, he found himself wrapped around as it were by a flame coloured cloud. . . into his brain streamed one momentary lightning flash of Brahmic Splendour which has ever since lightened his life.

Bucke spent the last twenty-five years of his life as medical supervisor of a lunatic asylum in London, Ontario, and the friendly correspondent in London England, was most important to him. Forman got him books and kept him *au fait* with the latest literary and intellectual gossip. Nevertheless, Bucke was important too, and provided Forman with a true friend to whom he could write without reserve (well not quite: I doubt he ever did that to anyone). Bucke's asylum was a backwater, but he was a pioneer of scientific psychiatry and it has become quite celebrated. 'With the publication in 1901 of his final book *Cosmic Consciousness* Bucke joined the groping but relentless search for a new medical understanding of the unconscious mind' a recent historian has it.

Bucke and Forman were both early Whitman enthusiasts and Bucke ended up as one of his most constant admirers and one of his three executors. He produced an adulatory book *Walt Whitman* in 1883; some portions were so heavily corrected by the subject as practically to rank as his own writing, a common habit with Whitman. Forman helped with general advice and actually had the frontispiece printed under his own supervision in London. He collected Whitman along with his other enthusiasms: besides an almost complete set of books, including a lovely first edition of *Leaves of Grass* 1855, he had Walt Whitman's hospital notebook, recording in manuscript the details of his civil war nursing. Rather later, in 1887, Forman wrote to Bucke that his son Maurice (by then 16) had read *Leaves of Grass*, 'It leads to awkward questions of course, but they are such a father ought to be glad of an opportunity to answer.'

Bucke and the Forman brothers probably met through their shared interest in Achille Comte. For Forman, this adhesion, intense in youth, somewhat dimming with age, influenced his whole life. Trying to read Comte now – wrestling with his turgid and involved prose – it is difficult to descry the attraction. There is, however, no doubt that the man and his work had a significant impact on nineteenth century free thinkers. Achille

No. G. 31

23, FARRINGDON STREET, E.C.,

London, _Nov 10_ 188/.

N H Buxton Forman Esq

To The TYPOGRAPHIC ETCHING Co.

| | £ | s. | d. |
|---|---|---|---|
| Photo Intaglio Walt Whitman | 5 | 5 | . |
| Printing 12 proofs on Whatman | | 15 | . |
| 1000 prints on Hand Made | 6 | 5 | . |
| Paper | | | |
| | £12 | 5 | . |

13. Bill for printing the portrait of Whitman in Bucke's book on him

Comte was born in Montpelier in 1798 and died in Paris in 1857. He left behind him a large body of work including the six volume *Cours de Philosophie positive* 1830–42 and the four volume *Systeme de Politique positive* 1851–54; a significant body of admirers and disciples; and the injunction in his will that his (thirteen) executors were to preserve his rooms in Paris as the headquarters of his new religion of humanity.

Comte's sweeping general view of human knowledge passes through three states: the theological, the metaphysical and the positive (or scientific). His readers could observe the gradual extension of science into new fields and the most important field remaining, in his view, was the study of society, which when achieved would provide a golden key to a new age. He thought that despite outstripping religion on a scientific basis, man would still retain religious instincts. He proposed that these be devoted to humanity in general, the agglomeration of human minds being labelled 'the Great Being'. After death, the only immortality was one's impress on the Great Being or, in other words, what other people remember of you. Comte even renamed the months – making thirteen of them – so a serious positivist might date a letter '24 Gutenberg 98' meaning 5 September 1886. He had an idea, which certainly influenced Forman, that miscellaneous and ill directed reading harmed the intellect. Comte's system was called (by a hostile critic) Catholicism without the Christianity. Although his church and much of his theory did not transplant wholesale, his ideas did have great influence, for instance in the Brazilian revolution of 1889. On a more literary and relevant level, Thomas Hardy drew diagrams to depict Comte's idea of progress and had a positivist heroine in *Jude the Obscure* (Comte had advanced ideas on the condition of women). J.S. Mill (utilitarianism – the greatest good of the greatest number), Harriet Martineau, G.H. Lewes and George Eliot (Dorothea in *Middlemarch*) were others who took on board part of Comte's cargo. Sassoon's *Credo* is not formally positivist but it does give some glimpse of the type of secular religion which many found inspiring.

### Credo

The heaven for which I wait has neither guard nor gate.
The God in whom I trust shall raise me not from dust.
I shall not see that heaven for which my days have striven,

Nor kneel before the God toward whom my feet have trod.
But when from this half-human evolvement man and
                                                        woman
Emerge, through brutish Me made strong and fair and free,
The dumb forgotten dead will be the ground they tread,
And in their eyes will shine my deathless hope divine.

Forman met his wife, Laura, at a positivist lecture: she was a
fellow enthusiast. He introduced her to George Eliot at another
such lecture on 5 May 1867 (serious people the positivists were).
George Eliot lived with G.H. Lewes at 21 North Bank, St
John's Wood (where else could she go, the world said). She moth-
ered the three Lewes boys, one of whom, Charles Lee Lewes
(1842–1891) was almost the same age as Forman and joined the
Post Office in the same year. He joined as a supplementary clerk
just like Forman, but his rise was much slower: he resigned in
1886 as a principal clerk, became a member of the London
County Council and died in Egypt in 1891 where he was buried at
Luxor with the full rites of the Coptic Church, 'a singularly
novel funeral for a London County Councillor' as his recent
biographer notes.

However, to come back to 1860, it was friendship with her
'stepson' that led to Forman's invitation to George Eliot's
Sunday 'at homes' and to Laura Selle's introduction to George
Eliot as Forman's future bride. She was the daughter of Dr
William Christian Selle, the son of an emigré German musician
from Hanover, who joined the Duke of Cumberland's private
band. Dr Selle continued the royal connection by becoming
organist at Hampton Court Palace and he was appointed
musician in ordinary to Queen Victoria.

Laura was born in 1841, the eldest of a family of four girls and a
boy: her mother Selina (née Underwood) was the daughter of a
Suffolk farmer. The family home was at 5 Old Palace Terrace,
Richmond, a most imposing Georgian terrace almost on the
Green. The couple were married at St Matthias, high above
Richmond, in February 1869; the witnesses being her father and
his brother Alfred. Perhaps they compromised their principles by
a church wedding, but doubtless family pressures, particularly on
her side, were very strong. It is difficult to get any clear idea of
Laura and we have been unable to discover any picture of her.
One has the impression, however, of a calm, comforting, sensible

and very healthy woman who was a great support to a husband who could be obsessive and hypochondriacal. The young couple moved out of the family house, briefly to Hampstead and then to a house in St John's Wood, 38 Marlborough Hill.

St John's Wood! The 'stuccoed villas in their bosky gardens' were just then being built and its comfortable verdant early Victorian character, never showy and never mean, was being developed and fostered by the landlords. The area had an unconventional reputation and Harry and Laura were making somewhat of a personal statement by living there. Herbert Spencer, Jane Williams (Shelley), Jane Clairmont (ditto), Madame Blavatsky and Charles Bradlaugh were neighbours (if not near neighbours) as was T.H. Huxley who was for a short time just round the corner from Forman. 'If your Wood continues to be a hot bed for Deists and doubters', someone wrote to Huxley, 'you should get its name changed from St. John's to St. Thomas's'. Harry and Laura moved into 38 Marlborough Hill in September 1870: he was to die there (1917); so was his widow (1932) and it remained the family home until his son left in 1946. The house was built about 1860 and Forman took over the lease from one Richard Farmer. As can be seen, it was an agreeable and spacious house: rather ambitious for a young post office clerk and the early years there were a financial struggle. Later, of course, he expanded to fill it and it seemed a very appropriate home for a senior civil servant. In 1870, it was at the edge of London and not far beyond were the open fields, soon to be built over, that are now Belsize Park and Kilburn. In 1866, the Metropolitan line was built and Forman probably travelled from Marlborough Road Station to the G.P.O. every day. The station is now a Chinese restaurant while the little school shown in the early maps at 24 has swallowed up all the west side of Marlborough Hill and what was once 38 is now the site of the school kitchen of the George Eliot Infants' School. The census of 1871 shows two domestic servants plus Eliot (son) 1 year and Gwendolen (daughter) 4 months. The third child Maurice (named after Mr Bucke) appeared the next year, increasing the financial squeeze, but there were no more, doubtless by design. In 1881, the household was: Harry Buxton Forman 38, Laura 40, Eliot 11, Gwendolen 10 and Maurice 9, together with a cook and a housemaid. Among the neighbours were a wine merchant, a ship owner, a silk

14.   46 Marlborough Hill, the Forman family house, *c.* 1950

merchant, a solicitor and a paper merchant (Yoannes Swaagman of whom we know nothing). The early corner had been turned and a comfortable prosperity set in for the family. Both the sons went to University College School in Gower St which was, by charter, non doctrinal. Eliot was there from 1883–88 and Maurice from 1885–88. Their later careers were initially in the city.

Most of Forman's acquaintances (he had perhaps only two or three friends) were from literary or Post Office circles. Positivist sympathies provide the link with a friend outside the general run, viz. Benjamin (later Sir Benjamin) Ward Richardson. He was a friend who had recommended Bucke for his asylum post in 1876. He was a well known doctor, who discovered a number of minor anaesthetics, one of them by observing that puff-balls (Lycoperdon giganteum) were used to quiet bees in country districts: *he* used them for putting down dogs and other unwanted pets in a special kennel. He believed in sound diet, clean air and abstention from alcohol: his best known book on these themes being *Diseases of modern life* 1876. He was also a minor literary figure and published a three volume novel *The Son of a Star* 1888, on Shimeon bar Kosiba, leader of the second Jewish revolt against the Romans in AD 130 and a less legendary figure now (due to recent discoveries at Masada) than he was then. Forman and Richardson were busy men who saw less of each other than they would have liked. Richardson seems to have treated Forman almost as another doctor in discussing medical matters (he was, after all, the son of one) and certainly as an intellectual and scientific equal.

One has the impression that Forman had one of those watertight compartment minds which kept the various strands of his life equal but separate. One strand – which was later to knit into a rope nearly enough to hang him – was the study of literature. The bachelor reading parties with Bucke and other friends gradually grew into a serious hobby and then a profession. He wrote to Bucke in October 1866 in the course of a nineteen page letter 'so much care is wanted in intercourse with women that our friendship there is to a certain extent damped by anxiety to keep at exactly the right pitch of warmth' and then

> you need not fear my becoming a renegade. . . . For "as long as the heart has passions as long as life has woes" I shall find in my books the most satisfactory of all resources. . . . The fact is that life is not what

it was in the glorious time we had with you, old fellow. Troubles and responsibilities increase on us all, I suppose; but at all events they have made not inconsiderable strides with us of late; and as I love the acquisition of knowledge of whatever sort more than anything else, I choose books for my anaesthesia.

It is an uncharacteristically revealing letter, even for Forman to his best friend. In November 1868, the goal is narrowed 'I have taken to literature, whereby to employ my time not wastefully and to add considerably to my income.'

This coincided with his first appearance in print, an anonymous series of articles published in *Tinsley's Magazine* and elsewhere on 'Our living poets'. Some of them caused a bit of a stir. First D.G. Rossetti dug out the author (1869) 'My Dearest Mother, I believe the author of the Tinsley articles is probably a man named Forman' and then W.M. Rossetti expanded in a letter to a friend (1870),

> The Mr Forman you mention is, I presume, the same who wrote the articles on Gabriel, Christina, & myself in Tinsley's magazine a few months ago. If so, I know that Gabriel met him soon after that at W. B. Scott's (& I rather think elsewhere also); & it appears to me the reasonable thing would be for him to address Gabriel direct, and ask whether and when his calling wd. be convenient.

Thus Forman gradually seeped into the literary scene of which he became a minor, if not greatly loved member. He published additional articles on literary matters (Ibsen, for instance, on whom he wrote four articles in 1872 for which he received no less than £19; or 'Poetry and Music'): his tastes were for poetry and drama; fiction did not attract him at all. From time to time he wrote to authors he had not met, posing erudite questions about points in their books. His first book was *Our Living Poets*, published by Tinsley in 1871, a revision of his periodical articles. But the wolf was not far from the door: as he complained to Bucke 'my style of writing is not what turns well to the making of pots of money' and in November 1871 he even besought a loan

> I want to borrow for a few months £30 or any less sum you can spare. . . . I lost months of writing over my book this year. . . . I have had some of my articles postponed so that the money is outstanding; and to crown it all, my expenses are just about going to have a sudden big increase in the matter of my wife's confinement.

While by December he admitted 'I don't think "Living Poets"

is doing at all briskly. I fear I shall get nothing out of it, though I don't believe Tinsley will *lose* anything.' The literary criticism in *Our Living Poets* is very detailed, very conscientious and rather difficult to read today. The poets are generally taken at their own valuations and the praise lavished on, for instance, William W. Story now reads rather embarrassingly. On the other hand, the account of Christina Rossetti was in advance of its time, and everywhere one notices detailed bibliographical application to find exactly what the poets wrote. It was his relationship with Richard Hengist Horne, one of the subjects of his book, which started him on a fatal path.

Horne was an eccentric poet who achieved momentary renown with his poem *Orion* 1843 – 'tis always morning somewhere in the world'. He directed that *Orion* should be priced at a farthing, which was very good publicity, and he was nicknamed Orion Horne. He disappeared from the English literary scene in 1852 and spent seventeen years in Australia much of it at the Blue Mountain diggings, the most lawless and primitive of the Victorian goldfields. He shed his wife in England, took a mistress, buried his bastard son, became Registrar of Mines at Blue Mountain and commander of the gold escort. He was also a big fish in the little pool of Melbourne's literary world. He gave many lectures, readings and recitals and he published various articles, reprinted *Orion* in Melbourne in 1855, an address to the Electors of Rodney in 1865 (he was not elected), and *The South Sea Sisters, a lyric masque* 1866.

When Alfred, Duke of Edinburgh visited Melbourne in 1867, Horne was commissioned to produce a welcoming *Galatea Secunda: an odaic cantata* for the lucky prince.

> But deem not, Prince, this land of gold
> Will change the impress of that mould
> Nor time nor distance can efface
> Derived from loyal Britain's race
> When thy sea-nymphs shall leave these shores
> Amidst saluting cannon-roars
> Bethink thee – while the silence comes –
> Where thou returnst *we* once had homes.

It was sung, in eight sections, to most prosaic music by one J. Summers. Most of it sounds like the dutiful enthusiasm of a very bad poet laureate and may be assumed to have bored Alfred silly.

He was not, in fact, a very satisfactory Royal Duke: it is said that he caused the royal yacht to anchor round the corner from Melbourne while the local prostitutes were sent on board, thus delaying the whole elaborate welcome by a day. We will meet *Galatea* again.

When Horne returned to England in 1869, he dined out for some time on his muscular tales of wild Australia, but seems to have found it difficult to settle down. He met Forman – perhaps at the home of Westland Marston, another *passé* literary figure – and soon came to depend on him for his practical abilities. Forman saw Horne's remaining books through the press, correcting proofs and selecting from a profusion of unpublished (and mostly unpublishable) manuscripts – 'my Hornucopias' the author coyly called them. Two of these printings were a bit odd. *Sir Featherbright* and *The two Georges* were both without date or imprint though modelled on pieces by Horne regularly published by Newman & Co. (e.g. *King Nihil's Round Table* 1881). Horne's annotations show that both pieces should probably be catalogued (London *c.*1881). Why not give the permanence of print to a piece you like? Well it may tempt you to gild the lily and take the final step into forgery as Forman did with *Galatea Secunda*. This unpublished piece was printed – perhaps in 1881 – with a false Melbourne imprint. There is no evidence that Horne ever saw it: but if he did he probably thought of it as no more than a quaint conceit. Being a Forman production the bibliographical details are very complex. It is only four pages but what a meal he made of it! The first issue (possibly a proof) has a mistake in a quotation from Virgil (hyems for hiems) and the imprint Melbourne, G. Robertson, H. T. Dwight, S. Mullen. In the second issue the quotation was corrected and various minor alterations made: this issue has three states of the imprint, 1) as above, falsely giving the names of Melbourne publishers but without a date, 2) falsely giving the date 1867 but without mentioning publishers apart from 'printed for private circulation' and 3) the same wording of imprint but reset on different size type.

These four varieties may be found, not quite randomly, on four different stocks of paper. One of them is watermarked 1858 and another 1873. All this finicking suggests not only a love of bibliographical complication but also a guilty conscience. Not all the issues print all the lies and if challenged, Forman could produce

the 1873 watermark copies and say 'well of course it was a mere
memento with a watermark to show that it was not really
printed at the date in the imprint: it pleased the poet in his last
years and was not intended to do more.' (Nor did it). On 13
March 1884, Horne died: Forman was left all his books and papers
and was appointed his literary executor. Among other bequests,
he left Gwendolen Forman, the daughter, a tract of land in
Australia but (characteristically) this proved to have been
repossessed long since by the crown, for unpaid rates, and he left
his estranged wife his blankets, linen, chest of drawers and bed
(doubtless he would have made it the second best if he'd had
one). On 12 November 1884, Forman sold many of Horne's books
and some of his own 'removed to make room for the Collection
bequeathed to him': the 377 lots made just over £200, not an
enormous sum but, as representing about half his yearly salary, it
must have been quite acceptable. Lot 108 comprised six Horne
pamphlets, the first mentioned being *Galatea Secunda* '4pp. privately printed Melbourne 1867' (but really London *c.*1881).
Horne was by this time dead and buried, both in fact and literary
reputation, so the lot made a mere two shillings. Nevertheless
Forman had started on his career as a forger and had invented a
new genre of book forgery – that of creative forgery. Book forgers
tend to copy the great books of the past – and tend to get
caught out when the original is compared to the forgery. But
Forman invented a book which had never existed so there was no
tell tale original for comparison. It was not literary forgery –
there is no doubt at all that Horne had written *Galatea* – but it
was bibliographical forgery, creating a book after the event to fill
a persuasive niche. Horne might so easily have had a rare Melbourne print made – so why not supply it? The idea is rather akin
to the Piltdown forgery. The missing link between man and
monkeys is predicted and then conveniently found. In Forman's
case the initial bright idea remained more or less dormant for
some five years.

## 4

## KEATS AND SHELLEY

In the meantime, while getting Horne out of his hair, Forman had found his real literary niche as the editor of Shelley. The poet's posthumous fame was slowly growing, but at the same time, a process of gentrification was setting in. The revolutionary and political poems were being smothered by skylarks. Consider *The Mask of Anarchy*, Shelley's terrifying reply to Peterloo.

> I met Murder on the way –
> He had a mask like Castlereagh –
> Very smooth he looked, yet grim;
> Seven blood-hounds followed him:
>
> All were fat; and well they might
> Be in admirable plight.
> For one by one, and two by two,
> He tossed them human hearts to chew
> Which from his wide cloak he drew.
>
> Next came Fraud, and he had on,
> Like Eldon, an ermined gown;
> His big tears, for he wept well,
> Turned to mill-stones as they fell.
>
> And the little children, who
> Round his feet played to and fro,
> Thinking every tear a gem,
> Had their brains knocked out by them.
>
> Clothed with the Bible, as with light,
> And the shadows of the night,
> Like Sidmouth, next, Hypocrisy
> On a crocodile rode by.
>
> And many more Destructions played
> In this ghastly masquerade,
> All disguised, even to the eyes,
> Like Bishops, lawyers, peers or spies.
>
> Last came Anarchy: he rode
> On a white horse, splashed with blood;
> He was pale even to the lips,
> Like Death in the Apocalypse.

And he wore a kingly crown;
And in his grasp a sceptre shone;
On his brow this mark I saw –
"I AM GOD, AND KING, AND LAW!"

No wonder Leigh Hunt did not dare to print it in 1817.

The standard edition of Shelley from its publication in 1870 was that of William Michael Rossetti. He put *The Mask of Anarchy* among the miscellaneous not the principal poems. His comment on our penultimate verse was

> "Death in the Apocalypse" is not pale, but Death's horse is pale. This might lead us to surmise that the line here should run "Like Death's in the Apocalypse". My impression however, is that there is no fault of print, but a haziness of memory or of phrase on Shelley's part.

This flat-footed comment seems first to have appeared in Rossetti's 1880 edition but is typical of his approach. He had a tendency to print what he thought Shelley should have written, rather than what he did.

Forman wrote to Bucke in September 1875

> I should just about like a chat with you concerning many things but mainly about Shelley who is occupying my whole available stock of mental powers at present. I am bent upon editing a good text of him with just what notes are necessary to support right readings and confound such blasted heresies as several of Rossetti's ... I am buying all the original editions where I can ... I have just given

> | | |
> |---|---|
> | for Rosalind and Helen | 35/- |
> | for Cenci (1st ed.) | 34/- [1988: £2500] |
> | for D. (2nd ed. very dirty) | 9/- |
> | for Prometheus | 25/- |

> and the "Rosalind" fetched the other day under the hammer £2.2s. When I die, mine will likely fetch £5.5s! You will see I am in earnest about editing.

Forman had to win the confidence of Sir Percy Shelley (nominally: but Lady Shelley was the power behind the throne and Sir Percy was more interested in his yacht than his father) and of Richard Garnett who had edited *Relics of Shelley* under their auspices in 1859. Even more difficult, he had to pacify W.M. Rossetti against whose edition he conducts a guerilla warfare throughout his text.

Forman called on Rossetti at Somerset House (he was Assistant Secretary of the Inland Revenue) and successfully proposed an exchange whereby each could print the pieces of which the other (or his publishers) held the copyright. Forman had just bought (for £10) the proof copy of *Laon and Cythna* extensively worked over in manuscript by Shelley to turn it into *The Revolt of Islam*. This demonstration of his combination of scholarly and commercial acumen was the first of many. He remarked at the time that the British Museum would give him an immediate profit and speculated that it would bring £100 or so in America.

In 1911 T.J. Wise offered Forman £1,000 for it *and* his other great Shelley manuscript, the extensively revised *Queen Mab* (Forman's answer was on the lines of 'don't feel I can do without the 2 books, tho' at present I can do without the sum they represent'). After Forman's death, *Laon* was sold in America in 1920, with the rest of his library, when it fetched $1,700. It is now in the Pierpont Morgan library in New York: its current value is difficult to conjecture but might be in the region of £50,000.

In 1876–77 the four stately volumes of Forman's edition of Shelley's poetical works appeared, to be followed in 1880 by four matching volumes of prose works. Forman arranged the texts in order of their original publication and put the unpublished pieces at the end in chronological order (as far as he could establish it). He collated the manuscripts and the printed editions, recording the variants as in a proper variorum edition, and included not only manifestly unpublished drafts but every smallest scrap which Shelley wrote. His edition, constantly tended and revised by himself, became the standard one for the next fifty years. As the editor of the Oxford Standard Authors edition observed in 1904

> For the first time Shelley's text was edited with scientific exactness of method, and with a due regard for the authority of the original editions. It would be difficult indeed to over-estimate the gains which have accrued to lovers of Shelley from the strenuous labours of Mr. Harry Buxton Forman C.B ... his untiring industry in research, his wide bibliographical knowledge and experience, above all his accuracy as invariable as it is minute have combined to make him, in the words of Professor Dowden, "our chief living authority on all that relates to Shelley's writings".

Contemporary reviews were not of course so complimentary and some wondered if Shelley was worth all the trouble. It was only in the course of time, that Forman's editorial methods were publicly vindicated and he is now seen as an important pioneer. Reeves and Turner, the publishers, printed about 1,000 copies and gave Forman 1s a volume sold, netting him about £200. He wrote to Bucke in 1874,

> You see the pay is not very big compared with the work, but the work is what I like doing; & I think the books are more or less of a property. I should feel very well satisfied if I could get quietly along putting a whole series of literary editions forth, and keeping them up to date. I should like to do Keats next (whole works), then Blake (whole works), then Wordsworth.

Forman took great care with the printing and appearance of his book. The contemporary editions are copied even to type facsimiles of the title pages so that nothing, even the original printer's imprint, is omitted. It may have been Forman who hunted up a D.G. Rossetti binding design commission in 1866 for a book on economics but which was never used. The design is appealing and much out of the usual run. It must have been Forman who suggested the twenty-five special copies on Whatman paper in a white rather than blue binding ('they will of course be eagerly taken up: "short issues" always are' he reported eagerly to Bucke) and one copy on vellum. These are, perhaps, expected bibliophilic flourishes. But Forman did not stop there and his further complications milked the book for all it was worth. For instance, Vol. II pp.363–88 of the *Poetical Works* contains *Epipsychidion. Verses addressed to the noble and unfortunate Lady Emilia V(iviani)*. This starts on pp.363–66 with type facsimile reproductions of the half-title and title of the original book, the latter with date 1821. The verso of the half-title, facing the title, has a long explanatory paragraph signed H.B.F. and pp.367–88 reprint the poem, line for line from the original, with footnotes by the editor. Forman simply took the original typesetting, added a leaf at the front:

Epipsychidion
Edited, with notes, by H. Buxton Forman,
and printed for private distribution
MDCCCLXXVI

ran off extra copies on fancy papers, got the thing up in facsimile original boards and had what may have been quite a saleable little

item for the bibliophile market. He produced no less than twelve
of these offprints (and one reprint) all available on different
papers or on vellum giving a total (if you worked it out) of some
thirty-five different variant issues. To cap it all, the illustrations to the *Works* seem also to have had an infusion of
private speculation, and the private prints could be further
diversified by adding plates from the book. Forman wrote to
Bucke in July 1877, sending a parcel of books he had ordered and
(oh yes!)

> I have put in six artist's proofs of the magnificent etching of the
> Cenci done by [W.B.] Scott for me (it is the frontispiece to Vol. II);
> and if you can sell those I shall be pleased, for I have lots of money
> locked up (in a small way) in those and the like: they will be 10s 6d
> each; and don't tell your friends you have six – produce them one by
> one!

Where the publishers (Reeves and Turner) or the printer
(Poetry: W. Bowden; Prose: Ballantine and Hanson) stood in all
this is unclear: weary tolerance for an obvious eccentric perhaps.
Our impression is, that fun though these things may have
seemed to Forman, he was not very successful at selling them.
The few contemporary prices recorded are tiny except for copies
on vellum (£3 or £4, not much more than the cost of the raw
material). This may be because he omitted that essential lure, a
notice of limitation. Obviously the market was not very large for
such trivia: most people would want only the eight volumes, the
more maniac Shelley collectors would want the offprints, and
the only way to stampede them was to print (or pretend to
print) a very few. Some ten years later in 1886, Forman produced
an excellent bibliography of Shelley wherein he described all his
little prints (indeed they supply about 10 per cent of the total)
giving elaborate and suitably small limitations for them, e.g. for
the *Epipsychidion* five copies on vellum: five on Whatman paper
and ten on ordinary paper. These limitations may even be correct: they are certainly far too late for the sales rush. All this may
seem unnecessarily complex: in fact the account given above is a bit
bowdlerized since Forman contrived to make things far more complex than we have indicated above (what about the cancelled preface for instance?). It does show his almost obsessive love of bibliographical creation, of making books without true cause, which was
to lead him into strange woods and pastures new.

His researches into Shelley led him in other directions. He knew that Claire Clairmont, stepsister to Mary Shelley and mother of Byron's Allegra, was still alive in Florence. She died in 1879 and her niece Paola Clairmont inherited her Shelley material. It comprised several notebooks, some 50 letters of Shelley, 110 letters of Mary Shelley, 50 letters of Trelawny and various miscellanea. Forman went swiftly out to Italy and swung into action. His rival was Captain Edward Silsbee, an American who had moved into the house in Florence while Claire was still alive. Silsbee had little ready money and, in the end, Paola preferred Forman's £150 cash to the Captain's promissory notes. Later gossip suggested that the one notebook Silsbee did get, was obtained by promising marriage to Paola, and was never paid for. Henry James transmuted the story to majestic effect in *The Aspern Papers*, changing the locale to Venice as he did so. His unnamed narrator – the 'publishing scoundrel' – is in some sense Silsbee and Forman rolled into one, and Forman did obtain a portrait (not of Shelley, but of Allegra) though he had to wait several years and follow Paola to Vienna to get it.

Forman sifted his purchases and after copying them, sold most of the letters on the open market, many going to C.W. Frederickson of Brooklyn. He can hardly have failed to get his money back on what he sold, while he kept much for himself, including the six best Shelley letters and a manuscript of notes on sculptures in Rome and Florence that he used in editing the *Prose Works*. The whole operation considerably strengthened his hand in the Shelley field while the Trelawny letters he kept to be edited in his retirement.

In the midst of all this, Forman took on another responsibility started by his friendship with Charles Lewes, who introduced him to John Payne. Payne was a solicitor and a 'modern' poet with a taste for languages: at his worst he should qualify for *The Stuffed Owl*, viz.

> Dear, have you forgotten how the roses
> Ran and revelled in the frolic green,
> Broidering the blooming garden-closes
> With their white and red and yellow sheen?

In 1877, Payne held a couple of parties at which he read his newly completed translation of Villon. At the second, it was decided to form a Villon Society to print the translation (some of his

15. Villon Society books, designed by Forman

verse is fairly free). Forman was production manager and turned out a striking volume in a decorated vellum binding, limited to 155 copies, which elicited a letter of congratulation to Forman from the author. Forman kept for himself alpha and omega, the first and the last, being No. 1 in the standard vellum cover and No. 155 in grey boards, but the only copy uncut or (so to speak) on large paper. He inserted some letters from the author and penned a long bibliographical note which ends,

> Payne's letter of delight, opposite, of course refers to the vellum-bound book. The device of dignifying the list of subscribers by the title of the Villon Society was confided by the Devil to me, and was destined to have wider issues for some of which I hope, I have no responsibility.

Quite what this gloomy pronouncement means is not clear, nor when it was written. The Villon Society produced a series of Payne's translations including an *Arabian Nights* and supplements running to thirteen volumes 1882–89. Partly because of the racy subject matters of some of Payne's translations, the Society became quite famous and its productions were eagerly subscribed. Perhaps Forman was writing from a moral point of view and deploring Burton's *Arabian Nights* 1885–88 and the works which followed. The Karma Shastra Society which printed these and several similar oriental translations certainly had a considerable similarity to the Villon Society in being not much more than a list of subscribers. Forman seems, unexpectedly perhaps, to have been very strait-laced. He was horrified when Bucke asked him to order Delepierre's *Un point curieux* which deals, for the first time openly, with homosexuality in Ancient Greece. (Could Bucke have wanted it for Walt Whitman?) The Villon Society books demonstrate Forman's growing confidence as a typographical designer, and his family feeling. Alfred Forman was brought in as secretary to the Villon Society and dealt with much of the administrative work.

The course of Forman's work on Keats started with the same methodical explorations as it had with Shelley. He began with Fanny Brawne's family. Ten years after the death of Keats, she married Louis Lindon, a wine merchant and one of the Secretaries of the Great Exhibition. She died in 1865, and her husband in 1872: their children Herbert and Margaret inherited the books and letters which she had from Keats. There was a long family connection with the Dilke family represented in Forman's time by the aristocratic and autocratic Sir Charles Wentworth Dilke, Bart. On the death of Louis Lindon, he bought various relics including Keats's annotated Shakespeare, and he thought he had bought Keats's letters to Fanny Brawne. It is not clear now, what exactly he had bought: it is quite clear he disliked Fanny Brawne and thought the connection demeaning to the poet and not fit to be exposed in the public prints. He seems to have bought the letters to prevent publication but he quoted one in 1875 and sent extracts to Lord Houghton, who quoted another in 1876 both with slighting references to Fanny. Herbert Lindon was annoyed and, perhaps maintaining that Sir Charles had broken his agreement, got them back. Sir Charles later commented

> I certainly thought I had in a vague way bought (them) for the purpose of preventing publication. They had been long in my possession but the son of Fanny Brawne had claimed them and I, having no written agreement, had found it necessary to give them up – although what I had bought and paid for, unless it was the right to prevent publication, I do not know.

Herbert Lindon, having got the letters back (all but two) sold them to Forman who may well have been the *éminence grise* behind their retrieval. A period of great activity followed as Forman plunged into Keatsian researches: the Lindons helped with stories of their mother; Fanny Llanos (née Keats, the poet's beloved sister) in Madrid and Joseph Severn in Rome all contributed. The latter wrote in September 1877

> Your letter is a joy to me – that you have received thirty-seven letters of Keats to Fanny Brawne astonishes me with delight for they must be even superior to his poetry & will be a boon to the world quite unlooked for – I will maintain your secret & now I proceed to answer all your questions.

Forman had decided to publish, and took significant risks, both financial and moral, in doing so. Sir Charles, from his magisterial pulpit of *The Athenaeum* pronounced an anathema

> If the publication is the greatest impeachment of a woman's sense of womanly delicacy to be found in the history of literature, Mr. Forman's extraordinary preface is no less notable as a sign of the degradation to which the bookmaker has sunk.

Forman's actions have an almost heroic cast when one considers the establishment stacked against him. But he would not be moved and, as with his Shelley, he regarded a pure text as a sacred mission: he was, in this, at least a generation ahead of his time. The preface, of course, does consider the ethics of publication in a guarded way but in his letter to Fanny Llanos soon afterwards, he defends his choice with the fire of conviction.

> I counselled and took part in the publication of those to me sacred letters on full consideration, and with the knowledge that I should have many people hotly against me . . . Those who have thought less about the matter than it has been my duty and my necessity to do, have not understood that this question of publishing your brother's letters was not one as between speech and silence, but as between perfect speech and imperfect speech; and in deciding for perfect speech I regarded the matter not only from posterity's point of view. I asked myself – 'If Keats had to choose between total oblivion and giving his whole story to posterity, which would he have chosen?' And I could not bring myself to answer but that he would *not* have chosen oblivion. Then I looked at all we had been told about him, and I saw only half the story, inaccurate in many particulars, and *not* – a thousand times *not* portraying the man's soul as it was. These letters, to my mind, set him right with posterity.

Dilke's grandfather, the friend of Keats, had not liked Fanny and was probably jealous of her. Our Dilke was devoted to his grandfather and determined to maintain his viewpoint. He may also have been particularly hostile to any freedom of expression in sexual matters, because his own position was not spotless. In 1885 he was cited in a sensational divorce and his political career was ruined. He was probably not guilty as charged, but there was some substance in the accusations. In 1890, in connection with Forman's new edition of the love letters, he revealed that he had held some of them back, and he tried to use these unseen words to convert Forman to his view of Fanny. Forman was, if he was anything, a devoted and even a fanatical editor, and he was in a most difficult position. If he moved too abruptly he would frighten Sir Charles away. He did his best

> My view of what I had to do in this matter goes beyond the aggregation of bare facts. I think the first duty in doing that kind of work is to get at the characters of the set of people concerned. Of the character of Fanny Brawne, both as a girl and as wife and mother, I formed a definite conception, from such documents and statements as were accessible to me . . . I am not obstinately bent on keeping

that conception; but as far as I have gone with fresh evidence, my view remains unchanged; and I think this revised introduction to the Letters expresses that view adequately, without making the lady out a saint or even a heroine. The passage you have been kind enough to send me at the close of your letter of the 2nd instant fits in with my conception of her character; but I cannot say what I might get to think if I saw the letters you mention in their entirety. At present I am doing nothing fresh about Keats; but if, for example, I had to write his life, I should feel compelled to ask for a sight of those letters, in order to give myself a chance of revising the fundamental conception of her character.

Alas he never saw the letters and late in life Sir Charles burnt them as he thought they contained things which should not be seen by anyone. Forman's failure was thus visited on us all. He did, however, gain access to most of the other Keats material; Sir Charles packed him off with a cab full of it.

The *Letters of John Keats to Fanny Brawne* 1878 shows Forman in a fine light, particularly with the benefit of over a century's hindsight. However, with the physical form of the book, he was up to his usual tricks. The book was at his risk, and he directed all the details. There is an elegant left-lining title page in italic capitals and the book is a fine early example of the 'aesthetic' taste in book design. There are three illustrations, one being an engraving by W.B. Scott after the celebrated drawing by Severn of Keats on his death bed, and another, a fine facsimile letter by G.F. Tupper, the acknowledged master of the craft. Not only was there an American issue printed from stereos, but also fifty copies on large paper, fifty copies on Whatman paper, two on pink paper, two on vellum, single copies on brown, yellow, blue, green and mixed coloured papers; and four different settings of the title, one limited to six copies. The creativity which found an outlet in all these variants was later to take a different path.

When Forman bought manuscripts, he took care, if he could, to buy the copyright as well (the necessary distinction between ownership of a manuscript and ownership of the right to print from it are often confused, they are quite separate and the first does not imply the second). Just before publication of the *Letters* Forman sold the letters themselves to F.S. Ellis, the well known antiquarian bookseller and publisher and a friend for many years, but he retained the copyright and two letters for himself. It was probably Ellis who tried (rather unsuccessfully) to sell them piece by piece at auction in 1885: it was this sale that prompted Oscar Wilde's indignant sonnet.

> These are the letters which Endymion wrote
> To one he loved in secret and apart
> And now the brawlers of the auction mart
> Bargain and bid for each poor blotted note . . .

But better that than silence.

In 1874, Forman was on £420 a year at the Post Office and his major advancement there was still to come. He had three children aged 4, 3 and 2. In June the two elder children had to go to Margate with a nurse for three months – 'this Margate business will cost like hell' – and in October he edited the Civil Service Review for ten weeks after contributing largely in the years before. Amid distractions like these, he produced the Shelley and Keats we have just considered and as well, started on his serious climb up the Post Office ladder. One feels that he paid for this intense application: 'Possibly so much rectitude in observing the letter of the law in matters of daily routine, required, psychologically speaking, release in another direction', as Nick Jenkins remarks of Warrant Officer Diplock in *The Soldier's Art*.

Forman's literary prestige increased, but he seemed to form no very warm friendships. He corresponded with D.G. Rossetti in 1880–81 about points in Keats, but despite their earlier acquaintance there was no great warmth in the exchange. His Swinburne correspondence, such as survives, has the same rather lifeless quality, only enlivened by the poet's private nickname for him – Fuxton Bor(e)man. Letters to Bucke plunge us back into real life.

> I am busier than ever, office work heavy – seven to ten hours still work a day – work in the train and at home – two or three hours in the evening. Health and spirits good – and two new editions of Shelley just ready – one the 4 poetry vols reprinted with many changes in detail but substantially the same book – the other 2 vols crown 8vo simple text of every scrap of verse & no notes. Keats going on same time but slowly. [May 1882]

The four volume Keats of 1883 was modelled on the Shelley being half poetry and half prose. It appeared to considerable applause: Edmund Gosse, for instance, reviewed it in *The Academy*

> In pure bibliography, then, Mr. Forman is a passed master; nay more, he has actually invented a method of arranging editorial material which is apparently the best known. His severest critics have never assailed his general accuracy; and I must confess that his scrupulous examination of documents, his taste in typography, his attention to the mint and anise and cummin of book-production, are delightful to me, and that he gives me not a note or an appendix too many.

Though, as is the way with reviewers, he then proceeds to suggest improvements. Forman replied to the review in generally genial tone, deflecting most of the criticism, but sounding a stern warning on textual details 'the missing lines and words and stops alluded to have not been dropped out by me; and I should wish to see MS. authority before making any of the changes suggested.'

A later letter to Bucke looks forward to the time they can talk on the telephone and even 'be able to see each other's faces across the Atlantic under some fresh combination not yet sketched out' (December 1883: perhaps he had been reading Robida's *Vingtième Siècle* 1883 in which television is predicted). In 1884, he wasted a good deal of valuable time playing the comparatively new game of lawn tennis, and in 1886 he told Bucke proudly that Eliot, by then 16 years old, was lawn tennis champion at his school. His editorial reputation was certainly riding high after Keats and Shelley and in 1885 John Murray vainly offered him £525 to edit Byron. However, instead of scaling new heights, he got closely involved with a rising young commodity broker, Thomas James Wise.

# WISE'S CHILDHOOD

Thomas James Wise was a Londoner – though actually born at Gravesend in Kent – and like many Londoners he kept to his own small area of the capital all his life. Thomas Wise, his grandfather, was born in Stepney in 1793 and lived most of his life there or in surrounding districts. He was a moderately prosperous silversmith in a small firm in Clerkenwell, the centre of the London watchmaking and jewellery trades. He was in partnership with Joshua Butler who founded the business. They specialized in small silverware, particularly pencil cases, and tortoiseshell ware. He may have lived over the business to start with, but by the time we catch up with him he had moved away to Barnsbury, a little to the north; it was a common pattern. He married Martha Butler, presumably Joshua's daughter, in 1826 and three sons followed: Thomas 1829, Joshua 1830 and George 1832. We find them in Barnsbury, a sub division of Islington, in the 1840s and it seems likely that their family house at No. 7 Richmond Terrace (later to become 60 Richmond Road) was bought new-built in 1841–42. There were sphinxes on either side of the door, presumably inspired by the contemporary disturbances in Egypt and the allied campaign which resulted in the capture of Acre from Ibrahim Pasha in 1840. Apart from a brief flirtation with Gravesend, Thomas and Martha lived at Richmond Terrace until their deaths some forty years later.

Gravesend was an ancient seaport which in the 1840s and 1850s was rapidly transformed into a seaside resort for millions of Londoners. They arrived by steamboat down the Thames and, despite Gravesend's resident population of 16,000 or 17,000, it seemed to support a million trippers a year by 1850. There were three piers, several bathing establishments, bathing machines, libraries, a theatre, numerous shops and pleasure gardens. The coming of the railways transferred much of the trade further east: but the town remained a favourite for a Cockney day out until the 1900s.

Gravesend is still an appealing spot, with the little church-topped mound looking down on Gravesend reach and with all the

16. Gravesend from the river, an engraving *c.* 1840

maritime bustle, now banished from further up river. An estate agent, writing in 1853 noted that it 'Is the nearest place to London where sea baths can be procured. The town and its vicinity are crowded with holiday-makers from the metropolis during the summer', but he added *'Not a place for fashionables'* (his italics). Probably the family had often holidayed at Gravesend and in 1854 the parents took a house at 37 Harmer Street, two rows of rather congested houses leading down to Royal Terrace Pier. Just before Christmas in 1854, Wise senior added a codicil to his will which favoured his second son Joshua as against his elder son Thomas (George had died in infancy). In 1855, the family moved back to Barnsbury and Richmond Terrace. Perhaps one winter had shown them that seaside attractions had a different complexion in wind and rain and snow (the streets were not to be effectively paved and lighted for some years yet).

In 1858, Thomas Wise, then aged 30, went up from Islington to Bury in Lancashire to marry Julia Victoria Dauncey aged 21. She was born at Uley near Dursley in Gloucestershire and was the daughter of a clothier. The marriage was on 9 December and by April 1859 the couple was established at 52 Wrotham Road, Gravesend, where the first child, our Thomas James, was born on 7 October. The house is quite a spacious three storey semi, built in 1852–53 on the main road south out of the town which traverses the North Downs and goes on to Wrotham Heath.

Again Gravesend did not suit the Wises and the young couple rapidly returned to Islington, giving up Wrotham Road in early 1860. Which address they moved to, we do not know, but by 1862 they had moved again and were at 37 Devonshire Road, Islington. This is a street of cramped terraced houses with minute gardens, which runs north from Seven Sisters Road, and is sandwiched with several others between Holloway Road in the west and Hornsey Road in the east. Holloway Road is the beginning of the old Great North Road out of London and the Mother Red Cap Inn was the halfway house between London and Highgate. Hornsey Road had only three houses in it in 1810 and Seven Sisters was not built until about 1830. The space between these main roads was filled with terrifying rapidity in the 1850s and 1860s when the green fields of Islington were swept away for ever.

Islington was mostly a mixture of lower paid white collar

17.   The Caledonian Road, near Wise's home, *c.* 1912

workers and better paid artisans, the two classes filling the streets round Devonshire Road. As an estate agent commented in 1853, 'On the whole Islington may be considered, *for unpretending persons*, a most respectable suburb. Its population in 1851 was 95,000; its assessment to the Income Tax 309,629L; and its number of acres 3,050, *too much built over.*' The real squash was yet to come: the population went up by fairly steady leaps to about 320,000 in 1891, about 100 head an acre. It is now down to about 60, though seen today you would not suppose that it could ever have been more crowded. Thomas Wise, the father, presumably followed in his father's footsteps since he described himself on his first son's birth certificate as a manufacturing jeweller: in 1862, when his second son George was born, he was a pencil-case maker, which suggests something of a decline, and in 1864 with the arrival of Henry Dauncey he baffles enquiry by calling himself 'independent'.

The first three sons were all baptised by the Revd Ebenezer Davies at the Caledonian Chapel, Islington. This was a non-denominational, evangelical, low church foundation, described in the directories as Congregational. It was built in 1851, an elaborate affair by Andrew Trimin, with a school room beneath. It was one of many valiant attempts to Christianize the inner city areas, a task at which the Church of England itself could hardly ever succeed, so closely was it associated with the ruling classes. The Caledonian Chapel was underfunded and overbuilt and spent most of its life with a millstone of debt round its neck. The Revd Davies seems to have been a lively character; ex. London Missionary Society, he wrote several books including *American Scenes and Christian Slavery* 1849 and *The "Mission House Letter"* 1855, the latter concerning an epic row over an intercepted pornographic letter alleged to be from him to his wife. The Chapel, as part of its outreach work, had various social clubs, lectures and so on and probably the Wise boys joined in. The Chapel is a good long way from Devonshire Road – perhaps half an hour's walk or so through hard and dusty streets – but is very near the grandparents in Barnsbury so we may well be seeing their influence at work.

In about 1865, the family moved again to 127 Devonshire Road and sometime after this, family troubles became apparent. Behind the rigid grid of census returns and rate books, one can

J. Vivian Arch[t].

M.J. Starling Del. et Sculp.

18.   The Caledonian Chapel, a lithograph, c. 1851

discern unhappy stirrings: but exactly what happened and why, is now impossible to say. The 1871 census shows the household at 127 Devonshire Road as consisting of Thomas Wise aged 42 – now a tobacconist – and his two sons, Thomas aged 11 and Henry aged 7. There is no wife, no son George (then aged 9) and there are no servants. This sounds an odd household: but in 1872 a new son Herbert arrived and his birth is registered by his mother in the normal way: his father is still a tobacconist.

The neighbours in 1871 included a journeyman coach trimmer, a compositor, and (moving on to the Wise stratum) a wine merchant's clerk and a poulterer's clerk. In fact skilled labourers, a coach trimmer might well be a good example, were often better off than the lower ranks of clerks, though they were below them socially.

We do not know how Thomas James was educated. In later life he was dismissive of biographical enquiries, 'All that's of interest about me is in my books. My life is in the bibliographies I've compiled and the books I've collected. The rest doesn't matter to anyone' he told Wilfred Partington, his biographer. In *Who's Who* he described himself as educated privately, on another occasion he wrongly claimed the City of London School and his brother said he had delicate health so he was educated at home. It seems improbable that he spent all that time at home and there were schools within reach if not very grand ones. St Mark's National & Infant School for teaching the poor, for instance, opened in 1863 in Tollington Park, only minutes from Devonshire Road. Thomas James may have just caught an early School Board of London, one of those lighthouses or beacons of the future which obtained such an encomium from Sherlock Holmes. If he did not, it seems very probable that his brothers did: one was open in Cottenham Road, the next street to Devonshire by 1877 and perhaps earlier.

On 4 October 1873, the final child was born, a little girl who lived only a month. Her birth was not registered until two days after her death, which may only indicate ill health. Officially she had no name (the family Bible calls her Julia after her supposed mother) and she was described as 'Daughter of Thomas Wise Tobacconist', without mention of the mother. By 1875 Thomas James was 16 and had started his commercial career as a clerk with Herman Rubeck & Co. This modest firm of merchants,

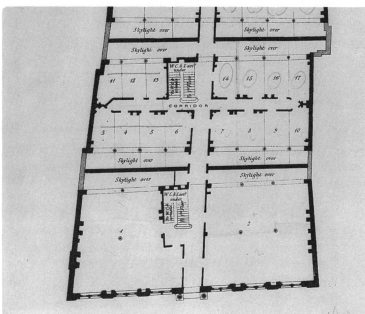

19.   9 Mincing Lane, a lithograph, *c.* 1860

successors to F. J. Price & Co of 12 Little Tower Street, were at 14 Mincing Lane in the centre of the London produce (we would now say commodity) trade.

Here was sold, either by auction or private treaty, a dazzling variety of goods: tea, coffee, cocoa, drugs, sugar, corn, pepper, ginger and other spices, mother of pearl, shellac, copra, hemp, sago, jute, essential oils for perfumery, frankincense, myrrh, honey, ivory, leather and even oriental curios. In their early years, we do not know what corner of this market Rubecks worked. They may have specialized by country – many German emigrés were in the East India trade – or by commodity. Until 1877 they were called simply 'merchants', after that, the designation was 'wholesale druggist' which would have included a vast range of animal, vegetable and mineral products – frankincense and myrrh for instance but not gold – most having a rather high unit value.

There were regular public drug sales at the London Commercial Sale Rooms. None of the lots was actually on the premises; they were to be viewed at the merchants' and brokers' offices all round about. Many of these were squeezed into the old courts and houses from which the original residents had been forced out: but purpose built office blocks were beginning to appear. These had a dignified and fashionable exterior with a flexible interior; basically lots of little boxes which could be run together if necessary. A reminiscence of many years later sets the scene,

high sloping desks, brass-railed to hold the books, tall stools graduated according to strict protocol, plain wooden seats for juniors, ditto but with rail backs for invoice clerks, and the same but with padded seats for senior clerks. The head clerk sat loftily aloof on a high Dominie style desk keeping vigil on the staff – not least on the sample room boys, always a mischievous lot, and of course a wary eye on the door to stimulate everyone into commendable activity should a partner walk in. Office boys nowadays are a vanished race – but what old office could do without them? The weary years from, say, 13 to 18, collecting and delivering letters, samples, copying, making tea, buying the head clerk his week-end kippers from Leadenhall Market and stacking up at night in the safe the multitude of books and ledgers. The hours – 9.30 a.m. to 6.30 p.m. except on mail nights when it could be 9 p.m. and a dash to the G.P.O. to catch the mail. Saturdays 9.30 a.m. to 3 o'clock. The wages – well, pre-1914 5s. a week would be considered reasonable, and by diligence to his master's affairs he would rise to 25s. or 30s. as a clerk, at which stage in his career top hats and stiff white collars and cuffs were *de rigeur* in many offices. Thereafter the sky was the limit and, happy to relate, a number reached it, by which time they had acquired a really impressive knowledge of contract, documents, arbitration and, of course, a note for market movements and crops which alone put them in a class apart from the "inside" office man. Appraisal of the quality of the commodities handled was vital and the skill with which the old Mincing Lane "hand" could detect inferiority, or value quality accurately was really impressive.

Wise started as one of those office boys. However, he was sacked after six months and only the remonstrances of his father caused Mr Rubeck to take him on again. Times were hard: Britain reached its imperial economic peak in about 1870: in 1873 exports fell, prices fell, there was a sharp decline into the great depression. Confidence was badly affected and the illusion of inevitable economic progress was broken. Wise weathered the storm and stayed on at Rubecks and in due course, as we shall see, acquired his top hat. In the meantime, Thomas Wise senior, his grandfather, died, aged 84, in 1878, leaving quite an elaborate will in which Thomas (Wise's father) and Joshua the two surviving sons, were each left annuities of £50 a year from the estate while their mother was still alive: in addition by the Gravesend codicil, Joshua was given 18 Albion Grove, Islington outright.

Perhaps as a result of the legacy, Thomas and the boys left Devonshire Road in the same year, 1878. We do not know where they went, though Thomas James Wise was to give his address as 412 Camden Road in 1880. By 1879 and perhaps earlier, Thomas James was attending the Camden Road Baptist Church, rather than the Chapel where he was baptised. The Church is much nearer Devonshire Road – the walk is less than half that to the Caledonian Road Chapel. Perhaps also the death of his grandfather had broken a link. The Church, by C.G. Searle, built in 1854, still stands, though the towers lost first one pinnacle then the other, which gives the architecture a rather odd truncated look. Standing beside the Church today on the corner of Camden Road and Hilldrop Road it requires a terrific effort to imagine the sunken way of hedges, elms and ditches winding up to Highgate Hill which the latter was only five or six generations ago. William Hone described it in 1825 as

well known to every botanizing perambulator on the west side of
London . . . The wild onion, wounds-wort wake robin and abundance
of other simples, lovely in their form and of high medicinal repute in
our old herbals and receipt books take root and seed and flower here in
great variety. How long beneath the tall elms and pollard oaks and
the luxuriant beauties on the banks, the infirm may be suffered to
seek health and the healthy to recreate, who shall say? Spoilers are
abroad.

Hone was making a political point, but still . . . all the lane yields
now is a little moss (Bryum argentium) between the paving slabs
and a few tufts of Poa annua, the commonest grass in the world.

The Church had a flourishing young people's group which produced a manuscript magazine *Pen and Pencil* of which volumes 1,
4, 5 and 6 have survived. Everyone contributed under pseudo-
nyms, though these were clearly transparent. Thomas James
Wise was 'Le Sage', and in the first volume (May–July 1879) he
contributed a vast poem *Isandula* of 55 stanzas.

> Who loves to hear the war-blast
> Re-echoing loud and shrill,
> Pealing the brazen death-notes
> Which make the bosom thrill.
>
> Long she reigns triumphant
> The mistress of the world
> Long as her stainless banner
> Floats for the night unfurl'd.
>
> Long as the nations round her
> Gaze at her form and see
> That the weak are strong when oppressed by wrong
> That the slave is for ever free.

He defended his poem against 'Eno' who claimed it contained
many words misspelt: 'I have looked through it and can find but
*one*.' He also posed the question 'Is it right for Christians to go
to the Theatre?' and received various opinions on the point. The
magazine is ambitious and quite impressive. It has printed rules
and printed titles and a half calf binding, both by William Fullford of 251 Pentonville Road, a local printer and binder we shall
meet again.

The last surviving volumes of *Pen and Pencil* belong to 1880.
The 'Mutual Improvement Society' as the contributors called
themselves was clearly in full swing, holding, for example, an
evening of impromptu speaking in February. Le Sage contrib-

uted a water colour of parrots (T.J. Wise watercolours have yet
to appear on the collector's horizon) and a most interesting long
essay on poetry. This quotes with immense approval Harry Buxton Forman (unattributed, but from the introduction to *Our
Living Poets* 1871). Wise had obviously just read the book and it
had made a great impact: he expounds Forman's views as the
complete key to the understanding of poetry. Wise and Forman
were to have a strange and fluctuating relationship, but on the
literary side Wise was often the disciple. 'I was somewhat
amused', he wrote to Forman in 1894, 'at your saying that *with*
your corrections, my par[agraph]s were passable as your own. It's
perfectly true: because, as I've told you, I learned Bibliography
from your eight Vols. of Shelley, & took you as my model when I
commenced to try & write myself. How then could I fail to echo
you!' Two other points can be gleaned from the membership list
of *Pen and Pencil*: first that it includes Wise's lifelong friend W.
B. Slater at 264 Camden Road, second that Wise's address is
given at 412 Camden Road, as from April 1880.

The census of 1881 shows Thomas senior and the boys at 3
Thornhill Grove. This is just two streets from Thomas James'
widowed grandmother in Richmond Terrace, and a slight step up
in the world. The house is a bit larger and the area was (and is) a
little more salubrious. To remind outselves how much the London streets have changed since then, we can turn to Edmund
Gosse's *Father and Son*. Edmund lived in Huntingdon Street,
about one minute's walk from Thornhill Crescent, from 1854 to
1857. He described life in another motherless Islington house
when he was eight and his father just widowed.

> When the milkman went his rounds in our grey street, with his
> eldritch scream over the top of each set of area railings, it seemed as
> though he would never disappear again. There was no past and no
> future for me, and the present felt as though it were sealed up in a
> Leyden jar. Even my dreams were interminable, and hung stationary
> from the nightly sky.
>
> At this time, the street was my theatre, and I spent long periods,
> as I have said, leaning against the window. I feel now the coldness of
> the pane, and the feverish heat that was produced, by contrast, in
> the orbit round the eye. Now and then amusing things happened.
> The onion-man was a joy long waited for. This worthy was a tall and
> bony Jersey protestant with a raucous voice, who strode up our
> street several times a week, carrying a yoke across his shoulders, from

the ends of which hung ropes of onions. He used to shout, at abrupt intervals, in a tone which might wake the dead:

Here's your rope. . .
To hang the Pope. . .
And a penn'orth of cheese to choke him.

The cheese appeared to be legendary; he sold only onions. My Father did not eat onions, but he encouraged this terrible fellow, with his wild eyes and long strips of hair, because of his 'Godly attitude towards the Papacy,' and I used to watch him dart out of the front door, present his penny, and retire, graciously waving back the proffered onion. On the other hand, my Father did not approve of a fat sailor, who was a constant passer-by. This man, who was probably crazed, used to walk very slowly up the centre of our street, vociferating with the voice of a bull,

Wa-a-atch and pray-hay!
Night and day-hay!

This melancholy admonition was the entire business of his life. He did nothing at all but walk up and down the streets of Islington exhorting the inhabitants to watch and pray. I do not recollect that this sailor-man stopped to collect pennies, and my impression is that he was, after his fashion, a volunteer evangelist.

The tragedy of Mr. Punch was another, and a still greater delight. I was never allowed to go out into the street to mingle with the little crowd which gathered under the stage, and as I was extremely near-sighted, the impression I received was vague. But when, by happy chance, the show stopped opposite our door, I saw enough of that ancient drama to be thrilled with terror and delight. I was much affected by the internal troubles of the Punch family; I thought that with a little more tact on the part of Mrs. Punch and some restraint held over her temper, naturally violent, by Mr. Punch, a great deal of this sad misunderstanding may have been prevented. . . .

Another joy, in a lighter key, was watching a fantastic old man who came slowly up the street, hung about with drums and flutes and kites and coloured balls, and bearing over his shoulder a great sack. Children and servant-girls used to bolt up out of areas, and chaffer with this gaudy person, who would presently trudge on, always repeating the same set of words –

Here's your toys
For girls and boys,
For bits of brass
And broken glass,

(these four lines being spoken in a breathless hurry)

A penny or a vial-bottell . . .

(this being drawled out in an endless wail)

. . . But on summer evenings I used to drag my Father out, taking the initiative myself, stamping in playful impatience at his irresolution, fetching his hat and stick, and waiting. We used to sally forth at last together hand in hand, descending the Caledonian Road, with all its shops, as far as Mother Shipton, or else winding among the semi-genteel squares and terraces westward by Copenhagen Street, or, best of all, mounting to the Regent's Canal, where we paused to lean over the bridge and watch flotillas of ducks steer under us, or little white dogs dash, impotently furious, from stem to stern of the great, lazy barges painted in a crude vehemence of vermilion and azure.

In later years, Thomas James Wise became a close acquaintance who was to exchange hundreds of letters with Gosse. He collected every one of Gosse's books; did he ever read *Father and Son* and ponder their Islington childhood? His Islington childhood must have been as shadowed as that of Edmund Gosse. The census of 1881 shows an all-male establishment at 3 Thornhill Grove, comprising:

| | | |
|---|---|---|
| Thomas Wise | 53 | Annuitant |
| Thomas J. Wise | 21 | Clerk Colonial trade |
| George J. Wise | 19 | Clerk House agents |
| Henry D. Wise | 17 | Clerk Silk brokers |
| Herbert A. Wise | 8 | Scholar |

George Wise has returned to the nest, but there is still no Julia. She is shown as the head of an all female household at 418 Camden Road and appears to be keeping a boarding house with two lodgers and (unlike her husband) two servants.

We have no evidence how long ago the split had occurred, though this second census does strongly suggest that the absence of a wife and mother in 1871 was not some isolated glitch in the system. Formal divorce was in those days an almost insuperable barrier for people of the class of Thomas James Wise's parents: yet it seems clear they were divorced in practice. One wonders whether the later children were not in fact Thomas James's half siblings and whether his father had a mistress and he an unofficial stepmother.

Wise was very sparing of family reminiscence (as we see now for good reason) but he did allow recollection of bedside readings to his invalid mother, who developed a partiality to Shelley. He

may have taken her side in the family disruption and when he
described his father (*de mortuis*) as 'a quiet old-fashioned Christian man, and death had no terrors for him' we may suspect that
he was describing what he wanted rather than what he got. The
fact that Wise senior died (at least partly) from cirrhosis of the
liver also seems a bit out of key with this pious epitaph. Thomas
James must have had early training at concocting a tale and
improving the lie of the ball. The calm and authoritative entries
in the family Bible conceal a good deal which we can never know.
The census enumerators had to record everyone who slept in the
house on the night of Sunday 3 April and there could be penal-
ties for inaccuracy: perhaps a woman moved out for the night.

Julia Wise died at 412 Camden Road on 9 May 1881 of con-
sumption and Thomas Wise married Hannah Waldock the very
next year. 412 Camden Road is the address Thomas James gave
at the Church Youth Club in 1880 and three doors from the
house his mother was in at the census. The houses have been
demolished but were at the northern end of the road, very near
the Baptist Church and not far from the old habitation in
Devonshire Road. Judging by the survivors, they were fairly
substantial stucco houses with quite imposing porticoes in a
wide and busy street. But why two addresses? Confusion is worse
confounded by the Islington directory for 1882 (but which
would normally describe the situation for the year preceding)
which for that year (and that year only) shows a solitary 'Mrs.
Wise' at 38 Freeling Street which is very near Thornhill
Crescent. Unfortunately the Islington rate books which might
have clarified all these addresses have been thoroughly weeded
and still more unfortunately, the only volumes retained are
those for each decade, 1870, 1880 and so on. As these more or less
coincide with the censuses they are little help in shedding light
on the dwellers in these mean streets.

Thomas Wise senior was present at his wife's death, and at
that of his mother which took place eight months later in the
house she had lived in for many years. As we have already
remarked, he married Hannah Waldock in 1882; it may be in that
year that he moved back to 127 Devonshire Road. His eldest son,
our Thomas James, accompanied him and presumably young Herbert, then aged 10. The area was just about respectable, but only
just. About five minutes walk up Seven Sisters Road was Camp-

bell Street, one of the most notorious slums in London: 'broken windows, dirty curtains, doors open, a litter of paper, old meat tins, heads of fish and stalks of vegetables. It is a street where thieves and prostitutes congregate', Booth described it some years later. Thomas James Wise was beginning to make his way in the world and he made the best of things. He had a room fitted out as a library by the local Harrods – Jones Bros of Holloway – and he set out to scale the peaks of the literary world.

# THE TWO FORGERS MEET

We have mentioned Wise admiring Forman from afar in his manuscript magazine *Pen and Pencil*. Forman was becoming a significant figure in the literary world; by contrast, Wise was still unknown. He had produced his first book, printed – like the title pages of *Pen and Pencil* – by Fullford of King's Cross. It was that most predictable production for an apprentice littérateur, an edition of his own *Verses*. The only unpredictable thing was the bibliographical complexity. There seem to be two issues of which the first (1882) exists on ordinary paper, lavender-coloured paper (five copies) and vellum (three copies) while the second (1883) exists on large paper (five copies) and vellum: one might infer an ordinary paper 1883 but none has yet been reported. In all this, of course, Wise was simply apeing Forman: witness, for example the *Letters to Fanny Brawne* referred to above.

*Verses* must have caused a stir among the Camden Road Mutual Improvement Society, not so much the poetry

> Full many a time and oft my soul
> Has nursed upon its faltering breast,
> The light of some long cherished goal,
> Yet vainly clutched the wished-for rest!
> Oft bursting on the heart's cold strand
> Hope's wave has borne a gladder ray;
> But full as oft my eager hand,
> Missing the wave, clasped but the spray!

but getting it printed. One copy was inscribed to a fellow member of the society and Wise's lifelong crony 'Walter B. Slater, with his friend's love. Xmas/82'. An inscription in one of his later productions (1886) reads 'To my dearest friend from his "Jonathan" ': was Slater the David? and did their friendship become more intimate than society would allow?

In 1882, Wise made his first sighting shot at Forman and enquired about his Shelley bibliography: he was told in formal terms that this 'will be published before long'. In the same year Wise joined the Browning Society. This had been formed by F.J. Furnivall in 1881. Furnivall, a celebrated oarsman, eccentric and philologist was a great founder of literary societies: the Browning was his fifth or sixth. In the same year he got involved in a furious row with Swinburne, partly about Shakespeare. A.C.S. called him an incomparable blackguard and a dunghill dog whose name 'it is degrading for a gentleman to pronounce, to transcribe, or to remember'; Furnivall published a pamphlet in which Swinburne was turned into Anglo-Saxon as Pigsbrook; A.C.S. retaliated with Latin, Brothelsbank (rather insecurely derived from Fornicis + vallum) for Furnivall; Browning to his great dismay was partly drawn into this mayhem. The Browning Society survived and by the end of 1881 had produced two publications, both printed by Clay and Taylor of Bungay, a firm we shall meet again. Forman was a founder member and may have recommended Clays.

Browning himself was not overly enthusiastic about a society dedicated to himself.

> The Browning Society, I need not say, as well as Browning himself, are fair game to criticism. I had no more to do with the founding of it than the babe unborn; and, as Wilkes was no Wilkeite, I am quite other than a Browningite

he wrote in 1882.

Wise, now having a sort of official position *vis à vis* Browning proceeded to pester him with naive questions about his poetry, supposedly submitted by members of the society, but probably composed by Wise. Again Wise was imitating Forman, but with much less finesse: the latter had written to Browning in March 1881 about 'Ah, did you once see Shelley plain' and got an excellent reply. Wise was clearly something of an Ampelopsis, as defined by Lord Peter Wimsey. 'Suburban plant that climbs by suction. *You* know – first year, tender little shoots – second year, fine show – next year, all over the shop.'

In December 1885, Forman wrote Furnivall a very prescient letter warning him of Wise.

> I do not think any printing ought to be put in hand without very serious consideration and the consent of the Committee. . . . when we have a full list of members representing a ponderable revenue, it will be time enough to launch out in large printing undertakings. I hope that, in annotating these articles, Mr. Wise will confine himself to correcting misstatements of fact in the simplest manner and avoid all such expletives as 'gross blunder' 'unpardonable inaccuracy' &c &c.

Wise eventually acquired the letter and may have smiled grimly to himself as he catalogued it: 'an A.L.S. of four pages quarto from H. Buxton Forman to Dr. F. J. Furnivall'. He misfiled it in a Shelley Society publication, supposing or pretending that this was the society to which it referred.

In 1886 the Browning Society employed the London branch of Clays to print a facsimile of Browning's rare early work *Pauline* 1838 and Wise was the editor. However, the author's reaction was not very favourable and the society printed little else apart from transactions. Clearly Forman's warning must have been heeded. The irrepressible Furnivall then founded yet another society. 'I resolved to found the Shelley Society – on the hill between Hendon and Hampstead on Sunday Dec. 6 about 1.30 p.m.' he declared.

> By Jove, I will; he was my father's friend!
> Thus Dr. Furnivall, in choice blank verse
> Replied when he was asked by Mr. Sweet. . .
> Why do not you a new communion found –
> "Shelley Society" might be the name –
> Where men might worry over Shelley's bones?
> By Jove, I will; he was my father's friend,
> Said Furnivall: and lo! the thing was done

was Andrew Lang's version of the same thing, in a spirited piece of blank verse (later pirated by Wise and Forman). The first formal meeting took place on 10 March 1886 at University College London. Shaw was present and commented many years afterwards on

> the pious old ladies whose subscriptions kept the Societies going. They followed him [Furnivall] into the Shelley Society in all inno-cence; and when I, at the first meeting in the lecture theatre of University College, announced that as a good Shelleyan I was a Social-ist, an Atheist and a Vegetarian, two of them resigned on the spot.

Behind the scenes things were moving with great speed. On 7 January 1886, Wise wrote to Forman

> Herewith I send you the short "Introduction" which I have prepared for the reprint of *Adonais*. I shewed it last evening to Dr. Furnivall, who approved of it in all ways, with this exception. . . By the way Dr. Furnivall told me that you had very kindly expressed your willingness to shew me sundry of your Shelley treasures. I need hardly tell you I should appreciate such kindness most highly.

Forman replied on 11 January

> the line you have taken in your introduction is the right one. This I

have gone over very carefully, & as an old stager in such matters, used to revising both my own work & that of others, I have ventured to look over yours with a pencil in hand... the first principle of our society should be to issue nothing that has not been very deliberately weighed, and nothing that has not received the sanction of the Committee. Accuracy, good taste, and finish, are of infinitely greater importance than hurry. In fact there *is no hurry*; & we have got the numbers together on the good faith of management by a committee of 'those who know' about Shelley. I shall be very pleased to show you my things. Will you call next Sunday between 4 and 6?

One can imagine Wise, dressed to the nines, waiting nervously on the doorstep of his hero. The acquaintance must have ripened with remarkable rapidity. We soon find Wise fulfilling Forman's veiled warning to Furnivall and publishing too many Shelley Society books too quickly. By the end of 1886, twelve separate books had been issued. They included reprints of Shelley's *Adonais, Alastor, Hellas, Epipsychidion*; a memoir of Shelley by William Michael Rossetti; and Forman's *The Shelley Library* Pt. I, an excellent bibliography, though Pt. II on collected editions did not appear.

Three books they were not allowed were *The Necessity of Atheism* 1811; *Posthumous Fragments of Margaret Nicholson* 1810 and *A Letter to Lord Ellenborough* 1812. Sir Percy Shelley was consulted (rather late in the day perhaps) and from the entirely appropriate address of the Grand Hotel, Nice, the old humbug pronounced his verdict 'I have reason to know that he [the poet] would have set his face entirely against the reprinting of these early essays.' The books had been set up, 'But for sufficient reasons, the book was never completed and issued', Wise said of the first, but he did have a few copies of each printed, and preserved one each of these rarities in his own collection. Not a very economical affair for the Society, since setting was a large part of the cost of an edition, yet it would have received no revenue for this. All of these were printed by the firm of Richard Clay of Bread Hill Street, London and Bungay in Suffolk.

Clays was founded in London in 1827 by the first Richard Clay: it took over the firm of Childs of Bungay in 1876 and by the 1880s was printing for most of the major London publishers. It also printed for Furnivall's Early English Text Society (from about 1877), then the Browning and then the Shelley societies and also Forman's first forgery – Horne's *Galatea*. All this antiquarian printing and reprinting certainly got them used to a) using their good range of type to mimic earlier styles, particularly in title pages and b) printing pieces in the 1880s with much earlier dates on the titles. Wise hijacked the Shelley Society printing programme and diverted much of it to his own ends. From the types set up and paid for by the Shelley Society he ran off extra copies on vellum or fancy paper. He removed mention of the Shelley Society in the imprints ('printed for private circulation' was the usual substitute) and sold these extra copies for his private gain.

Wise explained it all to Forman in November 1886. He had just reprinted W.M. Rossetti's *Lecture on Prometheus* from the Shelley Society papers

> This Lecture has cost me 50/- for the 25 paper copies, & 40/- for the 3 Vellums = 2/- each paper & 13/4 each vellum. I simply had them pulled from the forms as they stood for the Society's issue, & only had wrapper & title printed & the pagination altered.

In one case at least (and perhaps others) the entire cost of one of his own publications was charged to the Shelley Society. Wise was certainly the front man for all this: behind the scenes Forman was acquiescent if not encouraging. Forman was keeping up his own publishing programme and in the same year he reprinted Byron's *Fugitive Pieces*. This genuinely rare book (only four copies seem to survive) was printed for Byron in 1806 for circulation to his friends but suppressed by him in consequence of (in particular) the poem *To Mary* which was considered to be 'too warmly drawn'. The reprint is a most handsome book bound in gilt vellum and printed by the Chiswick Press and with all the ornaments etc. 're-engraved by that capital artist and fac-similist Mr Hooper'. W. H. Hooper certainly was all this and in 1894–96 cut in wood all the Burne-Jones designs for the Kelmscott Chaucer, that great monument of the English private press movement. Hooper was also responsible for several other Kelmscotts: there is no doubt Forman was a good talent spotter. As well as one hundred copies of the reprint, there were also seven specials on Jap vellum. According to Wise, writing many years later, the £70 profit Forman made on the venture was almost exactly what the original rarity had cost him – so in effect he got it free.

To return to the societies, Shaw summed up some twenty years later

The papers thought that the Browning Society was an assemblage of longhaired aesthetes; in truth it was a conventicle where pious ladies disputed about religion with Furnivall, and Gonnar and I (Gonnar is now a professor of political economy in Liverpool) egged them on. When Furnivall founded the Shelley Society I of course joined that; and we pulled off a great performance of The Cenci before we succumbed to our heavy printers bills.

It was the first performance ever and had to be shown privately as the Lord Chamberlain's office refused licence on the grounds that the performance might deprave the public. It was staged in May 1886 with Alma Murray as Beatrice. She was Forman's sister-in-law and this is perhaps the place to bring Alfred Forman, Harry's favourite brother, up to date. He had gone to a Naval School but did not follow his father into the service: like Wise he worked for a colonial broker in Mincing Lane and then from 1870 to 1882 he worked for two different firms of paper merchants, a speciality his brother was to find useful. He married the attractive young actress Alma Murray in 1876 when he was 36 and she 20. She gained a reputation for difficult roles and, having played in a couple of Browning Society revivals, she was a natural choice for the extraordinarily difficult part of Beatrice. She later created Raina Petkoff in Shaw's *Arms and the Man* in 1894, but was never a popular star and was often short of work. The *Cenci* was generally reckoned an artistic success but a performance of *Hellas* by the society in October of the same year was a financial and artistic disaster. The musical score by W. Selle (Forman's father-in-law) came in for much artistic criticism in town, and must, one imagines have come in for some moral criticism back in Richmond.

Forman was book collecting as hard as ever. In November 1886 he pestered Bucke in Canada for Walt Whitman books remarking that he had 'got the fever very bad' and in the same letter he made a remark very sympathetic to the present author 'Meredith – I never managed to read a book of his – looked one over and felt repelled'. His Whitman collection mostly acquired via Bucke, was certainly very impressive. It included all the major books and even the manuscript notebook recording the poet's nursing work in the American Civil War. By 1887 Eliot, Gwendolen and Maurice were 17, 16 and 15, and they all had a family holiday together at Hythe in Kent, swimming before breakfast and playing plenty of tennis. The next year both the boys left school and left home. They both got jobs with shipping companies in the city of London (their father may have used his connections). In the same year – 1888 – Forman's mother died and his sister Jessie was left alone in the house in Camberwell.

FUGITIVE PIECES BY

## GEORGE GORDON LORD BYRON

A FAC-SIMILE REPRINT OF

THE SUPPRESSED

EDITION OF

1806

LONDON

PRINTED FOR PRIVATE CIRCULATION

1886

20. Forman's reprint of Byron

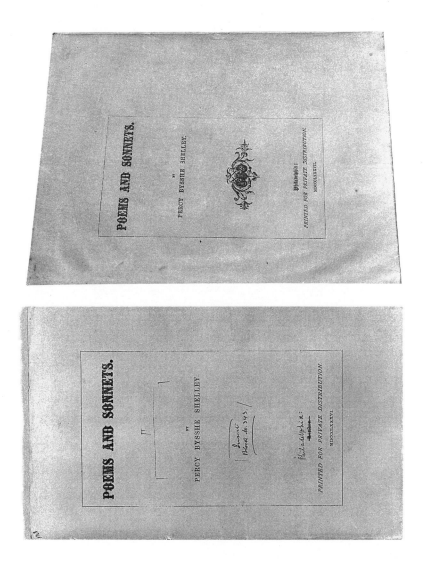

21.   On the left, the proof
and on the right the published book, a piracy

# 7

# THE FORGERIES BEGIN

In 1887 we see the first illegal printing by the two forgers, Forman and Wise. In November 1886, Edward Dowden, the noted Irish literary scholar, had published his great two volume biography of Shelley. It printed a considerable number of poems for the first time. These poems (plus one from a Shelley Society publication of 1887) were seized on by Wise and Forman. They decided to print them separately and invented Charles Alfred Seymour to edit them, making him a member of the mythical Philadelphia Historical Society. Proofs show that the book was originally intended to have a London imprint but a spurious Philadelphia was finally selected. Mr Seymour was allowed some pleasantries in the preface, including a comment on the necessity of importing the book's Whatman paper from England.

*Poems and Sonnets* is quite a substantial 4to, running to 76 pages and with elaborate typography to match: it has a limitation notice of thirty copies. It may have started as a learned leg-pull; indeed this is the line Wise took when he publicly described the book in 1924. However, Dowden's rights were ignored and considerable chunks of his text reprinted without permission; the imprint was false; and the announced limitation was probably exceeded. In short, *Poems and Sonnets* is a harbinger of worse to come. The types used show that it was printed by Clays in London; the false imprint seems not to have worried them.

Doubtless Shelley Society members were a useful market and our first evidence for the book is when Wise sent a copy to one of them, a Mr T.C. Abbott of Manchester in July 1887. Despite this, Dowden himself was not sent his copy until over a year later. His reply is polite but uncompromising; he calls Wise a highwayman.

A publication in some ways similar is *Letters from Percy Bysshe Shelley to Robert Southey* which, printed in London by Clays in 1888, is given the false imprint of New York, 1886. Both these Shelley pieces were the successors, natural or unnatural to Forman's and Wise's separate publication programmes which we have already considered. But they lead on to the forgeries proper, though differing from them not least in their higher production costs.

At some point in the next year or so, the full scale conspiracy developed, in which over one hundred fakes, forgeries or piracies were to be produced. Like most conspiracies this has left few written records. There are about seventy-five surviving letters between Forman and Wise, and with one or two exceptions, they tell us little directly, though they seem to be full of hidden meanings and hints we can only half guess at. There is also the historical evidence of when the forgeries were first recorded and the physical evidence of the books themselves. The former does provide evidence of dating (for reasons of simplicity we have dated many forgeries, but these dates are usually shorthand for 'not before' or 'not after'); the latter provides very little evidence for the chronological progressions of the forgers. Forman had certainly had the idea of creative forgery. Perhaps on one of Wise's visits to Forman's bookroom he showed him *Galatea*. Wise was an astute businessman and recognized a good idea when he saw it. He was a commodity dealer in the unregulated heyday of Victorian capitalism: here was an excellent product with which he could corner the market.

The cost of thirty or forty copies of a slim pamphlet might be £6 or £7; the unit cost therefore about 3s. 6d. or 4s.: and one copy could sell for as much as £100. What a lovely commodity! Wise certainly entered into his new role as a forger with alacrity and it is clear that Forman, though at first helpful, was later dragged kicking and screaming in his wake. But once in the secret, he could not get out: Wise had the drop on him. If the conspiracy had been exposed, Wise's fellows on the commodity exchange or at Rubeck's would probably have reckoned him culpable to be so careless as to be found out. Forman, as a civil servant and an established literary figure, would have been in a much more difficult position. He might well have been ruined, sacked from the P.O. without a pension and with his literary reputation in tatters.

The first mention of any of the new forgeries occurs in a diary entry (11 January 1888) by Bertram Dobell, the well known bookseller, 'Went to Shelley Society meeting. At this gathering Wise, Forman, Tegetmeier, Furnivall, Rossetti &c were there, but not Mr. Salt whom I had expected to see. Wise is still proceeding on his wild career of reprinting or pirating Browning, Shelley, Swinburne, &c.' Browning and Shelley we have accounted for. Swinburne is another matter, and this diary note must refer to one of the creative forgeries of Swinburne that were about to be loosed on the market. It is the first reference to them.

The second certain mention of any of the new ventures is in two letters of Swinburne to Wise written in April 1888. In September 1866, Swinburne published a short poem entitled *Cleopatra* in *The Cornhill Magazine* where it had slumbered ever since. The forgers disinterred it and printed it as a separate pamphlet with the date 1866 – just as if it had been published by John Camden Hotten in that year. Besides the publisher's imprint of Hotten the forgers also added a printer's imprint 'J. Andrews Clements Lane E.C.': this gentleman not only never printed anything else for Hotten, but was entirely imaginary and the pamphlet was actually printed in Bread Street, London by the firm of Richard Clay and Son. Having printed it, Wise (with his heart in his mouth no doubt) asked Swinburne about his recent 'purchase'. This bold attempt at a frontal attack was not very successful. Swinburne replied

> I did not know that Hotten had republished or reprinted my stanzas on Sandys drawing of Cleopatra which appeared with an engraving of that fine drawing in the Cornhill. . . . The verses were never intended for reproduction or preservation but simply scribbled off as fast as might be to oblige a friend whose work I admired. . . . If I were not a bit of a bibliomaniac myself, I should be shocked to think of your wasting good money on such a trumpery ephemeral.

Wise promptly gave him a copy and was told next day

> I am quite certain, quite positive, that I never set eyes on the booklet before nor heard of its existence. It is a fresh proof that the moral character of the worthy, Mr. Hotten was – I was about, very inaccurately, to say – ambiguous. He was a serviceable sort of fellow in his way but decidedly what Dr. Johnson would have called "a shady lot" and Lord Chesterfield "a rum customer". When I heard that he had died of a surfeit of pork chops, I observed that this was a serious argument against my friend Richard Burton's views of cannibalism as a wholesome and natural method of diet.

Wise pressed on and got another fine letter (and an invitation to luncheon) on 2 May. From this it appears Wise pretended to

Dear Mr. Wise

I know nothing whatever about the cut or uncut edges of the 'Siena' pamphlet — & care, I may add, considerably less than nothing; except inasmuch as I hope your copy may be 'all right,' on your account. I shall be most grateful for a sight of your 'Lyrical Ballads' — I want to have a transcript of The Convict.

Yours very truly
A C Swinburne

22.   Swinburne's letter to Wise about the forged *Siena*

have paid seven guineas for *Cleopatra* (perhaps he did – that would have been about the bill for the entire edition). Despite Swinburne's disclaimer of *Cleopatra* he had (more or less) accepted it – certainly he did not doubt the date. With further forgeries in mind, Wise tried to sound him out on *Dead Love*, a story he had contributed to *Once a Week* in October 1862. 'I need hardly say that I know nothing (and have never heard till now) of any such volume as you mention published or printed by Hotten under my name. I think it must be a myth' Swinburne replied.

The forgers were not deterred and in 1890 duly printed *Dead Love* as a separate pamphlet with the date 1864. Perhaps scared off by the reference to Hotten (see above) they produced John W. Parker and Son as publishers. This proved a frightful blunder as this style of the firm had been abandoned in 1860 and the firm itself had become wholly extinct in 1863. However, no one noticed the discrepancy until some forty years later. Finally Wise pestered Swinburne about *Siena*, a genuine pamphlet of 1868. By this time, Swinburne's patience was running out. 'I know nothing whatever about the cut or uncut edges of the 'Siena' pamphlet – and care, I may add, considerably less than nothing; except inasmuch as I hope your copy may be "all right" on your account.' (*c*.4 May 1888). This presages the forgers' less successful second string. *Cleopatra* and *Dead Love* were both creative forgeries with no original for comparison. With *Siena*, Forman and Wise attempted the much more difficult (and less imaginative) task of copying a rare original (six copies of *Siena* had been printed to secure copyright). They were quickly bowled out and J. H. Slater's *Early editions* 1894 mentions

> A pirated reprint is occasionally to be met with, and, having been very carefully executed, it is almost impossible to detect from the original. It is in every respect but one a masterly production, the only apparent defect being in the description of the paper, which it was probably found impossible to match exactly. There is no doubt that many of these forged copies are on the market.

The best that Wise could do, in a review of Slater, was partly to rehabilitate his production as the 'first published edition' and he later stated that Hotten readily sold copies at five or ten shillings a piece.

The best method of authenticating a forgery is to bamboozle

the author himself into it. Wise had failed at this so he tried other methods concocted, no doubt, with Forman. On 12 April 1890, Wise presented a copy of *Dead Love* to the British Museum: and on 13 May 1890, the British Museum bought a copy of *Cleopatra* for five guineas from one of his business colleagues, O. P. Rubeck. Being in the national collection and (incorrectly) catalogued as printed in 1864 and 1866 the pamphlets could be referred to as evidence for the doubters.

Another good method of authentication is to become the expert on Swinburne and effectively become judge and jury in your own case. This is just what Wise did: his first bibliography of Swinburne appeared in 1897, the second in 1919/20, the third in 1925 and the fourth in 1927. Once Swinburne was safely dead, his explicit statements about *Cleopatra* were swept away and Wise added some picturesque touches.

> Clearly Swinburne did authorise the issue of the pamphlet and revised the text of the poem for that purpose. This statement is supported by the fact that among the papers preserved at The Pines and acquired by me from Watts-Dunton was a set of proof-sheets of *Cleopatra*. These were pierced through the centre of the leaves, having apparently been thrust upon the point of an old-fashioned file

he stated in his second Swinburne bibliography. No one has ever seen these proofs which in the state described were a product of the forgers' imagination, spurred, perhaps, by the methods employed by the jobbing department at Clays. Swinburne was the earliest victim of the new team: in the same year (1888) we have the first evidence of others. Dante Gabriel Rossetti, the Pre-Raphaelite painter and poet was one.

On 7 July 1888, Wise wrote to a firm of booksellers, possibly Cornish of Manchester,

> Though you do not include *Rossetti* among the authors whose names you mention I send you two of his pamphlets, which (excepting the juvenile "Sir Hugh the Heron" of which I possess a copy) are the scarcest of all his writing. The handwriting in the "Hand and Soul" is that of W.M. Rossetti. A copy of this pamphlet was sold by Putticks some 3 or 4 years ago for between £4 & £5; I have seen no other sold. The printed slip inserted is from Robson & Kerslake's catalogue. Of the two pamphlets, the "Verses, 1881" is decidedly the scarcest. I am only acquainted with 4 fellow-collectors who possess it; 3 in L'don, & 1 in Torquay. Of the 12 poems contained in it the former "At the fall of the Leaf" has been included by W. M. Rossetti in the collected edition of his brother's Works. The

"Sonnet" which is extremely powerful has never been printed else-where. It was actually put up in type (I have seen the proof-sheet) for the Poems of 1870, but it was considered to be of so "Fleshly" a turn that it was deemed advisable to exclude it, & in 1881 when the "Poems" were again re-cast & re-published it was once more excluded, & in order that it might be preserved it was printed in the enclosed pamphlet. I cannot say how many copies were worked off, but I know that the number was very limited. I hardly know what price to put upon them, but I do not think that £7/10/- for the 2 is an unreasonable figure.

This is a most interesting letter and the forerunner of many others Wise was to write. We see him as the bookseller he always denied he was: what was he actually describing?

First he mentions *en passant*, *Sir Hugh the Heron* 1843. This is Dante Gabriel Rossetti's first book, printed by his grandfather on the private press in a house in Regent's Park. It *is* rare but a cache of copies did remain in the family.

*Hand and Soul* is a short *conte* about a thirteenth century (i.e. Pre-Raphaelite) painter in Italy. It was first printed in 1850 in *The Germ*, the pioneer magazine of the Pre-Raphaelites. It was reprinted in 1869 as part of the proofs of Rossetti's *Poems* 1870 but in the event it was not included. W. M. Rossetti explains

> My brother caused the poems [and *Hand and Soul*] in these sheets to be "privately printed" with a view to convenience in considering whether any and which of them should be published. At his death in 1882 I found in his house a very few copies of the printed sheets.

In 1886 William Michael Rossetti gave Forman, by then a friend for nearly twenty years, a copy of *Hand and Soul* (he still had twelve or fifteen of them in 1884). Soon after, Forman attempted to give them a title page 'Hand and Soul London Privately Printed 1870', a half-title, and a frontispiece, thus making more of a book of it. In typical Forman fashion the proposed title was ambiguous. It stated a fact that was correct (or nearly so: 1869 would have been more accurate) but would have been generally taken to be itself a product of the 1870 private printing. However, William Michael, a jealous if often flat-footed guardian of his brother's reputation, forbade the project. Next time he was not consulted and Wise and Forman printed *Verses* probably in the year of the letters (1888) as one of their earliest creative forgeries. Like most of their output it is a slight little thing, the two poems taking up only 12 pages. Unlike

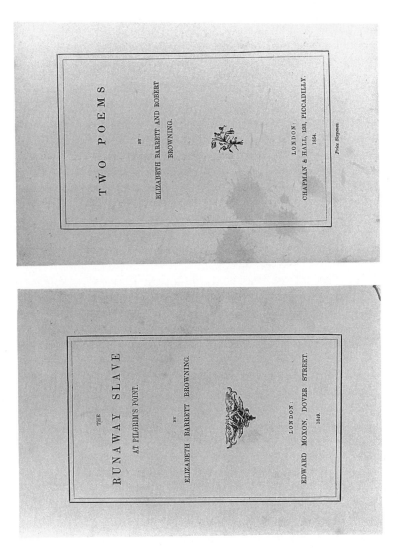

23.   The pamphlet on the right is genuine;
that on the left is a creative forgery modelled on it

almost all the rest to follow, it is printed on watermarked paper –
the bibliophiles' Van Gelder – which was probably abandoned as
being suspicious: it is not generally found in Dante Gabriel's real
books. The types are mostly the same founts as those used in the
*Poems* and the layout is a remarkably artistic effort, not at all like
the plain style that Rossetti used for *Poems* 1870.

Forman, in his own copy of the forgery, noted 'some friends of
Rossetti's had printed it . . . the whole issue must have been
extremely small'. One wonders for whom he was writing: presum-
ably for himself, to savour the delicious dramatic irony of 'some
friends' as an audience of one. Since we cannot trust the context, we cannot trust the date either, though that appended by
Forman (November 1887) is persuasive and may even represent
the true date of printing. Forman, as we have seen, had been a
Rossetti fan for nearly twenty years, and Wise got to know
William Michael pretty thoroughly as secretary of the Shelley
Society (they exchanged some twenty letters in 1888 alone).
Despite these favourable omens *Verses* never really took root. In
1890 O.P. Rubeck, Wise's stooge, tried to sell a copy privately
but was told 'it has been printed without any authority from
Rossetti, and must be the act of some bibliographical dilettante
for his own satisfaction or profit.' The informant was William
Michael who continued adamant: in 1902 and again in 1905, he
published a bibliography of his brother and (despite a renewed
attempt by Wise and Forman to convert him) he only noticed
the *Verses* as an unauthorized printing and did not give it a full
entry. This was unsatisfactory: in most later cases Wise (or
Forman) wrote the bibliographies themselves to make sure their
publications got proper billing. Book collectors can be rather like
stamp collectors: they like a full series. A dedicated Rossetti
collector would naturally consult the bibliography and try to
obtain all the items, which are numbered in sequence. Not having Rossetti No. 15 might seem serious: but he would hardly
worry about some obscure unauthorized printing with no
number.

The Brownings were the next to be visited. Robert Browning
and Elizabeth Barrett eloped and were married in 1846 after a
romantic courtship. In 1848 she published a poem *The runaway
slave at Pilgrim's Point* in an American anti-slavery charity book
*The Liberty bell* Boston 1848. The forgers produced a separate

pamphlet of this with the imprints of publisher and printer thus: 'London, Edward Moxon, Dover Street 1849' and 'London: Bradbury and Evans, Printers, Whitefriars': the two correctly would have read 'London T. J. Wise and H. Buxton Forman *c.* 1888' and 'London: Richard Clay and Sons, Printers E. C.'. There is a short note explaining the separate publication which is meant to be taken as by Elizabeth Barrett Browning herself: this is a (very minor) piece of literary forgery. She certainly did *not* write 'It is for a few "friends of freedom" and of the writer on this side of the Atlantic that the verses are now reprinted.'

Wise wrote to Robert Browning in terms we can partly guess from his reply (1 August 1888) 'I never heard of a separate publication, and am pretty certain such a circumstance never happened. I fear that this must be a fabricated affair.' Two days later, having inspected Wise's copy, he (like Swinburne) was overawed by the physical evidence.

> I daresay the fact has been that, on the publication of the Poem in America, the American friends (in London) who had been instrumental in obtaining it, wrote to the Authoress (in Florence) for leave to reprint it in England, and that she of course gave her consent – probably wrote the little advertisement. The respectability of the Publisher and Printer is a guarantee that nothing surreptitious has been done.

Forman gave the first bibliographical account of the authoress in *Elizabeth Barrett Browning and her scarcer books* 1896. He describes *The runaway slave* in great detail and slyly suggests that it was the model for another charity piece, the Brownings' *Two poems* 1854. This is perfectly genuine but the boot is on the other foot: *The runaway slave* was modelled on *Two poems*. But with the contrary account in the standard book of reference, who would be likely to doubt it? Another way to acceptance was to have a copy in the national library. The British Museum (now the British Library) is a standard benchmark for bibliographical studies, and the words 'I just want to check the B. M. copy' still rise to the lips of many booksellers and bibliographers.

In August 1888, the British Museum bought *The runaway slave* for five guineas from E. Schlengemann, the first entry of a creative forgery. Schlengemann was a fellow employee of Wise at Rubecks and it is an interesting illustration of Wise's force of character that he got his colleagues at work also involved. All these forgeries, and most of those to follow, were printed in London by Clays who must have been pleased by the volume of new business. In most cases, the evidence for this statement is circumstantial though overwhelmingly strong. In the case of *The runaway slave* there is a convenient piece of absolute proof. One copy, when still in sheets, was put down on an inked forme of type which, very lightly printed across four pages, part of the Shelley Society notebook published in 1888 and printed by Clays. So much for Bradbury and Evans and 1849!

The final act in the first year of full-scale operation was George Eliot's *Brother and sister* 1869 (a creative forgery of a group of sonnets which were first printed in *The Legend of Jubal* 1874). This (through Mr Schlengemann again) was sold to the British Museum for three guineas in October 1888: but with unpleasant results. It was catalogued with the note 'From "The Legend of Jubal and other poems" 1874 in which the Sonnets perhaps really first appeared.' The note was later removed from the British Museum catalogue on the ground that Mr Wise believed it to be quite unfounded, and the same authority was gaily assuring a fellow collector in 1896 'It is generally understood, and I think rightly, that twenty-five copies of "Brother and Sister" were printed.' As the publisher, he was, of course, uniquely qualified to pronounce on the print run: but since he still had twenty-four copies left in 1910, he probably understated it. In 1889, five more forgeries appeared: another George Eliot, two more Swinburnes and two of a new author – John Ruskin.

James P. Smart was secretary of the Ruskin Society of London, which was doubtless where Wise met him. He had done much work towards a bibliography of Ruskin and before he quite knew what had happened, he had acquired Wise as a collaborator. Their work appeared in nineteen parts from September 1889 to October 1893. Wise's role was mainly that of editor; he was particularly qualified to point out items that Smart had carelessly missed. The bibliography provided Wise with an ideal opportunity to survey the field of Ruskin's writings, notice the gaps where a creative forgery could be plugged in, and supply them. One of the Ruskins was *Leoni: a legend of Italy* 1868 which seems to be first described in the prospectus for the bibliography (?June 1889). It incorporates a minor piece of literary forgery in the guise of a preface signed JR which Ruskin never wrote, and aspires

BROTHER AND SISTER

SONNETS

BY

MARIAN LEWES

LONDON
FOR PRIVATE CIRCULATION ONLY
1869

24.   A creative forgery
with a bogus note of provenance in Wise's hand

to two different issues based on two letters dropping out of one word in the bogus preface. This last point is strangely reminiscent of the Formanian issue points in some of his Shelley reprints.

To provide additional evidence, Wise somehow persuaded George Allen – originally Ruskin's assistant and finally his publisher – to inscribe a copy of the forgery 'George Allen with friendly regards to T. J. Wise' and this inscription is clearly visible in the illustration in the bibliography. It is a reminder of how forceful and persuasive Wise was, face to face. Ruskin himself inscribed no copies: although he lived on until 1900, he had a mental breakdown in 1889, retired to the Lake District, and took no further interest in his work.

In 1890, there was a bumper crop of forgeries comprising four more Swinburnes, two more Ruskins, and some new entrants viz. two William Morris (Forman knew him well and he attached little importance to bibliographical details), three Robert Brownings (died 1889), and one each of Matthew Arnold (died 1888) Tennyson, D. G. Rossetti and William Thackeray (died 1863). Several of these were sold to the British Museum by O. P. Rubeck. Indeed Rubecks admitted much later to buying for resale a number of Tennysons and Swinburnes. Only Wise could have persuaded a wholesale drug dealer to stock modern first editions.

The year 1891 produced two more Swinburnes and a Dickens (died 1870), 1892 two more Ruskins, another Swinburne, another Matthew Arnold, a George Meredith and two Tennysons (died 1892), and 1893 another Swinburne and another Matthew Arnold.

It would be tedious to recite the circumstances of all these, but essentially it was the formula as before (only much more of it). There was much less of an attempt to confront authors with forgeries of their own work (surely a rather naive approach which must have owed much to Wise's impetuosity) and rather more of an attempt to adopt a circuitous round-the-houses approach and rely on death or incapacity of the victims. A number of the forgeries first appear in American auction sales and many of the essential British Museum copies were given, not sold (don't look a gift horse in the mouth, they may have thought).

There are a few of the fakes that are worth a special look. With George Eliot's *Agatha* (a fake of a genuine pamphlet) we find

# THE CONDEMNED FENIAN PRISONERS.

## "AN APPEAL TO ENGLAND,"

BY THE DISTINGUISHED POET,

### ALGERNON SWINBOURNE,

AUTHOR OF "POEMS & BALLADS," "CHASTELARD," &c.

**I.**

Art thou indeed among these,
Thou of the tyrannous crew,
The kingdoms fed upon blood,
O Queen from of old of the seas ;
England, art thou of them too
That drink of the poisonous flood,
That hide under poisonous trees ?

**II.**

Nay, thy name from of old,
Mother, was pure, of we dreamed ;
Purer we held thee than this,
Purer fain would we hold :
So goodly a glory it seemed,
A fame so bounteous of bliss,
So more precious than gold,

**III.**

A praise so sweet in our ears,
That thou in the tempest of things
As a rock for a refuge should'st stand,
In the blood-red river of tears
Poured forth for the triumph of kings ;
A safeguard, a sheltering land,
In the thunder and torrent of years.

**IV.**

Strangers came gladly to thee,
Exiles, chosen of men,
Safe for thy sake in thy shade,
Sat down at thy feet and were free.
So men spake of thee then ;
Now shall their speaking be stayed ?
Ah, so let it not be !

**V.**

Not for revenge or affright,
Pride, or a tyrannous lust,
Cast from thee the crown of thy praise.
Mercy was thine in thy might ;
Strong when thou wert, thou wert just :
Now, in the wrong-doing days,
Cleave thou, thou at least, to the right,

**VI.**

How should one charge thee, how pray,
Save by the memories that were ?
Not thy gold nor the strength of thy ships,
Nor the might of thine armies at bay,
Made thee, mother, most fair :
But a word from republican lips
Said in thy name in thy day.

*November 20, 1867.*

**VII.**

Hast thou said it, and hast thou forgot?
Is thy praise in thine ears as a scoff ?
Blood of men guiltless was shed,
Children, and souls without spot,
Shed, but in places far off :
*Let slaughter no more be,* said
Milton ; and slaughter was not.

**VIII.**

Was it not said of thee too,
Now, but now, by thy foes,
By the slaves that had slain their France,
And thee would slay as they slew—
"Down with her walls that enclose
Freemen that eye us askance,
Fugitives, men that are true ?"

**IX.**

This was thy praise or thy blame
From bondsman or freeman—to be
Pure from pollution of slaves,
Clean of their sins, and thy name
Bloodless, innocent, free ;
Now if thou be not, thy waves
Wash not from off thee thy shame.

**X.**

Freeman he is not, but slave,
Whoso in fear for the State,
Cries for surety of blood,
Help of gibbet and grave ;
Neither is any land great
Whom, in her fear-stricken mood,
These things only can save.

**XI.**

Lo, how fair from afar,
Taintless of tyranny, stands
Thy mighty daughter, for years,
Who trod the wine-press of war ;
Shines with immaculate hands ;
Slays not a foe, neither fears ;
Stains not peace with a scar.

**XII.**

Be not as tyrant or slave,
England : be not as these,
Thou that wert other than they,
Stretch out thine hand but to save ;
Put forth thy strength, and release ;
Lest there arise, if thou slay,
Thy shame, as a ghost from the grave.

25.   The genuine broadside

# AN APPEAL

TO

## ENGLAND

AGAINST THE EXECUTION OF THE
CONDEMNED FENIANS.

BY

ALGERNON CHARLES SWINBURNE,

*AUTHOR OF POEMS AND BALLADS,*
ATALANTA IN CALYDON,
Chastelard, &c.

*MANCHESTER:*
*REPRINTED FROM THE "MORNING STAR."*

1867.

26.   The pamphlet, a creative forgery

Forman directing Wise (6 May 1889) 'The enclosed proof shows how I fancy the new title page would look decent if properly done. I send you the book again because the imprint on verso should be given with all attainable exactitude.' Forman again acts as editorial director in a letter of 17 February 1890 telling Wise where to find the ingredients of the creative Morris forgery *The two sides of the River* '1876'. By 5 March 1890, this was in proof as Forman tells Wise not to delete 'Not for Sale' on the title. The 17 February letter also contains a mention of D. G. Rossetti's *Sister Helen* '1857' which made no public appearance until 1894 (typically Forman was cautioning Wise against printing an 1881 revised text in an '1857' forgery). One or two of the creative forgeries ran into the problem that after they were created, it was discovered that there was already a genuine separate edition occupying the place intended for the forgery. In such a case, Wise, like a cuckoo in the nest, usually managed to insert his creation as the true first and throw out the genuine article as a subsequent edition.

The 1890 Tennyson and the 1893 Matthew Arnold were out of the usual run. The first was a fake title 'Idylls of the Hearth' supplied to an extremely common Tennyson first (a cloth bound book in fact), with the real title *Enoch Arden*. The Arnold *Alaric at Rome* was a facsimile of a genuine 1840 pamphlet, but *most imprudently* was produced from the same setting of type as was used for an avowed reprint of this rarity edited by Wise and openly published as a reprint in 1893. One may guess that this slipshod opportunism was extremely distasteful for the much slower and more thorough Forman. But, as Wise was later to rebuke Forman, 'the moral position is exactly the same.' On the other hand, as one of P. D. James's characters points out, 'If you are proposing to commit a sin, it is as well to commit it with intelligence. Otherwise you are insulting God as well as defying Him.'

Finally the Meredith piece – *Jump-to-Glory Jane* '1887' produced another author's reaction.

> I have been told of the "leaflet" but I have not seen it. Of course it is piratical; whether issued by a lunatic or a profoundly speculative Yankee, I cannot decide. "Printed for a few friends only" is very amusing. The reason a poem of a writer whose verse is not popular should have been selected for fraudulent publication is not clearly seen.

# 8

# LITERARY AND COMMERCIAL LIFE

The first period of the forgery factory has covered six years, 1888–93, when a good deal else happened. For instance the poor old Shelley Society was in trouble. Wise had been elected Secretary in 1887 and (it will be remembered) had run off with the publications programme. In the two crucial years 1886 and 1887 when most printing was done, the society's two auditors were Alfred Forman (Harry's brother) and T. J. Wise himself. W. M. Rossetti summed up the situation accurately enough when he wrote to Wise in January 1890,

> As I understand it, the *moral* responsibility rests with you and Furnivall, and perhaps Potts as a third; while the legal responsibility rests with a rather large number of persons. You certainly can confirm my statement that all orders for printing were given, not only without any active cooperation on my part, but without my being in any way consulted or apprised as to details.

Furnivall was always keen on getting texts into print and doubtless gave a too hasty assent to Wise's plans. Wise made all the arrangements and when the crash came, partly paid Clays from his own pocket. No doubt he told them so and enhanced his reputation as the businesslike representative of a muddleheaded society. In fact the debt was shared among the committee and he was gradually paid off, not being cleared until 1902. In the end, despite his grumbles, W. M. Rossetti came nobly up to scratch:

> I don't quite like to think about our good friend Furnivall at his advanced age and burdened with literary researches, etc., unable to 'fork out' £8 odd with comfort and having to think about instalments. . . .I really should not mind adding his £8 odd to my £16 odd.

Wise profited from the affair in a number of ways:
1. He gained easy familiarity with printing procedures, the selection of type and so on.
2. He accustomed Clays to the complexity of facsimile setting in a good cause, so that they never noticed when this expertise was put to evil purposes.

3. The Shelley Society paid the typesetting (the major
   expense) for many of his private prints.
4. He gained a considerable foothold in the literary world. For
   some years after it folded, he was still using the impressive
   Shelley Society notepaper (listing himself as secretary) in his
   correspondence.

In 1890, Wise finally moved out of the family house, leaving his
father and his stepmother and getting married himself. His bride
was Selina Fanny Smith, born in St Pancras, but by 1890 living
with her family at 174 Leighton Road. This is only five minutes
walk from the Camden Road Baptist Church, so it seems likely
that they met there. At some point, Wise had clearly infringed
the code of conduct of the young people's group at the Church.
In later years they did not wish to speak of him or to him.
Whether this is because of his later conduct to Selina or for some
other reason is not known. A Baptist church was not a registered
building for marriage, so the fact that they went to the 'curious
Anglo-Norman Parish Church of Kentish Town' is not significant. Wise took up temporary residence at 33 Leighton Grove so
as to be in the parish. Selina was aged 22, the daughter of a
salesman, Thomas was 31 and described himself as a commercial
clerk. They moved into 52 Ashley Road, Crouch Hill, a larger and
more agreeable house than that in Devonshire Road and a little
to the north of it, in a more salubrious part of London. Both the
attractive red brick terraces and accompanying church of St
Mary were built about 1860. The latter is by the prolific A. D.
Gough, found all over this part of North London. 'His churches
are characterised by rather wild rock-facing and asymmetrically
placed thin spires' (Pevsner).

We have probably reached the end of Wise's churchgoing days
and he seems not to have attended St Mary's. He was only to
live in Ashley Road for about five years but was to use it to
christen both his library and his publications. The road itself was
named after Anthony Ashley Cooper, 7th Earl of Shaftesbury,
the great Victorian philanthropist and reformer: he might have
been rather surprised at the subsequent applications of his
second name. The collection of books which Wise was rapidly
building up was christened 'The Ashley Library'. He was, at this
stage, concentrating on the moderns, that is to say, nineteenth

century authors, usually poets, and some still living. He began with Keats and Shelley and continued through Browning, Tennyson, Swinburne and Ruskin. He was not afraid of giving high prices for really rare books and, being ahead of public taste, he made some outstanding purchases. In 1814, Shelley published (anonymously) a philosophical tract in the form of a dialogue viz. *A Refutation of Deism*. When Forman came to write *The Shelley Library* 1886, his marvellously complete and detailed bibliography, he knew of three copies. One was in the British Museum, a second was owned by Professor Dowden (of the *Life of Shelley*) who had bought it off 'a perambulating book-cart for twopence', and the third was owned by Richard Garnett, given him by the poet's son, Sir Percy. In 1888, Wise approached Dowden but he would not sell; in 1890 he had a correspondence with Garnett and, after offering less, he finally provoked Garnett into naming his price 'if you will give forty guineas it is yours'. Garnett did not really want to sell and may have supposed the price too high for the commercial clerk. Probably a year or two earlier it might have been, but income from the forgeries was beginning to come through and Wise snapped it up. £42 was, at the time, a year's wages for many people.

Wise and Forman were both avid collectors and the loosening of financial constraints secured by extra income from forgeries must have been a godsend. Also, by being so intimately involved with collecting, they were able both to conceive new forgeries and then market them among their fellow collectors.

The Ashley Library was also the name Wise gave to his bibliophile printing programme. He commissioned a special device – rather like a trade mark he may have considered – which is found at the end of almost all his legitimate printing. This is by Frederick Tilney, a minor artist, who was also responsible for Wise's bookplate and for the decorations to a particular edition of E. Barrett Browning's *Sonnets from the Portuguese* which we shall meet in a moment. In 1893, 1895 and 1897, was issued *The Ashley Library, a List of Books published for private circulation by Thomas J. Wise*. This lists a block of Shelley Society derived pieces still in stock, followed by 16, 25 and finally 33 other printings in the 1897 edition.

The two main groups are printings of Ruskin letters and Shelley letters, to a fairly standard formula: printed limitations

27.  59–61 Mark Lane, a watercolour, 1864

of about thirty copies plus a few on vellum or special paper; cloth bindings with deckle edges; and the letters split up and printed by groups, usually the correspondents concerned. It was obviously a fairly profitable way of milking the bibliophile market. However, Wise did not want to be seen as the covert bookseller he always was. The second list has the note

> The following list is printed as a Record, not by way of advertisement. Books printed in short numbers for private circulation become so rapidly and entirely absorbed, that it is exceedingly difficult to obtain information regarding them when such is required for bibliographical or other purposes. Hence the necessity for the present catalogue.

If Wise was busy printing, Forman was busy editing. His great eight volume Shelley (1876–80) and four volume Keats (1883) have already been considered. From the former, he excerpted and revised the far more popular poetry and published it separately in 1882, followed by a second edition in 1886 and a third in 1892. In the latter year he also produced the Aldine Edition of Shelley in five volumes to range with other standard authors in the series. As with Shelley, so Keats; he produced a *Poetical Works* in 1884, a second edition in 1885 and a third in 1889, together with a revision of the four volume poetry and prose in the same year. He was asked to contribute to Lloyd Sanders' *Celebrities of the century* 1887 and produced short biographies of some fifteen poets, including R.H. Horne, Keats, Shelley, William Morris, Walt Whitman ('the great prophet of the world's hope') and Ebenezer Jones. He patronized W.J. Ibbett, a minor poet of West Country origin who ran a private press at Epsom. *The Halfpenny Muse*, a series of forty-seven original poems, 1891–92, which included several by Forman and one by his wife, was printed there, as were two poems by Ibbett, *Rosamunda* 1890 and *A September Walk* 1891, both limited to twelve copies printed for Forman.

Meanwhile Wise was advancing on all fronts. Rubecks moved to larger offices at 59 Mark Lane in 1892. These were built in 1864 for the property speculators James and John Innes to designs by George Aitchison. 'It was a type of structure new to the mid-19th century – a block of lettable offices; a type which demanded a dignified and fashionable façade and a flexible interior.' Rubecks was on the second floor: in neighbouring offices were dealers in ships, tea, corn, brandy, seeds, phospate of lime, wine and even manufacturers of dog biscuits (Millington and Co.; which raises unsatisfied speculations about the history of pet food). At the same time, they took on a new office boy, one Herbert Gorfin, aged 14, who was to play an important part in Wise's life. Wise was by then cashier and manager of the firm and in complete charge of the outer office. He had become closely associated with Otto Portman Rubeck. Otto sold the British Museum two Ruskin fakes in 1890 at two guineas a piece, but it is clear from correspondence that he must originally have asked more. In 1892–3, he made several unsuccessful attempts to sell other books to the Museum. As we have seen in 1890, he tried to plant a Rossetti's *Verses* on a fairly wide awake collector and had to answer awkward questions in consequence. In all this, he was acting as Wise's catspaw: one is surprised how much he was drawn in and one feels he must have had some inkling of what was afoot. Wise thoroughly appreciated the fact that if you are peddling dodgy material there is an obvious utility in doing it at one remove.

Wise's bibliographical influence increased still further when, in May 1893, *The Bookman* announced

> Our readers will learn with great pleasure that Mr Thomas J. Wise, the well-known collector and bibliographer, has undertaken the editorship of our "Notes on Recent Book Sales" . . . [he] will add, out of the fullness of his knowledge and experience, such comments as will be interesting to all readers and particularly valuable to book buyers and booksellers.

Robertson Nicoll, the editor, was a prolific journalist and writer who lived not so far away from Wise in Hampstead (as Wise went up in the world, he became a nearer neighbour). He collected an enormous library but knew little or nothing about bibliography and the technical side of book collecting. Wise's new column was used to evangelize his own view of book collecting and especially to encourage collecting the moderns, in which field of course, he had a head start. His contributions are enthusiastic and readable – he was an excellent storyteller – but describe and authenticate many forgeries. Another, more considerable figure turned to Wise for technical help, viz. Edmund Gosse, who wrote on 10 May 1883:

My dear Mr. Wise,
A thousand thanks for your goodness, and for the gifts which have just reached me. I value both of them very highly. The Ruskin letters are charming. Your visit last Friday gave me great pleasure, but you left me quite depressed. I was positively humbled by your superior knowledge and acumen: I feel myself, by your side, a mere learner in this pretty science of bibliography in which you are a master.

Thus, the first of some 400 letters. Gosse, like Forman and Wise, was emerging from humble beginnings, to, in his case considerable literary eminence. The child of a strict Plymouth Brethren family, he had known Forman's Teignmouth and Wise's Islington. Gosse was an enthusiastic and stylish writer, producing a steady stream of books in a most readable style. He was a picturesque, rather than an exact writer: Forman despised his inaccuracy and lack of rigour, while Gosse could not really make Forman out and was probably even a bit frightened of him. In early youth both had celebrated Devon in verse, Forman writing an epic of 10,000 lines of blank verse, while Gosse wrote a series of poems on the legends of Devon. 'I want to drag my beloved county up to Parnassus with me if I can', Gosse remarked, a sentiment Forman probably shared though he might have expressed it differently. Relations with Wise were quite different. Unlike Forman, Wise relished personal contacts, personal salesmanship and he took great trouble with Gosse. He flattered him, fed him with books and information, and greatly benefited from his friends, his knowledge and his taste. In Wise's gallery, Gosse somewhat resembled Graf von Schwabing, who in Buchan's *Mr. Standfast*, was to be fed 'true stuff that don't matter so as they'll continue to trust him, and a few selected falsehoods that'll matter like hell'. One of these was about to emerge, the celebrated *Sonnets from the Portuguese* supposed to have been printed by Miss Mitford for Elizabeth Barrett Browning.

# SONNETS.

BY

E. B. B.

READING:

[NOT FOR PUBLICATION.]

1847.

28. Elizabeth Barrett Browning's Sonnets, "Reading, 1847", the most famous creative forgery

# THE READING *SONNETS*

Creating the *Sonnets* was a daring stroke which showed how high the forgers' confidence was riding. All the creative forgeries distort and falsify (if only by a little) the literary history of the author concerned. By forging Elizabeth Barrett Browning's *Sonnets from the Portuguese* '1847', Wise and Forman were tampering with the most celebrated literary love story of Victorian England. The romantic courtship in Wimpole Street under the eyes of her father, the elopement, the flight to Italy and the happy and poetic marriage all went to create a rosy glow about the whole affair. The sonnets were written by Elizabeth to Robert during the courtship and the title was supposed to conceal the intimate nature of the feeling which inspired them. It was this intense human interest, more than the intrinsic poetic value of the *Sonnets* themselves which raised them to an eminence in the literary world enjoyed by hardly any other poetry of the Victorian age. For more than forty years the first publication was believed to be in the second edition of Elizabeth's *Poems* 1850.

However, in March 1894, a preliminary note appeared in a rather obscure Philadelphia journal *Poet Lore* where, in an article entitled 'Browning Rarities', W.G. Kingsland announced that he had been afforded a sight of a tiny volume in which the sonnets, these exquisite gems of poetry, had first appeared. He regretted that 'Mr. Browning's attention had not been called to it while it was still possible for him to have spoken on the circumstances under which it was printed'. Kingsland was not, however, a very persuasive sponsor and his priority may have been accidental. In June 1893, Gosse had written to Wise 'I perfectly understand and while chronicling the existence of the Mitford volume [i.e. *Sonnets from the Portuguese*] I will do nothing to emphasise the value of it. Nor do I think I need borrow it from Forman. Like you, I hate borrowing valuable books.' The piece Gosse was writing, did not appear until November 1894 as the introduction to an edition of the *Sonnets*. The fairy story which follows was probably concocted by Forman and was then fed by Wise to Gosse.

It was in the second or 1850 edition of the Poems in two volumes that the Sonnets from the Portuguese were first given to the public. The circumstances attending their composition have never been clearly related. Mr. Browning, however, eight years before his death, made a statement to a friend, with the understanding that at some future date, after his own decease, the story might be more widely told. The time seems to have arrived when there can be no possible indiscretion in recording a very pretty episode of literary history.

During the months of their brief courtship, closing, as all the world knows, in the clandestine flight and romantic wedding of September 12th, 1846, neither poet showed any verses to the other. Mr. Browning, in particular, had not the smallest notion that the circumstances of their betrothal had led Miss Barrett into any artistic expression of feeling. As little did he suspect it during their honeymoon in Paris, or during their first crowded weeks in Italy. They settled, at length, in Pisa; and being quitted by Mrs Jamieson and her niece, in a very calm and happy mood the young couple took up each his or her separate literary work.

Their custom was, Mr. Browning said, to write alone, and not to show each other what they had written. This was a rule which he sometimes broke through, but she never. He had the habit of working in a downstairs room, where their meals were spread, while Mrs. Browning studied in a room on the floor above. One day, early in 1847, their breakfast being over, Mrs. Browning went upstairs, while her husband stood at the window watching the street till the table should be cleared. He was presently aware of someone behind him, though the servant was gone. It was Mrs. Browning, who held him by the shoulder to prevent his turning to look at her, and at the same time pushed a packet of papers into the pocket of his coat. She told him to read that and to tear it up if he did not like it; and then she fled again to her own room.

Mr. Browning seated himself at the table and unfolded the parcel. It contained the series of sonnets which have now become so illustrious. As he read, his emotion and delight may be conceived. Before he had finished it was impossible for him to restrain himself, and, regardless of his promise, he rushed upstairs and stormed that guarded citadel. He was early conscious that these were treasures not to be kept from the world; "I dared not reserve to myself," he said, "the finest sonnets written in any language since Shakespeare's." But Mrs. Browning was very loth indeed to consent to the publication of what had been the very notes and chronicle of her betrothal. At length she was persuaded to permit her friend, Miss Mary Russell Mitford, to whom they had originally been sent in manuscript, to pass them through the press, although she absolutely declined to accede to Miss Mitford's suggestion that they should appear in one of the fashionable annuals of the day. Accordingly, a small volume was printed, entitled Sonnets/by/E.B.B./Reading/Not for Publication/1847,/an octavo of 47 pages.

When it was determined to publish the sonnets in the volumes of 1850, the question of a title arose.

Furnivall's plain, unvarnished (and misspelt) account is nearer the whole truth: Furnivall was a closer friend than Gosse.

> Mrs Browning's *Sonnets* to her husband. She wrote these in London. One day she timidly hinted to Browning that she'd tried to express her feelings about him. He answered that he didn't think people should wear their hearts on their sleeves for daws to peck at, or something of the kind. This shut her up. When abroad she was one day late in putting on her bonnet to walk with him. He called to her. Spying about he saw a tiny roll of paper on her looking-glass or table, pounst on it and said, "What's this?" unrolling it the while. "Only something I wrote about you, and you frightened me from showing it to you,' said she (He told me this himself). And in her next edition the *Sonnets from the Portuguese* were printed.

The world preferred Gosse's story probably, like Gosse himself, convinced by the appearance of the book itself, by the authority of print.

Forman may have been rather vexed at Gosse being fed this important literary scoop and he was by now disenchanted with his partnership with Wise. In *Elizabeth Barrett Browning and her scarcer books* 1896 he mulls over the typography of the *Sonnets*

> The fact that it bears a Reading imprint does not necessarily imply production in Reading, as there is no printer's name and a Reading stationer, as well as any other might have employed a London house; but there is something of an indefinable provincial look about the thing, though certainly no reason why the printer need have been ashamed of his handiwork.

One has to remind oneself that the forgers designed the volume and had it printed by Clays in London! Perhaps Wise was taking over the reins too much and upsetting the more fastidious Forman. In fact, as the latter probably knew (and Wise probably did not) the natural printer would in the supposed circumstances have been George Lovejoy of Reading, a good friend of Miss Mitford's. Comparison of his output with the *Sonnets* might well have been fatal to the latter, which is perhaps what Forman is teasing Wise about. Forman was also sceptical of the Gosse story,

in three charming pages of picturesque writing we get brought
together the floating traditions of the episode, and over them is
thrown the glamour of the personal acquaintance between Browning
and his bright chronicler. Of course Mr. Gosse does not expect all
this to be taken too seriously or literally

and he later refers to 'some unknown circumstances leading to
the production of a few copies printed'.

Forman had come a long way since the innocent early days in
London when he was discovering English literature. 'Sonnets
from the Portuguese are not from the Portuguese at all but are
her own original love songs, addressed to Browning and published
under a title "de guerre" what I know of them are very beautiful', he wrote to Bucke in 1864. Little could he imagine then,
that in later life he would be manufacturing their first printing.

The forgers now had established *Sonnets* as a very marketable
commodity: how could they market it without arousing suspicion? This was a problem with all the forgeries which we will
consider later. It was particularly so with such a celebrity as the
Reading *Sonnets*. Wise, in his bibliography of Elizabeth Barrett
Browning published the year after Forman's death (did he
embargo it during his lifetime?) stated that the book was almost
unknown until a cache of ten or twelve copies were dispersed by
one W.C. Bennett, a friend of Miss Mitford's, in 1886. In 1929,
when Wise published *A Browning Library* the story was much
more elaborate. It ends

> Dr. Bennett has long been dead [he died four months before Gosse
> published the Reading *Sonnets* story] and most of the friends who in
> my early days were associated with me in admiration of Browning and
> in love of his books have also passed away. I am one of the few persons
> still living and I believe the sole remaining man who broke bread at
> Browning's table.

When the Reading *Sonnets* was exposed as a fraud some forty
years later, this lovely piece of embroidery caused Wise all sorts
of problems. Indeed Wise himself points out (in one of his typical
correctional notes) that in 1852 Miss Mitford confused Dr W.C.
Bennett with his brother Sir John Bennett and did not get to
know him any better in the three years of life that remained to
her. Why then did she entrust him with the remaining copies of
this very intimate book, which were in fact not hers to give?
Forman would never have been so rash, though Wise's story did

account for his possession of any copy that he cared to sell. It was a spare from his great haul.

Wise was an unofficial bookseller for many years, and must have found the forgeries a welcome addition to his stock. He used them to salt mediocre collections of books which he wanted to sell *en bloc*. Forman, being a much more discreet man all round, is more difficult to catch in action, but there is a little evidence that he used them as material for swops – from one collector to another so to speak. Quite a number of pamphlets were consigned to auction – that blessedly anonymous method of selling – and in some cases the forgers rigged a high price (put on a reserve and then bid against it: illegal but impossible to stop). Forman, at least, probably had contingency plans if he were to be detected and certainly intended to leave (if Wise had let him alone) a much more confusing trail. One defence was that of the 'remainder': the forgers had multiple copies of a perfectly genuine Browning pamphlet *Two poems* 1854. Moxon's publishing business had ended in rather a muddle and the various sales that followed its demise contained all sorts of bundles and lots that may have contained anything. Wise and Forman advanced the theory that they had contained bundles of forgeries, though this was only really convincing where they had faked Moxon's imprint. Another genuine remainder was Wordsworth's *Kendal and Windermere Railway* 1845. Forman had at least five copies of this which probably did come from a bundle in one of the Moxon sales. Between themselves, the forgers seem to have used 'remainder' as a code word for 'one of our forgeries'.

Another promising red herring was provided by Richard Herne Shepherd, a literary hanger-on, bibliographer and heavy drinker. He had printed a couple of Swinburne leaflets without the author's permission (but they are undated) and he did produce a piracy of Tennyson gleaned from uncollected periodical pieces. After some confusing lawsuits (and even more confusing bibliography) Tennyson stopped him. The forgers seem to have bought the unsold remainder of these pieces and distributed them with their forgeries after about 1892. Just to confuse matters thoroughly, Forman arranged that one set of Shepherd's Tennyson piracy with the single word title *Poems* should be overprinted to read *The New Timon and the Poets: with other omitted Poems*. Shepherd was known to be a bit of a bad hat and,

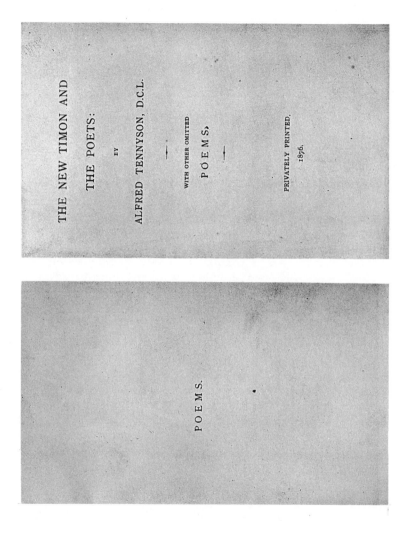

29.   Shepherd's piracy of Tennyson. On the left as published,
on the right with extra wording added by Forman

especially once he had died in 1895, was doubtless kept in mind by the forgers as a useful scapegoat.

Besides the Reading *Sonnets*, 1894 saw other forgeries emerging viz. two more Swinburnes, another Ruskin, a second Elizabeth Barrett Browning and the first R.L. Stevenson (died that year – in Samoa). There were now some thirty to forty forgeries about, not to mention Wise's bibliophile printings, the visible portion of the Ashley Library iceberg.

Just about this time, a fine new customer hove into view. This was John Henry Wrenn, a wealthy Chicago banker and broker and head of the firm bearing his name.

On the occasion of Wrenn's first visit to 52 Ashley Road, in 1892, it was the host, self-assured, shrewd, and aggressive, who took the lead in conversation. He discussed with enthusiasm his various bibliographical activities, referring with pride to his association with such men as Dr. F.J. Furnivall, Edward Dowden, Dykes Campbell, Richard Garnett, Harry Buxton Forman, and Edmund Gosse, even boasting of acquaintance with Swinburne and Browning. He brought out the crown jewels of his collection for the admiration of his visitor, enhancing their intrinsic interest by stories of their acquisition. The original manuscript of *Hellas* he bought from Sir John Bowring, who had it as a gift from Mary Shelley. A group of valuable Shelley letters came through Forman from the heirs of Jane Clairmont, together with Jane's own lurid diaries. His copy of *Oedipus Tyrannus*, one of the seven that survived destruction, was Shelley's gift to Edward Trelawny. For the precious Pisa edition of *Adonais* he had paid, he gloated, the record price of £40, and, mad as that price seemed to his competitors, they would live to call it a bargain. And indeed Wise himself saw the brochure sell for $6,000. It was his policy, this young collector declared, to buy only fine copies of desirable books, and he was always ready to exchange a good copy for a better, particularly if it had an "association interest." To Wrenn's hesitant question, as certain favourites were put into his hands, he gave a hearty, forthright promise that Chicago should have first call on these volumes should they be turned out of the Ashley Library to make place for larger or more interesting copies.

This account was reconstructed many years later by Miss Ratchford who had talked both to Wise and to Harold Wrenn the collector's son. One reason why Wise got on so well with people like Wrenn, who was a retired stockbroker, was because of his businesslike approach to the essentially subjective matter of book collecting. Many such men have rather a guilty conscience about spending serious money on their collections, but buying from Wise was reassuring. The first letters date from 1894 and mostly Wrenn was anxious to obtain Ashley Library private printings, showing what a useful bait these were.

> I think I shall be able to find you still a copy of Lang's "Tercentenary of Izaak Walton" and if so will forward it on. The "Lines on the Inaugural Meeting of the Shelley Society" [by Andrew Lang: a piracy] however I know I cannot send you. The book was issued in 1886, and that's a long time ago. Every copy went at the time it was printed, and it has now become a "scarce" book. Indeed my vanity was flattered a few months ago, when I saw a copy sold in the Sale Rooms for 3/3/-: it had been issued by me at 7/6!

The correspondence died away for a little to be awakened every now and then by the despatch of further private printings, but Wrenn was cautious at first about accepting Wise as a supplier of anything but new books. In April 1897, Wrenn jibbed at £80 for

> a copy of the first edition of "Paradise Lost" with genuine first title-page ... perfect condition, not washed or mended, not the slightest damage to any leaf; a large copy with wide margins to every page. In a fine old morocco binding of about the last decade of last century

and offered £70 which Wise accepted. He claimed he had just obtained Dryden's copy, with his lines to Milton in manuscript on the flyleaf. This latter has never surfaced and indeed sounds rather like a copy fabricated in a bibliographical parlour game. When sending the book off, Wise admitted the title had 'a tiny tear which Riviere has beautifully mended' he also mentions paying £60 for one of his own forgeries. In May, he received a letter from Wrenn objecting to the Milton: he put off replying *pro tem* and meanwhile wrote three further letters brimming with convincing bookish gossip and sold Wrenn a forged Tennyson. In his long and delayed explanation of Milton, he almost manages to convince Wrenn that black is white, or rather that his Milton with a corrected text is actually earlier than one with errors. To be fair, one has to say that *Paradise Lost* is a bibliographical minefield and even now the way through it is not charted with unambiguous clarity. In a subsequent letter, Wise admits to a corner torn off one of the leaves which he ought to have mentioned: and he suggests Wrenn may like to return the book. Despite this unpromising beginning it was not long before Wrenn was hooked and there was a steady flow of books and letters from London to Chicago. Wise, there is no doubt about it, was a crackerjack salesman, and time and again in his compelling prose one can watch poor old Wrenn being sold a gold brick in broad daylight.

There were other eager buyers for the new rarities including W.B. Slater (did he guess?) A.J. Morgan of Aberdeen, a wealthy Scot, Herbert T. Butler, Wise's relative, Colonel W.F. Prideaux the bibliographer, and William Harris Arnold (of whom we shall hear more). W.B. Slater deserves a little more than passing mention. He came from a silversmithing family and rose to become a partner in Holland, Aldwinckle & Slater, a very large firm of manufacturing silversmiths. This shared family background and their mutual membership of the Camden Road Mutual Improvement Society led to a lifelong intimacy with Wise.

All this activity did not lack critics, especially among the more crusted collectors of the old school who liked black letter folios and Elzeviers and nothing after 1700. Their spokesman was William Roberts who in *The Fortnightly Review* for March 1894 let loose a broadside. 'Now every little volume of drivelling verse becomes an object of more or less hazardous speculation, and the book market itself a stock exchange in miniature.' He had visited Wise at Ashley Road and may even have had him in mind when he fulminated against

> too-zealous persons who feed their own vanity by hanging on to the coat-tails of eminent men and claim the title of public benefactors by "resurrecting" from a well-merited obscurity some worthless tract or obsolete and ephemeral magazine article, and trumpeting it about as a masterpiece.

This was answered by Wise in his April *Bookman* article: he concentrated mainly on prices, instancing three of his Browning fakes as being worth ten or twelve guineas each and ending with a strong defence of Ruskin values (this was a falling market he was trying hard to prop up).

In the next month (May 1894) Wise had another fight on his hands. He reviewed *Early Editions: a bibliographical account of the works of some popular modern authors,* by J.H. Slater (no relation) and tried to right the many incomplete or inaccurate accounts of modern authors e.g.

30.  Forman visits Bucke in Canada, 1896

*Gold Hair* is stated to be "selling for about £5". *Gold Hair* is a privately printed pamphlet of the greatest rarity, and the sale of no copy has ever been recorded by Browning specialists. There would be no difficulty in finding buyers for half a dozen copies at *Twice* the £5 at which it is here reported to be "selling".

Wise is too optimistic since over the next twenty years or so, this forgery usually made between £3 and £8 at auction; and he sold nineteen copies at £1 each in 1910. There are similar puffs in his review, but what is really interesting is Wise's general criticism, which illustrates very well his attractions to businesslike collectors.

Mr Slater has attempted to do that which was impossible. No man can accurately and critically discourse upon a subject with which he is not perfectly familiar. Values in the book market are subject to niceties as fine, and to a large extent as indescribable, as those in any other branch of commerce. To appreciate such niceties, and to acquire the ability to estimate the worth of any article, requires a close and continued connection with it, and it is no more possible for a man to fix with any degree of accuracy the values of early editions unless he be a buyer or a seller, than it is for him to appraise the worth of parcels of goods in the produce market, or of shares upon the Stock Exchange.

He also pleads for the inclusion of collations, which is a shorthand way of describing the physical makeup of a book.

Forman meanwhile, was watching his children grow up. In 1894 Maurice, his favourite, departed for South Africa and a job in the colonial post office. His father missed him greatly since they had many shared tastes. In September of the same year, Forman wrote to Maurice Bucke in London, Ontario. 'Your letter and paper on Cosmic Consciousness came just as I was off to Devon with Laura and Gwendolen for a much needed annual holiday. I took the paper with me; and Laura and I both read it with great interest.' In 1896 he managed to visit Bucke in Canada. He makes a strange figure in the summer camp on Liberty Island, camping under the trees and feeding chipmunks. He was still collecting hard and, like Wise, had new money coming in from the fakes.

In December 1816, Harriet Shelley wrote her last letter addressed at once to her sister Eliza Westbrook, to her estranged husband and her parents,

My dear Bysshe let me conjure you by the remembrance of our days of happiness to grant my last wish – do not take your innocent child from Elizabeth who has been more than I have, who has watched over her with such unceasing care.

Harriet was found drowned: after a legal dispute about Ianthe and Charles her brother, Shelley was given limited access which he never exercised and he never saw his two children again. The letter was probably left behind in Marlow and came into possession of Shelley's landlord. It then appeared in London in 1895. The story of its sale is told by W. Courthope Forman, Harry's youngest brother.

> The story of the re-appearance of Harriet's last letter is rather a curious one – It was told me by Mr George Suckling the second-hand bookseller, & print-seller in Garrick Street – One day a woman came into his shop & asked if he bought autograph letters – He said "Yes", & she produced a packet of letters written by William Godwin – These do not command a large price, but he made her a fair offer for them which she accepted – When she had gone (leaving her name & address) he went over the packet again, & found among the letters that one signed Harriet S – He came to the conclusion it was Harriet's last letter – "Your brother Buxton" he said to me "should have this I thought, so I went to the General Post Office & showed it to him" He read it – How much he said, I answered £20 – Too much Suckling, no I won't give it – So I took it away & walked back to my shop by Holborn in a leisurely way – On arriving there was your brother! I'll have the letter Suckling he said, & drew me a cheque for £20 – I sent the woman on a proportion of my profit, & later much regretted my honesty – She worried me continually like the daughters of the horse leech crying out for more – At last I had to threaten her with proceeding if she bothered me any more – The purchase was a good one for my brother, or rather for his widow – When his library was sold in New York it realized some £350: for there is no doubt it was written by the despairing wife of the poet

Wise's next collecting exploit was carried out in conjunction with Clement Shorter, another crony of his. Shorter had come from a similar background to Wise. His father early left home and he had an impoverished non-conformist upbringing in North London. He became editor of the *Illustrated London News* but left in 1902 to found *The Sphere* which he ran for twenty-four years. In later life he lived at 16 Marlborough Place, just round the corner from Forman. The two were poles apart in character and never struck up any kind of friendship, if indeed they ever

met. Wise, however, thoroughly enjoyed his company, and in
later life they had weekly lunches. As described by Wise himself,

> On the days that it was Shorter's turn to pay, he would tell the
> waiter to make out the bill "all on one". Then, while this was being
> done, he would take out his wallet from an inside pocket and carefully
> select a letter he had received from Thomas Hardy, or George Mere-
> dith, or some other author, and – holding it high between finger and
> thumb – slowly advance it to me, saying "Well, Tommy, if you settle
> the bill and I give you this, we shall be quits – eh?" This became a
> regular thing; and so I nearly always found the cash for our luncheons.

The difficulty about this friendship was that Shorter and Gosse
hated each other. On one occasion Shorter went into print with
'Personally I do not like either Mr. Gosse or Sir Sidney Colvin'.
Quick as a flash E.V. Lucas burst into poetry in *Punch*, of which
we give two verses.

> Alas, alack for Sidney C!
> Alack, alas for Edmund G.!
> On both must History's verdict be
> That Shorter did not like them.

> In vain poor Edmund's enterprise
> In baring Putney to the skies,
> And linking up with T.J. Wise,
> For Shorter doesn't like him.

On another occasion, Shorter called Gosse 'the so-called critic'
causing Gosse to write furiously to Wise, 'Will you explain to me
why I have suddenly received over my head and shoulders this
bucket-full of Mr. Clement Shorter's bedroom slops?' Wise was a
considerable diplomat and he remained on good terms with both.
Shorter did a good deal of literary hack work (which is not how he
thought of it, however) in providing introductions and notes to
reprints of classics. Indeed for Ward Lock's Nineteenth Century
Classics he got Wise to edit Browning's *Bells and Pomegranates*
1896. Shorter also wrote biographical studies of the Brontës and
Borrow: his own opinion of the last was that it was one of the
best biographies ever written. From about 1912 on, he followed
Wise's lead and printed a number of limited edition pamphlets of
such authors as Conrad, Barrie and Meredith. The latter's view
of him was

> The type of literary man who would print a famous writer's
> blotting-pad in a limited Edition if he could get hold of it, though

according to his lights and limitations he did his best to further the appreciation of the good literature.

Shorter also collected a substantial library, again following Wise's footsteps, though many miles behind.

Back to 1895 when, following initial detective work by Forman, Shorter, accompanied by Robertson Nicoll, went over to Banagher in Ireland to seek out the Revd Arthur Nicholls, a struggling farmer. He had been the husband of Charlotte Brontë from June 1854 to March 1855. Shorter bought for £400, in conjunction with Wise, not only a large parcel full of manuscripts and letters by the Brontë children, but also copyrights. Wise had the manuscripts bound, very mixed up in some fifty or sixty thin volumes. Some he kept and others he sold, thus for example dispersing bits of the Angria cycle all over the place. Wise left some of the private printing of this cache to Shorter, since he had other fish to fry. He had undertaken a commission from George Allen (first met over Ruskin) to edit Spenser's *Faerie Queen* published in nineteen parts 1894–97 with illustrations by Walter Crane. He followed this up with another George Allen commission, an edition of Ruskin's *Harbours of England* published in 1895. He was also busy preparing a new group of forgeries; Rubecks had just moved; his stepmother was ill and died in 1896; he was servicing orders from his Ashley list of 1895 (all his life he packed and addressed many of his own book parcels); he was very busy. He was in fact so busy that he had little time for his pretty and lively young wife, whom he may have valued mainly for social reasons. When asked the inevitable question, he is said to have answered, 'Children! I can't afford children. They cost a thousand pounds each; and what a lot of books I can buy for that!'

Selina took to going often to a local tennis club, and one day in 1895, simply walked out on him. It must have brought back disquieting memories of his mother's flight and he was very upset. He obtained a decree nisi on 28 October 1897, on the grounds of his wife's adultery with one Lionel Rogers (curiously enough, Rogers was the maiden name of Selina's mother). It must have been exhausting, depressing and expensive to obtain the evidence; yet it is said that when Selina later fell on hard times, and he had remarried, he did help her out with money.

Wise faked his family background in his resumed correspondence with Wrenn. In December 1897, he explained that he had
hoped to have completed his Tennyson bibliography 'by the end
of the New Year, but the loss of my wife in the early summer
prevented me from devoting to it the time necessary to its rapid
progress'. This upset caused Wise to move house, and he left
Ashley Road for 15 St George's Road, Kilburn. This is much
nearer Forman, only a ten or fifteen minute walk, and the house
and neighbourhood look like a pale imitation of Marlborough
Hill. It was just as well Forman and Wise were close together, as
a new forgery promotion was in train. This was *Literary anecdotes
of the nineteenth century* published in two volumes in 1896–97.
The title harked back to Nichols's celebrated *Literary anecdotes
of the eighteenth century* and it was intended as a similar compendium to run to ten volumes (only two appeared, however). It had
the hidden purpose of bringing many forgeries before the public.
Forman contributed several of the separate articles (including
*Elizabeth Barrett Browning and her scarcer books* quoted above
which was also issued separately). He was not credited in *Literary
Anecdotes* which appeared as edited by Wise and W.R. Nicoll (the
sleeping partner). Forman boiled over:

Dear Wise,                                         29 Sept. 96
   I return the advertizement slip, as requested. My doing so means
nothing – that is to say, in any discussion which may take place
hereafter, I do not expect to be told "Well! You passed the advertizement slip ".
   When I made in regard to Vol.I some remarks about my things
going forth to the world under Nicoll's name & yours, you repudiated
my suspicions (or something of the sort that you called them), said
you thought I "must have been treated very scurvily" sometime or
other, & under what I suppose was strong enough compulsion,
arranged to have some of my contributions credited to me: – with a
distinct understanding of ultimate credit of everything through a
list in Vol. x.
   Now the distinct understanding is a perhaps, & the anonymous
system is actually said to be the universal rule, & to have been so
from the first! Well! Well!
   I think I said at the time that your suspicions were correct, &
that, just as gratitude is a sense of favours to come, so the old sense
of smart resolved itself into expectancy of scurvy treatment in the
future.
   But perhaps it is good trade & literary morals for two men to rest
almost entirely on a third in making a serious claim to literary

THE LAST TOURNAMENT

31.  Tennyson's *The last tournament*,
a creative forgery with an inscription by the supposed printer


honours, and adopt the attitude that if it suits their purpose they
will in ten years time tell the public what they have been doing!

I enclose a few scrappy remarks that can be taken in any order you
like.

Yrs.                                                    H.B.F.

### JANE CLERMONT

As it is a mere reprinted scrap from the Bookman, Dr N. cannot
attach any importance to the question of whether it goes in Vol. 2 or
3. It should therefore be kept over for his reconsideration. N. *has not
been told the truth*; & the par. ought not to appear at all in L.A.

H.B.F.

To me personally it is most annoying. I know *why* the lies have been
told: they should be repented of – not reblazoned abroad.

### CERTIFICATES

As to the certificates, thanks for your long story about Mrs Severn –

with whom you *do* seem to have put yourself in a difficulty. There is more than an appearance of *dishonesty*. The appearance is this – that you are reluctant to say how many are printed; & say "a few" because some will understand that to mean, some 10 or 12, some 20 or 30, & so on. There cannot on the face of it be an honest reason for wanting the number printed to be differently conjectured by different people; and it turns out that the appearance is borne out by the fact that, printing 30 (more or less), you want some one to think you only print 10 or 12. However, that is all your affair; and I have done on it, so far as your Ruskin Letters go. But what has that to do with *Browning* Letters? As to the 'Ashley List', it does not affect the question – has absolutely no bearing upon it.

Wise annotated this outburst at various points for return to Forman. After 'only print 10 or 12' he added

Quite so. And we print "Last Tournament" in 1896, and want "some one to think" it was printed in 1871! *The moral position is exactly the same!* But there is no "dishonesty". Mrs. Severn does not *buy* her copy under the impression that only 10 or 12 are printed: I *give* it to her *gratis!*

This document, known as the Pforzheimer document from its owner, is the only cast iron evidence that the conspirators themselves left behind them. It would have been difficult to explain away if they had been confronted with it, and would have been a decisive piece of evidence in a law-suit.

# THE
# LAST TOURNAMENT

By ALFRED TENNYSON, D.C.L.
POET LAUREATE

STRAHAN & CO.
56, LUDGATE HILL, LONDON
1871

32. *The last tournament*, from Lord Brotherton's library

# SUSPICION AROUSED

The Pforzheimer document introduces the forgeries of 1896 which include (of course) Tennyson's *Last Tournament* mentioned above. Tennyson (who died in 1892) was to prove a very lucrative new line and the proof that has such revealing annotations was Forman's *The Building of the Idylls: a study in Tennyson* published as a chapter of *Literary Anecdotes*. This chapter introduces five new Tennyson forgeries including *Morte D'Arthur* 1842, ('So all day long the noise of battle rolled/Among the mountains by the winter sea;/Until King Arthur's table man by man/Had fallen in Lyonesse about their Lord,/King Arthur'), *The Last Tournament* 1871, and *The Promise of May* 1882. The first two look much too much alike (placed side by side) to be separated by thirty years.

Tennyson is a tricky author, bibliographically speaking, since he loved to revise in proof: and sometimes these proofs can be elevated to the status of a 'private edition' and sometimes not. His revisions and further revisions, sometimes on different states of proof, sometime restore lines once discarded, thus making a considerable chronological tangle. Wise and Forman, needing to insert their fakes into an already complex genealogy, produced such intricate bibliographical accounts that few people read all the details and fewer still understood them. When Wise, after examining the tangled skein, pronounced a verdict then

AUTHOR'S PRIVATE EDITION.

**The Last Tournament.**

By Alfred Tennyson, D.C.L., Poet Laureate.

F'cap. 8vo, *handsomely bound by Riviere in full crushed levant morocco extra, uncut, t.e.g.*

*Strahan and Co., 56, Ludgate Hill, London,* 1871. **£26**

This little volume is of great rarity. It was printed for circulation among a limited circle of the Author's friends, and in a copy in Mr. Wise's possession, the Publisher Strahan, has written the following note :—

" Of this private Edition of the Last Tournament not more than 20 copies were printed."

33. A cutting from the Maggs catalogue
from which the book was ordered

34.   A bill from Maggs to Wise
for one of his forgeries

most people sighed with relief and accepted it. The consequence
was, of course, that they accepted first editions which were
nothing of the sort and of which a ready supply could be released
from Wise's cupboards or Forman's back rows of books. As William Harris Arnold observed some years later, 'Through the kind
offices of my new, but now dear old friend, the distinguished
collector and bibliographer, Thomas J. Wise . . . I obtained one
Tennyson rarity after another, most of which at the time, were
unknown to American collectors.' The forgers also made a final

sweep of Swinburne by printing no less than five creative forgeries, many described in *Literary Anecdotes*.

1897 brought the last big crop of forgeries, the last big crop
because the year also produced the first of several disputes. The
authors selected were Ruskin (1), E. Yates (1, really a Thackeray
item since it concerned a memorable row with him and the
Garrick Club), Swinburne (2), Stevenson (2), Tennyson (5) and a
special group of Morris which will be described later.

We might at this point stop, and consider one of these forgeries a little more closely, Swinburne's *The Devil's Due*. This story
starts with a fine row caused by an article in *The Contemporary
Review* for October 1871. This was entitled 'The fleshly school of
poetry: Mr. D.G. Rossetti' and purported to be by Thomas
Maitland, actually a pseudonym for Robert Buchanan, a poet
and author. Swinburne commented to W.M. Rossetti 'I believe
it is a habit with the verminous little cur to sneak into some
other hide as mangy as his own and pretend to yelp at himself as
well as his betters, to keep up the disguise.' In December 1871,
D.G. Rossetti answered 'Thomas Maitland' (as he formally was)
with an article 'The Stealthy School of Criticism' and in the
same issue of *The Athenaeum* was a note from Buchanan's publisher implying that he (Buchanan) had nothing to do with 'The
fleshly school' and one might 'with equal propriety associate
with the article the name of Mr. Robert Browning or of Mr.
Robert Lytton or of any other Robert'. William Minto, the
editor, rubbing his hands with glee, no doubt, was able to print
in the *same* issue a letter from Buchanan acknowledging his
authorship. In the next issue, his explanation was that he was
far out of reach, cruising in the Western Hebrides when T.
Maitland was affixed to his piece. Swinburne kept the pot boil-
ing with *Under the Microscope* a pamphlet published in July 1872.
This is a torrential denunciation of Buchanan and other critics in
which he is called a skunk and a dung eater.

In 1875, an anonymous book called *Jonas Fisher* stirred up the
mud again. Swinburne assumed it was Buchanan renewing his
attacks (it was actually by the Earl of Southesk) and published
in the *Examiner* his *Epitaph on a Slanderer*

> He whose heart and soul and tongue
> One above ground stunk and stung,

Now, less noisome than before,
Stinks here still, but stings no more.

The following week the *Examiner* reviewed *Jonas Fisher* and remarked that it was rumoured to be 'the work either of Mr. Robert Buchanan or the Devil' and Swinburne returned this lead and indeed all the others. He wrote a letter to the *Examiner* as Thomas Maitland and called it 'The Devil's Due'. The postscript gives a good flavour of it,

> The writer of the above, being at present away from London on a cruise among the Philippine Islands, in his steam yacht (the "Skulk", Captain Shuffleton, master) is, as can be proved on the oath or the solemn word of honour of the editor, publisher, and proprietor, responsible neither for an article which might, with equal foundation be attributed to Cardinal Manning, or to Mr. Gladstone, or any other writer in the *Contemporary Review*, as to its actual author; nor for the adoption of a signature under which his friends in general acting not only without his knowledge, but against his expressed wishes on the subject, have thought it best and wisest to shelter his personal responsibility from any chance of attack. This frank, manly, and consistent explanation will, I cannot possibly doubt, make every thing straight and safe on all hands.

The upshot was a lawsuit in which Buchanan claimed £5,000 damages and received £150 (those were the days!). The quarrel then slumbered on, unremembered save by a few, though the periodical publication of 'The Devil's Due' was listed in R.H. Shepherd's *Bibliography of Swinburne* (last edn: 1887).

For the forgers, the first thing was to find the text: probably this was Forman's job. He seems to have enjoyed sorting through odd volumes of periodicals for his favourite authors. A book collector pursuing an author always has troubles with periodicals. He is, by definition, a book collector: what does he do with the *Examiner* 1875 ('The Devil's Due') or come to that *Harper's Bazaar* 1891 (Tess of the d'Urbervilles) or *Good Words* 1877 ('Why Frau Frohman raised her prices')? The conventional collector ignores them but to anyone seriously interested in Swinburne, or Hardy or Trollope this is unthinkable. Even if the texts and illustrations do appear in book form, they are never the same. One can imagine Forman's rows of untidy envelopes containing odd pages marked up in blue pencil (as was his wont), a scruffy assemblage. Printing the contributions separately is one way of tidying up the mess and sorting your author out from the surrounding clutter. Feelings such as these may well have started Forman on his creative forgeries.

Wise was now a dab hand with printers. He would set off, copy in hand, from his office in Mark Lane to Bread Street Hill where he would come through the main door of Clays imposing building, tip his hat to Cecil Clay or one of the other governors, and go straight through to see J.R. Maylett, the foreman. Maylett may have known something was amiss (did Wise bribe him?) but to Cecil Clay, Wise was just a steady customer printing lots of little pamphlets.

In those days, Wise could arrange to pick up first proof in less than a week (*The Devil's Due* only makes nine pages of text even with a half title), show it to Forman, take it back and after another week or so have a neat parcel of thirty or forty Devil's Dues. The types used are all perfectly possible for the date and the pamphlet does not look out of place. However, the paper on which it is printed can be shown by chemical tests to be not before 1883. This little quirk of paper making history was not to be unravelled for many years but when it was, it caused Mr Wise grave embarrassment.

The next stage was to prepare the ground. In *Literary Anecdotes* Vol. 2 (published in December 1896) Wise has this to say

> It is said that concurrently with its appearance in the columns of the *Examiner, The Devil's Due* was printed in pamphlet form for private distribution, but was rigidly suppressed in consequence of the unexpected result of the libel action brought by Mr. Robert Buchanan against Mr. P.A. Taylor M.P. the proprietor of the *Examiner*. If such a pamphlet does exist, it must be of the utmost rarity, as no copy is known to the editors of *Literary Anecdotes*, who have instituted a lengthy search in the hopes of finding a stray example. In any case, if printed at all, it must have been distributed at the instance of the editor, as it was certainly not issued upon Mr. Swinburne's initiative.

Swinburne was still alive, and the forgers were doubtless chary of involving him. However, both P.A. Taylor the proprietor of the *Examiner* (died 1891) and W. Minto the editor (died 1893) were not available to comment.

In February 1897, Wise reverted to the subject in one of his expansive letters to Gosse:

Walter Theodore Watts-Dunton
from Algernon Charles Swinburne
April 1900

THE
DEVIL'S DUE
——
A.C.SWINBURNE
1875

35.   Wise's two copies of a creative forgery,
one with an inscription added from elsewhere

# THE DEVIL'S DUE

A LETTER

TO THE EDITOR OF "THE EXAMINER."

BY

THOMAS MAITLAND.

1875. For Private Circulation.

36.   A creative forgery of a piece by Swinburne ('Thomas Maitland')

My dear Gosse,

Thanks for your note. I wonder *you* did not know of "The Devil's Due". It only shews how very circumscribed is the knowledge of even the best of us when such trifles as the minute points of Bibliography are in question.

I knew of the tract years ago: – or rather *I had heard that such a tract was set up in type*, for until a month ago I had never been able to *see* a copy. It was Fairfax Murray who first told me of it. I have now seen and handled it, and am quite satisfied that it is in every way "all right". But it is a miserable little scrub and hardly worthy of even being dignified by the name of "tract". It was shewn to me by a gentleman, who called upon me in consequence of having read the note regarding it at p.355 of "Literary Anecdotes", v.2. Its owner believes (though possibly it is only a case of 'the wish being father to the thought') – that it is just a stray survivor of a few copies cheaply and roughly printed to use at the trial, that the "Letter" might be read, and its harmlessness appreciated by persons concerned with the legal proceedings.

It may of course be that such an issue was commenced, and never carried out, as was the case with the Rossetti–Buchanan pamphlet, of which you may have heard. Of this only 2 copies were preserved (Counsel's opinion having been taken, and the pamphlet declared to be libelous), – one of these 2 Wm. Rossetti has; the other Ellis burnt at Torquay 2 years ago.

If this copy of "The Devil's Due" remains unique, & no more turn up, it is of course of great value, and I should much like to purchase it. But until time has proved it to be unique, or at least one of 2 or 3 survivors, I don't feel inclined to give the £15.15 at which its owner values it – though I don't even *know* that he would sell at all. The "Letter" is such a wretched little scrap that if 20 copies were extant I should think 18/- each quite enough for them.

It really is vastly strange how things do crop up.

In about March 1897, Wise offprinted the Swinburne portion of *Literary Anecdotes* and was able to announce publicly that a copy of 'this most interesting brochure' had come to light. In October 1899, Wise dangled a copy before J.H. Wrenn, his invaluable American customer. 'I have heard of another copy of the very rare "Devil's Due". It belongs to a gentleman (Mr. Joseph Howell) at Cambridge. If I can manage to get it at a reasonable figure I will buy it for you, as it is a very desirable item.' In November 'No success yet with regard to the "Devil's Due", but Hope still lifts her head.' Wise finally managed to wrest a copy from his stock and sold it to Wrenn for £12 10s. Other copies must have been sold, though the next of which we have a record is in 1907 when Quaritch bought a copy at auction for £12 10s.

Swinburne died in 1909 and Watts-Dunton in 1914 so in 1919, Wise was able to rewrite the story in a much more satisfactory way. He records sending his initial bibliography to The Pines, where Swinburne and Watts-Dunton had their strange ménage; with the result that

> I was informed by Watts-Dunton that he had found a copy of the pamphlet, and was invited to call and inspect it. This I did, with the result that I was enabled to add to my *Bibliographical List* a *Postcript* in which the little rarity was described in full. The, as I then imagined, unique example I purchased from Watts-Dunton for £21. Three years afterwards, one Sunday afternoon, Watts-Dunton surprised me by asking whether any friend of mine was desirous of obtaining a copy of the First Edition of *The Devil's Due*. Upon my expressing curiosity as to his reason for making such an enquiry, he informed me that he had found a small packet containing a number of examples of the original pamphlet. This packet he then produced. There were in all some fifteen copies of *The Devil's Due*. One of these was handed to Swinburne; the remainder I carried away with me, having acquired them from Watts-Dunton at the rate of three guineas each. The copy handed to Swinburne was entrusted to a local binder, who put it into a commonplace cover of black roan. Swinburne then wrote the above inscription [*Walter Theodore Watts-Dunton/from/Algernon Charles Swinburne/April 1900*] upon the recto of the first leaf, and presented the tiny volume to his friend. The date of this inscription, *April* 1900, fixes approximately the date when the little 'remainder' came to light. In the autumn of 1909, after the death of Swinburne I purchased this inscribed copy also for the sum of £21, the identical price I had paid for the first recovered copy in 1897. The book has since been bound in levant morocco by Riviere.

Wise was a jolly good embroiderer: one observes the stray gentleman of the Gosse account turning into Theodore Watts-Dunton and Wise selling a copy of the remainder to Wrenn before he had discovered it. The evidence of Watts-Dunton's own copy is nil, since the presentation inscription is not on the book but on an inserted piece of paper bound in, which was lifted by Wise from some other source. The remainder suggestion is particularly interesting: it is another precautionary tale which could explain the ownership of so many little clean and fresh pamphlets, all without contemporary evidence of provenance. It is worth noting that Wise's Swinburne is still the standard bibliography of the poet and was reprinted in that guise as recently as 1972.

William Morris was clearly a Forman speciality, as Swinburne was of Wise. Forman had been on nodding, if not on intimate terms with William Morris for some twenty-five years: he was known as a keen and punctilious collector of his works and as a useful literary type who could safely be entrusted with a set of proofs to read. He certainly admired Morris greatly, so it was in the natural course of things that he would write the standard bibliography and forge the productions of his hero. Morris died on 3 October 1896 leaving behind him a literary corpus including books of poetry, translations from the Norse and Icelandic, political poems, tracts and manifestos and the two Wise–Forman creative forgeries (one of which Forman persuaded him to sign!)

Forman began picking up the threads of his bibliography and consulting his own collection. He could not resist tinkering on an extensive scale (approximately 10 per cent of the contents of his Morris bibliography are his own productions, authorized and unauthorized). He started off by reprinting *The Pilgrims of Hope*, a poem which had originally appeared in *The Commonweal* 1885–86. He set the title so that the date of publication of the poem in the periodical could be taken (and was intended to be taken) as the date of publication of the booklet. In fact the imprint date is about ten years too early, the book not being published until Morris's death in 1897. It has no printer's name but the surviving proofs show it was another Clay production. So a standard creative forgery? – not quite since Forman added a signed foreword. In this he stated that the reprint had been mentioned to Morris and he had not demurred – 'being unforbidden I had it printed' was how he put it. However, the reason they dared not submit this reasoning to Morris himself is suggested by a letter from Morris to Wise inserted in the latter's copy. 'As to reprinting in any form my callow productions, I beg your forgiveness for saying no in the flattest way. I want them forgotten as completely as it seems likely they will if they are left alone' (23 July 1894).

Forman then knocked off four new creative forgeries all with the same ambiguous title page as *The Pilgrims of Hope*: one of these though dated by implication 1885 had some copies printed

on paper watermarked 1896 (compare his first ever creative forgery *Galatea* of which this is also true). Was this a sop to his
conscience, a marker for later researches or a very present alibi in
time of trouble? He then provided Morris pamphlets (perfectly
genuine) with *fake wrappers*. These wrappers made the rather
insignificant originals look more exciting, pointed up the name of
Morris, and in one case added '250 copies for the author'. It is
hard to take these fake wrappers too seriously and their place in a
shadow land halfway between forgery and reality is typical of
Forman. The feeling that he was in close touch with Lewis
Carroll, increases when we notice that he arranged for one of the
complete fakes to be available in a second class state without its
wrappers.

The pamphlets that Forman treated were produced for quite
other purposes than gracing the shelves of collectors – inciting
revolution or preserving ancient buildings. They therefore did
not necessarily conform to collectors' taste – so Forman dressed
them up a bit. It is a curious fact that a number of creative
forgeries once had wrappers which were removed before they were
marketed – for example the Reading *Sonnets*. In other cases
almost all copies are without wrappers save for one or two in
specially selected libraries. The William Morris *Sir Galahad* fake,
for instance, has no wrappers even in the Ashley copy (ruby red
morocco instead) yet the W.B. Slater copy is in a blue green
wrapper. Similarity of colour between pamphlets that should
not have been similar at all may have driven the forgers to last
minute second thoughts. Forman's fascination with wrappers
did not end at Morris. He had a copy of Christina Rossetti's
*Verses*, a genuinely privately printed piece of 1847. It is bound in
full brown morocco by Tout and has Forman's manuscript note
'I never saw an uncut copy with a wrapper like this.' The reason
for his single sighting of the wrappers is that they are apparently
his own insertion. He may also have added a wrapper to one of his
copies of Wordsworth's *Kendal and Windermere Railway*, another
genuine pamphlet we have already considered (see page 109).

Some of Forman's file copies of the Morris group have survived
with his annotations. We get three layers of reality: the published account in the bibliography; what Forman wrote on the
file copies; and the approximate truth revealed by later research.
In his *Books of William Morris*, Forman notes the wrappers but

not his connection with them. A typical example is *Under an Elm-tree* 1891, where his printed account reads: 'It was sold without a wrapper; but special copies are occasionally found with a pale green printed wrapper added.' In manuscript with his file copy he went further: 'Having bought a small parcel of copies for myself and friends, I had 50 wrappers printed.' To cap the story, one can show that he added these fake wrappers to the wrong edition, not the first, an unexpected slip. But he stopped short of annotations admitting a forgery, and even deepened the mystification. *The God of the poor* is a creative forgery with a red wrapper, *The Voice of toil* ditto with a yellow one. However, he had one of each in each other's colour with the manuscript note

> This is the only copy of "The God of the Poor" that I ever saw in a primrose coloured wrapper. This pamphlet and "The voice of toil" having both been printed at the office of "Justice", there must have been an accidental transposition of coloured papers through having the two little prints in hand at the same time. This accident tends to fix the date of the "God of the poor" pamphlet.

Reading such notes, one seems to be a spectator at some abstruse private charade, a theatre with the puppet master as his sole audience. We christened such mixtures of true pamphlet and fake wrappers chimeras, by analogy with the graft hybrid or Chimera. The best known of these is + Laburnocytisus adamii which consists of laburnum with a skin of broom, the two tissues growing side by side in one plant, but distinct and producing flowers of both species. Chimerical wrappers were used to create collected editions of socialist pamphlets which never existed (though the constituents were genuine enough). The most complex chimera of all was *Gossip about an old house* 1895. This article by Morris on Kelmscott Manor appeared in *The Quest, The journal of the Birmingham Guild of Handicraft* for November 1895. Instead of reprinting the whole thing to produce a genuine creative forgery, Forman extracted the six relevant leaves from the magazine and added a title, half-title and colophon which claims that fifty copies were done in the separate form. The Birmingham Guild were a careful lot who even insisted in setting all the advertisements in their magazine in their chosen Caslon typeface. They must have been very puzzled when they read Forman's Morris bibliography and he had at least one awkward letter on this point. It was from another Morris specialist, H.C. Marillier 'May I ask, by the way,

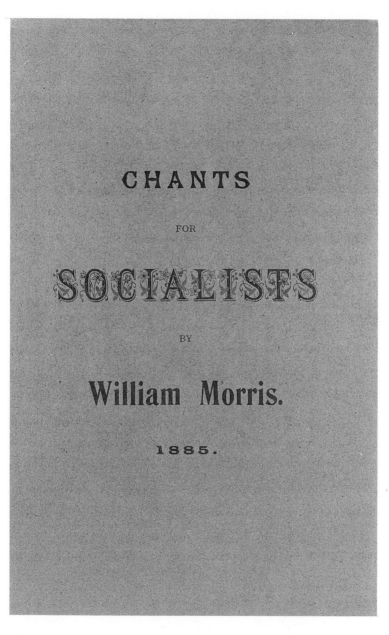

# CHANTS

FOR

## SOCIALISTS

BY

## William Morris.

### 1885.

37.  Chimerical wrapper added by Forman to a Morris pamphlet

This demy 8vo. pamphlet is the first edition of "Chants for Socialists," although "The Day is Coming" had appeared by itself under that heading in 1884, and was followed by "The Voice of Toil and All for the Cause: Two Chants for Socialists." Unlike most of the Socialist penny pamphlets of Morris, the demy 8vo "Chants" was issued uncut and simply folded with no stitching or metal-sewing. It had no wrapper as published. But it happened to go to the Office of "The Commonweal" just as it had been sold out all but a handful and the second

38. Account by Forman of how he forged the wrapper

edition with a seventh poem
was just ready. I bought the
handful and had the red
wrapper printed to protect
what seems to me still to be
a very agreeable and sightly
title-page. I should not have
chosen these ornamental
types, but had to have what
I could get. I had fifty of
these wrappers done, and
ultimately got copies enough
for all of them.

The pamphlet as issued,
wrapperless, is by no means

easy to obtain. It had a large
and quick genuine sale among
folk not given to cherish things
of the kind; and the chances are
that the bulk of the edition has
gone the way of wastepaper.

I am assured that the note-
worthy paragraphs of prose on
the verso of the title are a quotation,
not from some undiscoverable
author, but from a street-cor-
ner utterance of the poet's own,
one of his earliest Socialist
speeches.

how one may come by the reprint from "The Quest" of Morris's article on Kelmscott Manor. You seem evidently to have got the book, but the Birmingham people strenuously deny its publication, in spite of the colophon which you quote.' (4 January 1898).

More serious trouble had already started *vis à vis* some of Forman's other Morris forgeries. The forgers' luck seemed to have run out. One of Morris's executors was his former secretary, Sydney Cockerell, alive, alert, intelligent, a good bibliographer and rather a pest: the other, F.S. Ellis, was a retired antiquarian bookseller, the publisher of Morris's earlier works and an old acquaintance of Forman's. The forgers tried selling some of their new publications in a Jones and Evans Catalogue of 1897. This bookshop was run by F.H. Evans, best known as a photographer. The shop was in the city, very near Rubecks and Wise knew Evans pretty well. However Cockerell read the catalogue and descended on Forman at once.

> Do you know anything about a privately printed *Pilgrims of Hope* advertised in Jones and Evans' Catalogue? I have never seen a copy and begin to wonder whether it may not be an unauthorised reprint. I have asked Evans to let me see it. Nor have I seen *The God of the Poor* in a red wrapper. I shall be glad when your little book comes out to tell us what does exist, & what does not. I have great doubt about the *Sir Galahad* which W.M.'s old friends don't ever seem to have seen – What do you think about it?

Attached to this letter is Forman's pencilled draft reply on two pages dated 10 September:

> I too shall be glad when my book is out! Meanwhile I send you slips of what I have said about the three pamphlets you mention. For *The Pilgrims of Hope* you see I am personally responsible; and I have much pleasure in sending a copy for your acceptance. Whether when you have read my note on it you will clarify it as "unauthorised" or "unforbidden", I wonder.

Cockerell immediately replied on 11 September,

> Many thanks to you for the copy of *The Pilgrims of Hope* which I need not say I am exceedingly glad to possess. I think that it contains many fine things, but that it could not now be reprinted as W.M. decided against it, & took three of the best chapters for *Poems by the Way*. Thank you also for the notes on *Sir Galahad* and *The God of the Poor*. I shall not believe in *Sir Galahad* until I find someone who saw a copy before 1860. As to *The God of the poor* & another pamphlet offered by Evans *The Voice of toil: All for the Cause* can you tell me whether these

GPO

16·9·97

Dear Cockerell,

Many thanks for the additional
information sent in your letter of
the 14th. As to the pamphlets
you mention I think it unlikely
that they were sold in any
quantity — especially if, as
Walker thinks, they were run
off expressly for me. Of two
things I am sure — (1) that I
have additional copies
of most if not all of them, &
(2) that you are heartily welcome
to anything that can be supplied
from my duplicates & parcels.
So don't buy any of these things

39.   Draft of a letter from Forman to S. C. Cockerell
with a partial admission of guilt

were ever offered for sale in any quantity at the Justice offices or
elsewhere? Walker had never seen either of them, & there were no
copies among W.M.'s odds & ends. – nor yet of *The Socialist Ideal of
Art* which appears to have been printed at the same place ... I will
send you the other particulars on Monday.

Monday was 13 September and on the following day Cockerell
sent the 'other particulars' and apparently some comments by
Emery Walker, in a letter which was not preserved.

On 16 September Forman drafted a two page reply to Cockerell.

Many thanks for the additional information sent in your letter of the
14th. As to the pamphlets you mention I think it is unlikely that
they were sold in any quantity – especially if, as Walker thinks, they
were run off expressly for me. Of two things I am sure – (1) that I have
additional copies of most if not all of them, & (2) that you are heartily
welcome to anything that can be supplied from my duplicates &
parcels. So don't buy any of these things that you don't happen to
have; & when I am through my book – if not sooner – I will hunt
through my cupboards & back rows – which I know are pretty rich in
Morris tracts, especially of the Socialist period, & ask you to accept
anything I have which you have not. Walker of course will be welcome
too where three copies will go round.

Cockerell replied to Forman on 17 September, asking for a clearer
statement of his responsibility:

Many thanks for your generous promise to let me have any duplicate
Morris tracts that you can spare & that I have not got. If, as you hint
in your letter, you are responsible for the existence of some of these, I
think there ought to be some statement of it in your bibliography or
elsewhere, in order to separate these artificial rarities from duly published & authorised reprints – what do you think?

If Forman replied to this letter, he preserved no copy of the draft.
The sequel to this exchange of letters was a markedly less urbane
notice printed in *The Athenaeum* for 20 November 1897:

A Warning to Collectors
As executors of the late William Morris, we think it right to warn
collectors that unauthorised reprints of some of his contributions to
the weekly and monthly press are now being offered for sale at high
prices. It would be well for those concerned in the manufacture of such
"rarities" to remember that they are engaged in an act of piracy and
that they lay themselves open to proceedings under the Copyright
Act.
F.S. Ellis
S.C. Cockerell

Forman's bibliography itself is an attractive book. Rather like his *Shelley Library* it attempts to make bibliography more popular by telling it as a chronological story, so that it becomes a sort of biography. It has a rather touching dedication to Maurice in Cape Town which (especially the bracketed verse) seems to have several possible meanings.

Dedication to Maurice Buxton Forman of Cape Town, South Africa.

> Dear Son,–In this poor gift there's fitness;
>   For when into the world you came,
> You got–and let this leaf bear witness–
>   A twice associated name.
>
> Our well-belov'd friend Bucke's prenomen
>   We gave you–and the letters show it:
> Still, we'd an eye upon the omen
>   That that same name described a poet.
>
> 'Tis naught but simple truth I'telling–
>   Two sponsors' names in one we found,
> With some slight difference in the spelling
>   And none whatever in the sound.
>
> While yet a lad you loved to walk about
>   The book-room mingling lore with chaff;
> And well you knew some tomes I talk about
>   In this my biobibliograph.
>
> Later, the "midnight lamp" has seen us
>   In that same book-room all alone;
> But since the Atlantic heaved between us
>   Those Morris rows have grown and grown;
>
> And still with every teeming year
>   That made the listening world his debtor
> I grew to hold the man more dear
>   And ever loved the poet better.
>
> (Ah! Morris, it was well to know you–
>   Whatever comes of it, it was well–
> Though dry the sprigs of bay I throw you,
>   Right fain were I to be your Boswell!)
>
> So long, dear Boy! The ship's in port
>   That scores the Atlantic east and west:
> Those rollers huge she'll make her sport,
>   And bring you this at my behest.

Forman ambiguities are also found in the text, for instance in the description of *Sir Galahad* '1858' which he and Wise had printed, perhaps in 1890.

> It is but a thin little pamphlet and cannot be traced in the books of Messrs. George Bell and Sons, the imprint of whose predecessors, Messrs. Bell and Daldy, it bears. Neither is it traceable at the Chiswick Press, at which *The Oxford and Cambridge Magazine* and Morris's first two volumes of poetry were printed. It does not, however, look like Chiswick Press printing; and so small a thing may have been got done anywhere.

Forman's *Books of William Morris* got 'done' by Billings of Guildford. They printed some of the Morris forgeries; Clays printed the early ones; and a third printer, the socialist Twentieth Century Press printed others. There is one final point about the Morris fakes. They use quite a lot of different coloured paper for the wrappers, (remember the multicoloured papers used for *Letters to Fanny Brawne* 1878?). One of the fake Morris wrappers survives in a proof with Alfred Forman's initials on it. Having spent twelve years in the paper trade he supplied all the paper needed for most of Harry's legitimate prints and (presumably) for the forgeries as well. He may have had some inkling of what his brother was up to; but it is going too far to christen him the third forger. Still, a useful adjunct for any forger, a friend in the paper trade.

All the Cockerell fuss did not go unnoticed and stirred up further mud. Robert Proctor was a disciple of Morris who became a typographical expert of international standing. He himself seems to have projected a Morris bibliography but he did not complete or publish it. However, his researches led to another announcement in *The Athenaeum* (22 June 1898, some seven months after Cockerell and Ellis):

> Mr. Temple Scott and Mr. H. Buxton Forman, in their bibliographies of William Morris, agree in assigning the place of honour among his works to a separate edition of "Sir Galahad, a Christmas Mystery," which is assumed to be earlier in date than the "Guenevere" volume, in which it is included. Mr. Forman further distinguishes two editions of "Sir Galahad," a genuine original, and a later unauthorized reprint. I have recently had the opportunity of examining a copy of the former, which purports to be published in 1858, the year of "Guenevere," by Bell & Daldy, the publishers of that volume. All that is known about it seems to point to its being itself an unauthorized and later reprint from the "Guenevere" of 1858, the imprint being taken bodily from that work. The types in which it is printed differ wholly from those used by the Chiswick Press for "Guenevere"; and, after what Mr.

Forman has said on p. 33 of his book, it may be considered certain that it was not printed there. But for all Morris's other literary ventures at this period he employed the Chiswick Press; and it is therefore extremely improbable that different printers should have been used by him for two books so intimately connected, and both published, as is alleged, by the same firm in the same year. Moreover (Forman, p. 33), the books of Messrs. Bell do not, any more than those of the Chiswick Press, contain any trace of such an edition having been ever undertaken by them; and, what is even more convincing, neither Mr. Morris's family nor any of his most intimate friends had ever seen or heard of the tract before the publication of Mr. Aymer Vallance's "Art of William Morris" last spring.

R. Proctor.

There was no reply to either of *The Athenaeum*'s announcements. With so many hostile and accurate experts rallying round, the forgers must have wished they had kept their fingers out of the Morris pie. Shortly after these imbroglios, Wise went out to bat for the team, on an equally sticky wicket. One of two Stevensons mentioned above was a creative forgery of *Some college memories* 1886 which R.L.S. contributed to *The New Amphion* 1886. This time the correspondence was all in public in *The Athenaeum* (again) starting on 8 January 1898.

Messrs. T. & A. Constable write from the University Press, Edinburgh:–
Application has been made to us from two sources for information about a pamphlet, at present being offered for sale at extraordinary prices, entitled 'Some College Memories,' by Robert Louis Stevenson. It contains eighteen pages, and is stitched in a purple-grey wrapper, which is ornamented with a vignette of the late Prof. Kelland, pirated from an etching by Mr. Hole. The pamphlet has neither publisher's nor printer's imprint, but it is stated on the title-page that it has been printed for members of the Edinburgh University Union Committee. 'Some College Memories' was first contributed by Mr. Stevenson to a little volume called 'The New Amphion,' which was printed by us for the Edinburgh University Union in November 1886. This paper was reprinted in 'Memories and Portraits' (Chatto & Windus, 1887), and in the first volume of the Edinburgh edition of Mr. Stevenson's works. The origin of the grey pamphlet is unknown to us as well as to Mr. Colvin and Mr. Baxter. Its existence was also unknown to the editors of 'The New Amphion,' who were the secretaries of the University Union Committee. It appears to have been printed to catch the collector of first editions and can doubtless be multiplied indefinitely. But it is not a first edition – merely a pirated reprint, of which the sale is illegal.

Messrs. Constable are, we fancy, in error. Stevenson, if we mistake not, had some copies printed off in 1886 for distribution among his friends connected with the University. We are informed by a bibliographer of note that he has seen one copy of the grey pamphlet bearing an inscription of some length in Stevenson's handwriting, which he is persuaded is quite genuine.

From *The Athenaeum*, 22 January

University Press, Edinburgh, Jan.11. 1898.
The authenticity of the grey pamphlet is but a small matter to continue a correspondence about, yet we think it a duty to collectors to reply to your remarks on our former letter.

We have compared the text of 'Some College Memories' as printed in 'The New Amphion' with Mr. Stevenson's original manuscript. We find that the printed text differs in several places from the manuscript from which it was set up, showing that Mr. Stevenson had revised the proofs of 'The New Amphion' and had made alterations on them. The text of the grey pamphlet is exactly the same as that of the 'Amphion,' showing that it is a reprint from that little book.

We must repeat our conviction that the grey pamphlet is merely a pirated reprint, and was not printed for Mr. Stevenson, for the following reasons, among others:–
1.  It is difficult for us to believe that between November 30th (the date of issuing 'The New Amphion') and December 31st, 1886, Mr. Stevenson would, unknown to Mr. Colvin and Mr. Baxter, have commissioned any Edinburgh printer other than ourselves to reprint his article.

2.  It is impossible to believe that Mr. Stevenson would have stated that the pamphlet was printed for the University Union Committee when, on the authority of the secretaries, it was not printed for that Committee, and until now its existence was unknown to them.

3.  It seems preposterous to believe that Mr. Stevenson would have secretly photographed and reproduced a portrait which was the work of one friend and the property of another, if for no higher reason than that he could have had the original plate if he had wanted it.
T. & A. Constable

In *The Athenaeum*, 5 February Wise replied:

15 St. George's Rd.N.W. Jan. 31, 1898
"It might have been supposed that the editorial note appended to Messrs. Constable's first communication would have sufficed to settle the question of the position in Stevenson bibliography to which the separate print of 'Some College Memories' was to be assigned. But since Messrs. Constable have thought proper to reopen the question, it may be as well to state clearly what was the genesis of the little book.

After having made its first appearance in 'The New Amphion,' 'Some College Memories' was reprinted in Edinburgh at Christmas 1886. It was produced under the distinct direction – or permission – of Robert Louis Stevenson, and was seen through the press by Mr. W.H. Hepworth, Examiner in Art at South Kensington, and – outside that inner circle of close companions which included Mr. Edmund Gosse, Mr. Sidney Colvin, Mr. Charles Baxter and others – one of Stevenson's most valued friends and correspondents. That the distribution of the little book was never carried out to the extent its author had intended was no doubt due to Mr. Hepworth's very indifferent health; added to which in 1886 there were probably not more than a dozen persons who would have troubled to preserve it, even had it reached their hands. Possibly, also, the festivities of the season may have served to interfere with the despatch or receipt of copies of the tract.

Briefly, the book is no 'piracy,' as it was printed under its author's direct instructions; neither is it in any way a 'spurious print,' as it was printed in 1886, as duly set forth upon its title-page.

Messrs. Constable's suggestion that because the pamphlet of 1886 was not printed by themselves, therefore it must be spurious, can hardly be serious, although, of course, had it been printed by direction of the Committee of the University Union, no doubt Messrs. Constable would have been employed to produce it. But it was not printed by direction of the Committee. It was printed by Stevenson himself, in conjunction with Mr. Hepworth, for distribution among members of that Committee and other friends, and it was open to Mr. Hepworth to have the work executed at any printing house he chose. The most natural course for him to pursue would be to commission, not Messrs. Constable, but the printers who in 1886 and the surrounding years were producing the majority of Stevenson's books.

Messrs. Constable's further remark – that because the text of the separate print agrees with that contained in 'The New Amphion' and does not follow the original 'copy,' therefore the separate print was unauthorised – is also difficult to follow. Had the pamphlet been printed by Messrs. Constable themselves, they would naturally have set up its pages from the revised text as contained in 'The New Amphion' and would never have gone out of their way to revive the cancelled readings of the manuscript. It cannot, therefore, be conceived as possible that Stevenson, when arranging with Mr. Hepworth to issue the private print, would have instructed him to go to Messrs. Constable and obtain the original (and discarded) copy of a text which he had already sufficiently revised. Unquestionably the only reasonable plan to adopt would be to work from a copy of 'The New Amphion.' Messrs. Constable's collation of the original manuscript is of considerable value to the bibliographer, as showing that Stevenson was given the opportunity of revising the text of his essay during the passage of 'The New Amphion' through the press, and that he availed himself of the opportunity afforded. To myself, as the

bibliographer of Robert Louis Stevenson, this fact is of peculiar interest; I had always regarded these 'Memories,' delightful as they are, as
entirely lacking revision. But the result of such collation can have no
bearing whatever upon the genuineness of the privately printed booklet. Fortunately the position of that book is unassailable, and its
validity is beyond dispute.

Thomas J. Wise.

A final sarcastic reply came from F.T. Sabin, an antiquarian bookseller.

From *The Athenaeum*, 26 February

Could Stevenson, forsaking awhile the fellowship of the immortals,
revisit a world he has so much delighted, would it be fair for Bibliography (while strewing flowers in his path) to ask a simple question or
two?

"Did you in December, 1886, the month following the copyright
publication of 'Some College Memories' by Messrs. Constable & Co.
(in 'The New Amphion'), direct Mr. Hepworth to print a separate
issue, with the following words on the title-page and cover: 'Edinburgh: printed for Members of the University Union Committee,
1886'?"

Stevenson: "My object in producing this private issue, without
informing any of my Edinburgh friends, or taking any notice of Messrs.
Constable's copyright interest, must remain an undiscoverable secret.
I might easily have obtained Messrs. Constable's consent to reprint
the "Memories"; I might also have borrowed their block for the
portrait; but I did neither of these things. You may observe that the
printing is anonymous – that it is inferior to the work of the better
houses. That no copies ever reached the members of the University
Union Committee, for whom the booklet was professedly printed, is
not to be wondered at. I took precautions to prevent it! Purposely
avoiding everything that was easy, natural, and inexpensive, I have
entirely succeeded in the attainment of my object – to create a
mystery and confuse and puzzle everybody."

"Can you state who did the printing for Mr. Hepworth; how many
copies were done; and if any copy has ever been in your own possession?" These are questions I leave to be answered by the Wiseacre
bibliographers.

Frank T. Sabin.

In the same year (1898) came another more general attack in a
magazine issued by the great American bookseller G.D. Smith and
edited by A.J. Bowden.

There is an uneasy feeling among collectors on this side regarding the
numerous little privately printed pamphlets by celebrated modern
authors that are being offered from England. Grave suspicions are
entertained that some of these are being manufactured – but that

£2175.

29

70   163. ENGLAND AND AMERICA IN 1782.   1872
     Printed solely for copyright purposes, exceedingly
     rare

120  164. BECKET.   A TRAGEDY.   1879
     Trial Edition

52 10/ 165. THE FORESTERS.   1881
     Trial Edition.   This is the only copy known

315  166. THE CUP AND THE FALCON.   1882
     Trial Edition, with author's corrections

30   167. TO H.R.H. PRINCESS BEATRICE.   1885
     Privately printed, only three examples known

100  168. MS. OF "THE BIRTH OF ARTHUR"

5    169. LUCRETIUS.   1868
     Printed for private circulation at Cambridge, Mass.

105  170. THE PROMISE OF MAY.   1883
     Second Trial Edition

33   171. BALLADS AND OTHER POEMS.   1880
     Inscribed to Henry Irving

10   172. STANZAS ON THE MARRIAGE OF THE PRINCESS
     ROYAL.   1858
     The only copy known

3015.   10/-

40.   Wise insures his Tennysons for an exhibition:
      the first two are forgeries

these suspicions are well grounded cannot be said. One thing is certain, however, the rarity of these ephemera has been much exaggerated. Maybe "The Last Tournament" by Tennyson *is* worth $300, but it is curious that every Tennyson collector of note has been supplied with one lately.

The attack was renewed from the same source in 1901.

Does the reader remember a period about two years ago when "rare" privately printed little pamphlets by Tennyson and Swinburne were being "Boomed?" At least one inexperienced collector in New York was misled by a perfectly reputable firm into buying thousands of dollars' worth of these things. The firm had taken the word of the London sharks for gospel and themselves paid high prices. What was the result when a market was found to exist? Such items as "The Window", "Laus Veneris," "Gold Hair," and a dozen other small books of that ilk, cropped up with distressing frequency. Now they are selling at about one third of their record prices. It is significant that all these high-priced and "rare" privately printed items are of the pamphlet variety and of modern date – few being over 20 pp. and of an earlier date than 1865. They are easy of fabrication and we believe they have been fabricated. Is such a book as "Poems by Two Brothers" any rarer than a genuine "Laus Veneris"? Yet the latter occurs for sale three or four times to the Tennyson book's once. The reason is the "Poems by Two Brothers" is too old and too bulky to forge and "Laus Veneris" is neither. Buying books by bulk is the point of many a joke against the ignorant buyer, but by the Lord Harry bulk is at least one guarantee against fraud. The collector's best safeguard is to buy through or from a dealer not only of personal integrity – most American booksellers have this attribute – but able in his trade – as most of them are not. The possession of respectability, some capital, a bookstore and a keen desire to do business does not constitute a bookseller. One might just as well assume that ordination to the priesthood would be an unvarying guarantee of a man's virtue. History tells another story – take the case of "the unfortunate" Dr. Dodd.

Wise grumbled in private to Wrenn

I am interested to observe the name "A.J. Bowden" at the foot of the typed memos you sent me. I suppose you know who this person is? His name is still sometimes heard here, muttered by his unfortunate victims. I know he had absconded to the States, but I did not know what had become of him.

Despite this comment no public reply was ever made. These, and a few other rumblings, never got near to unmasking the conspiracy. They made a few titles dangerous and unsaleable but made no general accusation.

# 11

# ILL-GOTTEN GAINS

The forgers, meanwhile, had other irons in the fire. Forman was probably very shaken by the Morris denunciations: he hadn't Wise's toughness and sheer brass. From this point he began to retire more into his shell and one senses the shadow of his partner falling more darkly upon him. He busied himself with legitimate literary work. As we have seen, John Murray suggested that he edit Byron. He did edit several of Dent's famous 'Temple Classics' series including Elizabeth Barrett Browning's *Aurora Leigh* 1898 and Robert Browning's *Sordello* 1902. Alfred H. Miles was plodding through his ten volume compendium *The poets and the poetry of the [Nineteenth] Century* 1891–97. The major entries comprise a biographical and critical account followed by a selection: it is still a work of great interest particularly for minor figures. Forman contributed Charles Wells, R.H. Horne and Thomas Wade to Vol. 3 and William Morris to Vol. 6 (W. B. Yeats contributed William Allingham to Vol. 5).

Forman's plain text of Keats reached a fourth edition 1895, a fifth 1896, a sixth 1898 and finally a seventh edition 1902, all published by Reeves and Turner. Forman kept his own copies of all of these and his bibliographical notes add extra information and complications. In his copy of the 1902 edition, he wrote 'The paper was not got through my brother Alfred, as that of all the other editions was; hence its inferiority – thick and clumsy as it is.' In 1895 he produced, in similar format to Keats's works, his complete letters, a text which was to remain family property for another fifty years or so. He teamed up with the Glasgow publishers Gowans & Gray and contributed a Keats to their complete library series: it appeared in five volumes, 1900–1901. Judging by the errata lists, he found them somewhat careless in textual matters. The popular cumulation of his Keats scholarship came when he was commissioned to produce the Oxford Standard Authors edition. This first appeared in 1907 and was reprinted many times, being almost continually in print until after the Second World War. For hundreds of thousands of people all over the English speaking world, the OSA Keats *was* Keats: and Forman was the editor. He grew less happy with Shelley as he grew older. The Reeves and Turner *Poetical Works* did not go beyond the third edition of 1892, though as already mentioned, he did contribute Shelley to George Bell's new Aldine Edition of the British Poets (5 volumes 1892; several times reissued). When the OSA Shelley appeared in 1904, it was edited by Thomas Hutchinson though with a glowing tribute to Forman in the foreword.

Forman's health was not good (he would be 60 in 1902) and pressure at work was still quite intense: he went to Washington in 1897 for another postal congress and worked in a visit to Bucke in Canada. In 1899, Eliot, his eldest son, was home 'now my Boy has gone back to Japan, I shall not begrudge, as I have done for six months, every hour spent out of his company seeing they all have to be so' he wrote to Wise. The latter was also pretty busy. In 1897 he produced the first two bibliographies on his own, viz. *A bibliographical list of the scarcer works and uncollected writings of Algernon Charles Swinburne* and *A complete bibliography of the writings in prose and verse of Robert Browning*. Both of these were limited to fifty copies, or at least so the colophons stated. Both represented a considerable investment of time and money – the printing by Clays is quite impressive. Both, of course canonized all the forgeries so far produced. Wise's other literary volume at this time was a curious affair indeed. He edited the first seven parts of *A reference catalogue of British and foreign autographs* 1893–1900: he wrote Charlotte Brontë and Dickens, while Forman did Keats. Otto Portman Rubeck makes a ghostly appearance alongside W. B. Slater as a member of the committee of the 'Society of Archivists' who produced it. He was down to write on the autographs of Sir Walter Scott, but luckily for him, the series never got that far.

Meanwhile, Wise and Wrenn were in full flow, exchanging letters every two or three weeks and Wise was beginning to take the position of sole supplier. In May 1898 he offered Tennyson's *Carmen Saeculare* 1867 for £20. This is a badly researched fake in which a periodical poem is supposed to have had two author's private prints, the revised text (Wise & Forman) being followed by a later printing of the unrevised text (the real thing). Wrenn cabled a refusal (Wise used W. B. Slater as his address) then on second thoughts an acceptance. He had consulted two fellow American collectors, one Beverley Chew (who could not help), the other William H. Arnold who urged acceptance: he may not have been an impartial guide. Wise wrote to Wrenn

> I know for a fact that the number of copies printed was extremely small – just a mere handful, and it is honestly worth a long price. The last copy sold in London was bought by B. F. Stevens for £46. . . . This same I consider an extremely high price – too high in fact, just as high pitched as the copy of The Falcon which Mrs Rylands bought for £120. But £20 is just as cheap as £46 is dear, and I think you have done well.

To put the record straight, we may mention that the first auction record is £31 in November 1899 (note how Wise implies but does not state an auction) and *The Falcon* is another fake and Mrs Rylands never bought a copy. A month or two after peddling the Tennyson, Wise was selling to the same Arnold two very rare and genuine Tennyson pieces printed at Canford Manor by the Guest family and bought direct from Hallam Tennyson the poet's son. They were not mentioned to Wrenn. A few years later, Beverley Chew received a letter from a fellow collector (Marshall C. Lefferts) which suggests that not everyone shared Wrenn's view of Wise.

> My Dear Chew
> Wrenn is "stung" again – he has written that he has received from Wise – who has had it bound by Riviere – a copy of Tate's "Character of Virtue and Vice – 1691" and quotes from Wise "It is not included among the series of books by Tate described in the Hoe catalogue; it is not mentioned in the Grolier Club's 'Poets Laureate' Bibliography and it is not to be found in any of the catalogues I possess – if this signifies that you possess the only copy owned in America I heartily congratulate you for the book holds an important place in literature, &c., &c."
> I have written Wrenn thanking him and Mr. Wise for having called my attention to it and enclosing a cutting from Pickering's last cat. offering a copy "sewn" @ £1.4. Cheap for such a unique book.

But after May 1898, Wrenn never again seems to have taken outside advice and henceforth was Wise's dazzled and compliant customer. A more personal note is struck by Wise's comments on the Spanish American war. 'The devilments of Modern Spain are bearing the ripest fruit in that they are drawing John Bull and his brother Jonathan together in a bond of truest friendship.'

Since Wise was soon to make his fortune in Spain, this comment strikes a slightly unpleasant note.

Winfield Schley, an American naval officer who was second in command of the blockade of Santiago in Cuba, had just destroyed the Spanish fleet. Bernard Shaw's view was that there ought to be 'a howling protest against this war, especially after the impassioned confession of faith by Commander Schley after the roasting of the Spanish sailors'. The war suggested some further reflections to Wise

> For a century or more, the United States was used as a dustbin, a place in which to shoot the scum and refuse of Europe. You've largely – and rightly – put a stop to that now by your immigration laws; but you've still got a mess of undigested rubbish which makes the national stomach roll and rumble a bit at times. But in a generation or two all this stuff will become absorbed, and America; no longer filled with a scratch-crew but inhabited by a homogenous people, will take her place among the foremost nations of the world.

This exchange of bar room politics seemed to cement the relationship which was to remain constant until Wrenn's death in 1910.

August 1898 saw Wise in Moscow investigating some business complications and then staying on to take a holiday there: doubtless his house in Priory Terrace was lonely without a wife. He was soon to remedy that, however, for on 27 June 1900, he remarried and moved house. His bride was Frances Louise Greenhalgh of Southend; he was 41 and she 25: her father was a banker. It may be that they met through Forman's agency. Frances Greenhalgh had two uncles; one, Frederick Higginbottom, was a journalist, the other, Herbert Higginbottom, worked in the secretary's department of the G.P.O. Both were to become quite close friends of Wise, and 'Bertie' was to be one of Wise's executors. The couple were married at the Registry Office at Rochford, just outside Southend: the witnesses were John Greenhalgh and W. B. Slater. She was a nice girl and Tommy and Louie remained happily married to the end of their days. She made the most of the social pleasures of bibliography and submitted with good grace to Saturday afternoon rounds of the booksellers – if not the necessity of sitting and knitting outside every bookshop in Europe, the complaint of another book collector's lady. On Sunday morning she went to church while her

41.   Louie, Wise's second wife

husband wrote bibliographical letters – often to Wrenn. The new house was 23 Downside Crescent, Belsize Park. This is quite a thin narrow house in a terrace but is nearer the fashionable hills of Hampstead than St. George's Road. The pair were to spend ten 'very happy and prosperous years in the tiny house at Downside Crescent' as Wise wrote to Wrenn in 1910. It was purchased as a skeleton, half built, and the Wises took charge of the completion of the building and the decorating and furnishing. Wise seemed to have enough energy for everything. The correspondence with Gosse was gathering strength: in 1986 Wise gave him a copy of the George Eliot forgery *Brother and Sister* '1869' and Gosse responded 'These little pamphlet rarities are my special weakness'. When told of the impending marriage, Gosse congratulated him but finished the letter 'Alas! for the ravages of time. I am 50 today. It is like hearing the first tap of the gravedigger's pick. Come to see me before I am too old to see or hear or talk or think.'

The final three or four years of forgery production until about 1903 produced about another twelve legitimate pamphlets and only another twelve fakes. These comprise one each of Kipling, Thackeray, G. Cruikshank and Wordsworth (very rash, this latter, the typography does not look, as it should, Kendal 1846), two more Stevensons and no less than six Tennysons. Some of these, particularly the Tennyson may well have been forged for one particular customer – J. H. Wrenn again.

Throughout the period of production, selling was going on both at auction and privately. Auction records up to the end of 1903 suggest that about £900 was obtained in England and about double that – £1800 – in America. These are very rough figures and would not for several reasons (Auctioneer's commission, cost of the occasional posh morocco binding, items sold at second- or third-hand and not directly) represent pure income. Private customers are not so easy to log, though we know that Wise had an extensive American acquaintance. From 1897, for about ten years, Wise supplied Wrenn with some 75 forgeries at a cost of about £800 or £900 (again a rough figure). It is difficult to translate this total of £3,500 into present day terms but it is perhaps equivalent to £175,000. Looked at another way, Forman's gross income as second secretary at the P.O. was £1,000 a year. But Forman was in a very responsible position. In the fifteen or so years of American auctions, the forgers were making about the income of an average American ($500) every year. The money received from the forgeries – and yet to come – must have been a most welcome addition to book collecting funds and partly explains why both Wise and Forman collected such impressive libraries on what were (at least initially) shoestring resources.

In 1901, William Harris Arnold decided to sell his American literature (New York, 30–31 Jan. 1901) and he followed it up by selling most of his English literature (New York, 7–8 May 1901). This latter sale caused rather a stir: Wise professed ignorance to Wrenn 'Do you know if Mr. Arnold is selling all his Tennyson books?', but if Wise had not arranged that all his letters to Arnold were burnt, then there might well be evidence that the two were hand in glove. There were two other sales with the same auctioneer in February and April preceding the Arnold sale. The first had fourteen Wise–Forman productions, the second nineteen. Suspicion in the New York trade reached a new height and in *Prices Current of Books* (March 1901) was printed the article which we have already mentioned. Arnold's sale was, despite Smith's warning, reasonably successful. Wise commented on the prices to Wrenn.

> The two Tennyson plays sold fairly cheap. They'll bring a lot more before very long, as indeed everything by Tennyson will. I am told that there has been some absurd nonsense talked or written, by a second rate New York bookseller who cannot get copies of the rarer Tennyson pieces and so tries to put his customers off them by crying "sour grapes", and asserting that they have been reprinted, to the end that they shall confine their purchases to such goods as he may have to sell. Well, this may have the effect of putting inexperienced collectors who cannot judge for themselves off the books for a while until time proves the stupidity of the statement, but the effect will be that presently they will have to pay pretty heavily for waiting!

George Smith was the greatest antiquarian bookseller in New York at the time, so Wise did not lack courage.

The two fakes Wise mentions, viz. *The Falcon* and *The Promise of May*, made $410 and $430 respectively. Arnold caused some offence in bookish circles by reprinting the auction catalogue in September 1901 with his cost prices printed in red to contrast with selling prices in black. He claimed that the two Tennysons cost him $350 and $330 which seems improbably high (the dollar was then about five to the pound). Incidentally Arnold's final summing up showed that he had paid $10,066.05 and received (gross) $19,743.50.

Wise was now really getting into his stride with Wrenn. In the same year as the Arnold sale, he sold Wrenn one of the Thackeray fakes: one cannot resist watching him at work.

> I have bought the very rare Thackeray's "Leaf out of a sketch book" for you for £47.10.0. I offered £42. for it some weeks ago, and this is the best I have been able to do. The only auction record I have of this book is in regard to a copy sold in the early weeks of 1895. This was bound in morocco, uncut, but it had no wrappers, and one of the illustrations was mended. It sold for £63. I have notes of two copies uncut in wrappers like yours. One was sold for £60., and one for "about £70." So this price of £47.10.0. is quite safe.
>
> There is rather an interesting pedigree to your copy. It once was the property of George Dolby, who was the Secretary to Charles Dickens in America during the whole of the series of Dickens's Readings in the United States. Dolby died not long ago in the workhouse, having sunk into abject poverty, the result of Drink. Before he went into the Workhouse he sold his poor property – probably only for a few shillings value. Amongst the things he sold was this copy of the Thackeray book. He set, it seemed, some store by it; but neither he nor the original buyer had any notion of its monetary value. I find that the book has passed through at least two hands before it came to me. Thus it is by no means improbable that Thackeray gave this copy either to Dickens or to Dolby. I will give the book to Riviere to have a case fitted to it. I would advise you to allow me to have a neat slip of paper printed to insert at the commencement of the book detailing the above particulars. May I do so? The cost will only be 2 or 3 shillings, and it will add a lot of interest to the book. It seems almost pathos, does it not? that a poor devil should go to the Workhouse to die, and at the gates almost of the Workhouse sell for practically nothing a valuable piece of property. I enclose a scrap out of the proofs of my Tennyson Bibliography, in which the book is described at length.

What a lovely story! The only point that needs a gloss is the reference to the Tennyson bibliography. The *Leaf* . . . was supposed to be a separate print from *The Victoria Regia: a Christmas miscellany*. This has a Tennyson contribution, *The Sailor Boy*, which was also forged, hence Thackeray could be authenticated from a Tennyson bibliography. This bibliography, incidentally did not appear until 1908 so perhaps the proof was specially set for Wrenn. At nearly £50 it would have been well worthwhile.

In August 1901 Wise mentioned it again

The Thackeray's *A leaf out of a Sketch book* came home this morning. It will go to you by next mail. Please advise receipt directly it reaches your hands, as I shall be anxious about it. Although we got it as a bargain I consider it would run to close upon £100 in the auction room, and it makes one a bit nervous to put hundred-pound books in the post.

It never did reach £100 at auction, the highest auction price recorded being £45 in 1903, sinking to £21 in 1922 and a pound or so once the forgery was unmasked. There are many similar examples in the correspondence: often Wise cloaked a miscellaneous collection of discards and forgeries with a phoney provenance to make it more palatable. In these capers he often used his clerk at Rubecks – Herbert Gorfin – as a stooge. From about 1898, he often acted as an agent for Wise, selling books on commission; packing up parcels of books; typing lists and no doubt doing Wise's work in Rubeck's time. In the fictional world which Wise created for Wrenn, he would sometimes buy books from 'Gorfin' on the one hand and then ask 'Herbert' his clerk to type the list up; Herbert Gorfin, however, was just the one person. In his role as clerk, Wrenn several times tipped him two gold sovereigns for his trouble – Wise probably threw him a few scraps too.

The amount by which money has depreciated is difficult to grasp and robs the £42 Thackeray of its proper impact. In the produce market then, one could expect an office boy for eight shillings a week or a junior clerk for £2 a month. Gorfin may perhaps have made £3 a month. Wise's price for the twenty-four page *Leaf from a Sketchbook* takes on another aspect when assessed as twenty months' wages for a junior clerk. What is that today?

In 1899, Wise sold Wrenn one of the Tennyson forgeries – *Morte d'Arthur* – for £40. He did not, however, just send it with an invoice like any second-hand bookseller – he built up the dramatic tension most artistically.

March 22
A few days since I learned that Mr. Walter Harrison (a nephew of Edward Moxon) possessed a copy of the very rare Tennyson trial-books "Morte D'Arthur." etc., 1842, which he was disposed to part with.

I have seen both him and his book.

It came, he tells me, directly into his possession from the hands of his uncle, Edward Moxon, Tennyson's publisher.

It is quite sound and uncut, but has no binding. This, however, is no matter, as a couple of pounds paid to Riviere would cover it perfectly.

It is, of course, a tiny bit faded with age, but is very much cleaner than might have been anticipated. There is not a tear – or a damage – or a serious soil throughout. It is on the same thinnish wove paper which Moxon (or rather Bradbury and Evans) employed for their proofs; this paper is the same as used for "Enid and Nimue," "The True and the False," and the early Dickens numbers.

This question of paper may appear very trivial, but it is of more importance from both a Bibliographical and a monetary point of view than is apparent at first sight.

Had "Morte D'Arthur" been printed off in any number – that is had the book been worked off for the purposes of sale – it would have been pulled upon the thicker and more expensive rag paper employed for the "Poems" of 1842. The fact that it is pulled upon the thin cheap "proof" paper is evidence enough that only a handful of "revises" were struck off for the use of author and publisher. This precludes the possibility of any "remainder" being brought to light at any time, and renders this book perfectly safe regarded from a monetary standpoint.

Had any such sum as £25. or £20. been asked for the present copy I should have bought it for you without troubling to cable you, because in the very unlikely event of your not wishing to have the book I could readily have disposed of it here at a big advance. But the price suggested by Mr. Harrison was £70., and this was too much for one to think of giving. I do not mean to say that £70. could not be got for the book – it very likely might – but £70. was more than I could advise you to pay, besides which I quite thought that if I shewed Mr. Harrison a telegram from you making a distinct offer, and told him that he must either take your price or cease to regard me as a probable buyer, he would close. I therefore cabled you yesterday asking for a limit. This morning I received your reply: "Rely your judgment cable price and your advice." To which I responded that Harrison asked £70., but I should advise you to offer £40., as I thought that sum would get the book. Further I advised you to purchase. At four o'clock came your message: "Offer forty." I will see Mr. Harrison tomorrow, and try and conclude the transaction. I will write you the result, and hope to be able to post you the book by next mail. I will ask Harrison for a formal receipt, as a note in his handwriting to keep with the book would be an interesting scrap of pedigree.

March 23

I have seen Mr. Harrison today, but regret that I have not been able to settle with him regarding his copy of Tennyson's "Morte D'Arthur!"

I shewed him your cable, and told him that I considered your offer to be a very fair one.

He said that he had been given to understand that the book was worth £70., and that he had anticipated receiving this sum for it, but that if I would meet him half-way he would accept £55.

This I refused to do, and told him distinctly that he must either accept your £40., or look elsewhere for a buyer.

Finally he has taken two days to consider the matter, and promises to give me his decision on Saturday night. For these two days I have given him the firm offer of £40.0.0. But I have caused him in the meantime to leave the book in my hands, taking my receipt for it. This I have done to the end that he may not avail himself of the delay to offer it elsewhere. I told him plainly that if he took the book out of my hands our offer was void, and once recalled would not be renewed.

Well, I've done my best, and can only hope that the spirit of greed will move our friend to close with me on Saturday.

March 25

Up to now Mr. Harrison has not turned up, so I send you this hasty line, as the mail leaves at noon on Saturdays. But I don't despair and am full of hope that next mail will carry you the book!

March 28

Mr. Harrison only called yesterday, and, after some further attempt to wring a better ransom out of me, he accepted our offer of £40. for his "Morte D'Arthur."

Here it is, and I feel sure you will be pleased with your acquisition.

I asked Harrison to give me a receipt for the money, and to state clearly upon it that the book came directly from Edward Moxon.

I thought it would be interesting to retain this note of the pedigree of the volume, but if you don't care to bother with it you can easily pitch it away. After being properly bound (with a very little dry-cleaning – no washing is needful) the book will make a splendid copy.

The receipt supplied appears to be in the hand of Herbert Gorfin.

By now, Wise knew Wrenn very well and sold him several examples of a much more traditional kind of fake. A 'sound uncut copy' of Shelley's *Epipsychidion* appeared in March 1901. It has a half-title printed on old paper but in fact from the same type as the Shelley Society facsimile of 1887. Presumably Clays ran this off for Wise. They may also have helped with another Shelley, a *Queen Mab*. This 'exceedingly fine copy . . . fresh as it could be from first page to last . . . "right" in every way' has three leaves in printed type facsimile: Wise sold it to Wrenn in March 1907.

Even stripping out the fakes, Wise overcharged: a check on twelve plays supplied 1901–1903 suggests he charged a bit over double current auction prices – thus acting exactly the part of the bookseller he always swore he was not. He also had a very free hand with attributions, falsely attributing anonymous or doubtful pieces to known authors and thus increasing their value. Some of his attributions were quite reckless and in one or two cases he even succeeded in attributing the same piece to different authors in succeeding years.

Wise, of course, had customers other than Wrenn though none nearly so well documented. He sold many pamphlets to John A. Spoor for example, another Chicago businessman, who ended up with an even more complete set than Wrenn. He also had a copy of Wise's *Verses* (Wrenn never did) which suggests considerable intimacy. In England the circle included Stopford A. Brooke, R. A. Potts, Alfred Crampon and others. He also used booksellers to promote indirect sales. One he regretted using was W. T. Spencer who had an enormous bookshop on Oxford Street and a shady country house in the Isle of Wight where indentured young ladies were said to improve plate books with modern colour and engage in other doubtful bibliographical sophistications. Wise and Spencer being birds of a feather (though differently disguised) came to hate each other. There was little Spencer did not turn his hand to: bogus provenance (Dr. Johnson's teapot; Dickens's chair); books imperfect or made up with facsimiles; modern colouring; facsimile wrappers for his favourite Dickens in parts; and so on. He must have guessed what Wise was up to and he decided to take a hand in the profitable game himself. Wise and Forman produced a creative forgery of Swinburne's *Dead Love* in about 1890; and in about 1904 W.T. Spencer copied it. In fact like most such copies it was not quite exact and when Wise described the two editions he pointed out the differences. He added, 'The whole thing proves once more that, easy as it appears to be to fabricate reprints of rare books, it is in actual practice absolutely impossible to do so in such a manner that detection cannot follow the result.' Some years later, the celebrated collector Richard Jennings bought a copy of *Dead Love* from Spencer for seven guineas. He showed it to Wise who became very angry and persuaded him to swap it for a copy of the genuine edition which he happened to have by him (he still

42.    On the right, the creative forgery;
on the left, the forgery of it

had twenty copies in 1910). It was this affair which prompted Wise (apropos several of his genuine private prints) to comment to Wrenn

> Of course Mr. Spoor will have copies in due time, but he will not get them through Blank [i.e. Spencer]. I would not let one of them pass through Blank's hands on any account. I should expect, were such to be the case, to hear of forged reprints being in circulation very quickly.

This excursion on Spencer has taken us a little way from forgery prices. In December 1907, Spencer sold Alexander Turnbull of Wellington (a passionate collector and virtual founder of the New Zealand National Library) several fakes including *Dead Love*, presumably in his own edition, for £8/5s. and *Siena* for £3/10s. A month later he was quoting Browning's *Cleon* and *The Statue and the Bust* for £70 the pair and claiming he could find no records at auction for the last four years. He was strictly accurate since this pair of fakes made their first appearance at auction in June 1903 when, bound in calf, they made £13/5s. together. Wise used several other booksellers including Jones and Evans of London and J. E. Cornish of Manchester, selling the latter several cases of his discards salted with forgeries.

One is struck, reading the endless letters to Wrenn, by what a vast quantity of rebinding went on. Also when one views the Ashley Library *en bloc*, the general effect is of gleaming morocco: at least two-thirds of the 5,000 or so items have been rebound or put into cases. Wise, no doubt, obtained trade terms from Zaehnsdorf or Riviere. As a major customer, he was on matey terms with Mr Calkin, manager of Riviere and Mr Marlow, manager of Zaehnsdorf: relationships perhaps analogous with his intimacy with Maylett of Clays. Did he claim a commission on the Wrenn binding bills which he supervised? Did he turn his attention to leather, although there is nothing in the whole field of commerce more surprising than the fluctuations of the leather market? Its sensitiveness may be described as morbid, but that would be an attraction for such an experienced commodity hand as Wise. Did he buy his own hides wholesale at the London Commercial Saleroom? There were many sales in Mincing Lane of tanned morocco and other leathers. Like Harley in the eighteenth century he could have ensured the quality of the leather and reduced the binder's cut. Wise, in his efforts to

London April 27th, 1917. 19

T.I. Wise, Esq.

# Bought of MAGGS BROS.,

⊰ Dealers in Books, Prints and Autographs, ⊱

## 109, STRAND, LONDON, W.C.

LIBRARIES PURCHASED OR VALUED FOR PROBATE.　　CATALOGUES POST FREE.

### BOOKBINDING EXECUTED.

"Books Wanted" not in Stock, sought for, and reported Free of Charge.

*Telegraphic & Cable Address—"BIBLIOLITE, LONDON."*　*Code in use—"Unicode,' & A B C 5th Ed.*

*Telephone "GERRARD 4664."*

| | | | | |
|---|---|---|---|---|
| 19 | A Mememto of Mr. & Mrs. R. Browning. To binding in full levant morocco super extra, lettered on side and back, also tooling poem on leather fly-leaf, providing and inletting glazed frames for two locks of hair, supplying silk wrapper for sonnets by "E.B.B." and card mounts etc. also cloth case to hold volume. | | | |
| | Paid Binder for same. | 15 | 16 | 6 |
| | Plus 10% our commission. | 1 | 11 | 6 |
| | | 17 | 8 | |

736　　109. STRAND,
LONDON. W.C.

Recd. the sum of £ 17 : 8 : —
ON ACCOUNT OF

## MAGGS BROS.

Date

43.　The bill for binding the Reading *Sonnets*

promote the pamphlets often spent much more on binding a fake than on printing it. Few of his bills have survived, so the cost and chronology of his moroccos cannot be properly recovered. For his worst effort, he deserted Riviere and went to Sangorski and Sutcliffe, renowned for bindings of great skill and elaboration, but little taste. To his annoyance (no doubt) he had to order through Maggs, which cost him an extra 10 per cent. Sangorski did Wise proud with his 'matchless association volume' of the Reading *Sonnets*. This is encased in a mausoleum of crimson morocco with green morocco doublures elaborately gilt and lettered. Inset in each board are locks of Robert and Elizabeth's hair. Had the Reading *Sonnets* not been a fake, the volume would still be distasteful: as it is, the effect is extremely bizarre.

44. The ground floor of the London Commercial Salerooms, wash drawing *c.* 1891

# 12

# WISE ON THE COMMODITY MARKET

The Edwardian era saw Wise's apotheosis as a commodity dealer.
There is a romantic side to the trade but also a ruthless one.

> Under the brown fog of a winter noon
> Mr. Eugenides, the Smyrna merchant
> Unshaven, with a pocket full of currants
> C.i.f. London: documents at sight,
> Asked me in demotic French
> To luncheon at the Cannon Street Hotel. . .

The currants were quoted at a price carriage and insurance free
to the Port of London, as were many of the drugs which Rubecks
bought. London was still the centre of the commodity trades
and drugs were shipped in from all over the world. Much was sold
by private treaty but auctions were still important. The only
drug sale catalogue we have been able to trace is one of 1811 held
in the old East India House in Leadenhall Street. This repre-
sents a tradition going back a couple of centuries when the John
Company ships brought spices and other merchandise from the
East to be sold in London. Mark Lane and Mincing Lane were
the direct route between the Pool of London and the Royal
Exchange, which once housed all the merchants. The Exchange
rapidly became too small and the trades spilled out into streets
and coffee houses. The Commercial Hall, Mincing Lane, was built
in 1811 for the sale of Colonial Produce: it probably represented
an earlier coffee house tradition. By 1818, it was the Commercial
Sale Rooms and soon became one of the centres of the produce
market, dealing mainly (tea and coffee excepted) with the non-
food side. Continual extensions were made, but the trade out-
grew them all and in 1890 the building was completely rebuilt
(sales moved temporarily to the New Corn Exchange in Mark
Lane). At the same time it was incorporated as a limited company with about 1,500 subscribers – who alone had the right of
admission, though they could select nominees. It acted as the
produce market's private club and place of business combined. A
new Mincing Lane man would join when he was put on the

45.  A commodity sale in an upper room of the London Commercial Salerooms, 1909

market and be taken round and introduced to the porters at the doors who kept out non-members by sight.

The Commercial comprised a subscription room and restaurant on the ground floor and numerous small sale rooms upstairs. One of these was permanently occupied by tea sales but others were taken over by different brokers to sell a vast variety of different produce. Drug sales were every other Thursday through the year. The Commercial provided the venue, but nothing else. Each individual broker provided a catalogue, samples to be viewed in their own premises (they were banned at the salerooms), an auctioneer and a clerk. A typical morning would have seven or eight brokers in succession – they drew lots to arrange the order. Unlike, say, a fine art sale at Sotheby's, there was no central control and each broker would issue and advertise his own catalogue. This was very much in the form of the earlier catalogue we have illustrated and might well be arranged by cargo. New firms were exploiting a changing market, an example being Samuel Figgis & Co. which was established in 1880 when its energetic founder broke away from Lewis and Peat and soon made a success of it.

A typical sale took place on 20 February 1901, when Figgis offered the following:

10 Cases Rhubarb
22 Bales Ipecacuanha
34 Bales Jamaican Sarsaparilla
16 Cases Gum Benjamin
10 Cases Gum Eleni
15 Cases Cardamons
72 Mats Madagascar Wax
53 Bales Zanzibar Wax
10 Cases Eucalyptus Oil
50 Cases Castor Oil
24 Bales Bucha leaves
50 Bags Cascara Sagrada
6 Bags Aveca Nuts

The next day's *Public Ledger*, the Bible of the produce market, had a long comment on the sale which began 'The moderate supply offered, met with a generally slow demand. Aloes Cape firmly held. Bucha Leaves slow and easier. Colomba Root quiet.

*"Luke Howard Jewell & Gibson*
*Nangh Court*
*Bawden & Co*

## ( 69 )

# DRUGS, &c.

FOR

# SALE

AT THE

*East-India House*

On Tuesday, the 28th May, 1811.

Every Person who shall be declared the best Bidder for any Lot or Lots of Goods at this Sale, shall make such Deposits with the Company, in Money, within Three Days from the Day of Sale, as are herein–after expressed, and shall make good the Remainder of the Purchase Money, on or before the 23d August, 1811, without Discount.

The Buyers are to pay Warehouse Rent for every Lot of Goods sold at this Sale, that shall remain in the Warehouses Three Months after the Prompt Day (unless otherwise herein–after expressed), the following Rates per Month, until the same shall be taken away.

For every Lot not exceeding 1 Cwt. Gross, Three-pence.

For every Ditto above 1 Cwt. and not exceeding 3 Cwt. Six-pence.

For every Ditto above 3 Cwt. and not exceeding 5 Cwt. Nine-pence.

For every Ditto above 5 Cwt. and not exceeding 8 Cwt. One Shilling.

[ 18 ]

## ( 110 )

PRIVILEGE

Mats
Frankincense, 25 br ov

## Per Marian

| Mark | Lot | Deposit per Lot |
|---|---|---|
| M◊ | 2110 | £3 4 7/ |
| | 2111 | {2 {4  5/ *Griffin* |

35

CAMPHIRE OIL, at ℔ to adv. 1d.

## Per Wm. Pitt, 1810

| | Chests | Foreign Quart Green Glass |
|---|---|---|
| SHG | 825 £3 3 | 98 |
| | 826  3 *out* | 94 |
| | 827  3 | 103 |

9

SENA, at ℔, to adv. $\frac{1}{8}$

## Per Marian

| M◊ | 2112 | 6 Mats 5/4 |
|---|---|---|

LONG PEPPER, at £2 ℔, to adv. 1s.

## Per Fairlie

| FG&C◊ | 2113 £4 10 Bags | *Tucker* |
|---|---|---|
| | 2114  10 | 7s/ |
| | 2115  11 | |

31

---

46.   A commodity sale catalogue of 1811

Dragonsblood bought in. Ipecacuanha quiet and easier.' The subscription rooms on the ground floor, meanwhile, were used for 'rings' to settle prices, and for innumerable private deals. Ground rules for both auctions and private deals were laid down by the General Produce Brokers Association which was founded in 1876. This mirrored the situation in other areas where specialized trade organizations gradually codified their practice and arbitrated disputes.

Rubecks were wholesale druggists and standard buyers at such sales, selling on the raw material to retail chemists, drug manufacturers, soap makers or perfumers. The bulk of each lot was stored in Thames Warehouses or at the Cutler Street Warehouse taken over by the Port of London Authority on its foundation in 1909. After arranging payment, warrants were issued allowing the goods to be released from the warehouse. These were tantamount to certificates of ownership and if you lost the warrant, you lost the goods. The gradual development of warrants from dock warrants for a particular piece of cargo, into general warrants for a particular quantity of a particular commodity is the beginning of sales of 'futures' (terminal sales was the original English expression).

The brokers charged 1 per cent to the sellers plus an extra charge 'lot money' to allow for catalogue printing and auction expenses. They also charged the buyers ½ per cent. Wise had a very shrewd commercial instinct: whether he had also the desirable attributes of well developed senses of sight, touch, scent and taste we do not know.

We cannot resist a brief glimpse of some of the material available on other days, often auctioned by the same brokers who dealt with drugs on Thursdays. There were auctions of isinglas, bristles, straw plait, shells, vanilla, horns, bones, goat, rabbit and sheep skins, bird skins (Albatross wing quill feathers, red humming 3d. to 3½d. each, red tanagers 4¼d., cock of the rocks 2s. 10d., amethyst humming ½d. to 2d.), furs, tallow, cinchona bark, woolled sheep skins, ivory, ostrich feathers, canes and sticks, and many other commodities. Distance lends enchantment to the bustling offices, busy salerooms and horse drawn streets. It was a small and self contained world in which everyone knew everyone else and such personal acquaintance played a very important part in commercial life.

**H. RUBECK.**

TELEGRAM ADDRESS:
RUBECK, LONDON.
TELEPHONE NUMBER 2204, AVENUE.
A. B. C. CODE USED.

59, MARK LANE,
LONDON,
E.C.

2 DEC 1902
190

SOLE AGENT for
Messrs. PASCAL & LAFOND, Succrs.,
MANUFACTURERS OF
FRENCH ESSENTIAL OILS,
SOMMIÈRES.

PROPRIETOR of the
"EXCELSIOR" BRAND
OF ESSENTIAL OILS,
AND
SOLE AGENT for
"CATANZARO" LIQUORICE JUICE.

*My dear Wrenn,*

*Just a few lines to let you know that I bought three small lots for you at Puttick's Sale yesterday.*

*(1) About twenty volumes of Tennyson, the later green books, almost all First Editions, in first rate condition,*

Telegram Address: Rubeck London.
Telephone Nº 2204 Avenue.
A.B.C.Code used(4ᵗʰ & 5ᵗʰ Editions & Lieber's)

*Established* 1856.

**H.RUBECK**

**DISTILLER**
OF
*Essential Oils.*

Proprietor of the
"EXCELSIOR" Brand
OF ESSENTIAL OILS
Distilleries
LONDON and in SPAIN
Importer
OF SPANISH SAFFRON

59, MARK LANE,
LONDON, E.C.

22 FEB 1911
19

*My dear Wrenn,*

*Please give me credit for the enclosed Riviera a/c. —*

*Yours always*

*Thos. J. Wise*

47.    Letters from Wise to Wrenn, on Rubeck notepaper

Rubecks and their able cashier Mr Wise, were on the verge of considerable expansion. They had, for instance, acquired a telephone (2204; United Telephone Co.) by 1885. This was a far sighted move: at the time there were only about 6,000 subscribers in the whole of London. Gradually the round of morning visits to find out what was available and at what price, gave way before the telephone. For many years, Rubecks had been wholesale druggists: in about 1905 they announced a specialization which had been developing for some time and became essential oil merchants. This was a particular corner of the drug trade. Essential or volatile oils are oily substances obtained from plants or fruit which have a taste or perfume. Traded in the London drug markets were oils of cinnamon, cloves, jasmine, juniper, lemon, peppermint, sandalwood, wintergreen, pink blossom, rosemary, bergamot, sage, ylang ylang, patchouli, geranium, lime, cedar, birch, attar of roses and many others, and they were imported from all over the world. They were used in perfumery, for the manufacture of soaps and other toilet preparations and for flavouring food. There were plenty of expanding markets here. For instance the rapid growth of a taste for fizzy drinks (and the availability of cheap glass bottles to put them in) led to a great increase in the demand for lemon and orange oil as flavourings. The mass market for cosmetics was just beginning to reappear. Up to the 1890s Eau de Cologne with its lavender scent was all that could really be admitted to. But, first under medical guise, cosmetics gradually gained respectability. Helena Rubenstein's career, for instance, began in New York in the 1890s. She started with borrowed capital and a cosmetic cream which contained almond essence. Naturally essential oils vary somewhat in composition and strength; variation might be due to change in soil or climate or changes in preparation. Little glass sample bottles circulated constantly and an able buyer could tell not only if the oil was good and its composition, but also exactly where it came from. But the sample would still be sent out for analysis mainly to determine specific gravity and optical activity. A sample book was the essential record and would contain technical details of all samples, with notes of origin and destination of every parcel dealt with.

The different national pharmacopoeias attempted to set standards but these were often contradictory or incorrect. To complicate matters further the artificial oils were beginning to achieve some importance and obviously affected the market for naturals (artificial oil of peppermint from Germany is one example). Despite occasional triumphs, however, they never made the massive inroads that at one time seemed likely and they are still only of minor importance.

48.   An advertisement by Rubecks in the trade journal, 1919

As well as technical decisions, one had to judge the probity of both buyers and sellers and try to anticipate the inevitable market fluctuations. 'One of the shrewdest buyers on the produce market' was how Wise was described by a close associate. Not only was Wise a good buyer, but he was a powerful personality, good at arranging a deal, extracting a debt or pacifying an angry customer.

In 1904, he asked Wrenn to verify the standing of an American firm seeking to order 5,000lbs of oil of sandalwood @ 10s. per lb. Before quoting (a quote was binding) they asked for references but 'these three firms are not houses in whom we have any very great confidence.' In the same year the two businessmen arranged a joint fortnight's trip in France with their wives. They started from Paris, hired a car, and toured the French provinces. It was evidently a great success in 1906, for Wise wrote to Wrenn,

> Join you in another jaunt? Rather! We had contemplated, for business considerations, taking our little trip on the Continent in September this year, but June will suit me very nearly as well. Say the middle of June, or the last two weeks of that month. During July and August I shall be closely tied to business, the reason being that during those two months our Oil business in Spain will be claiming all attention. (Essential Oil of Lavender, of course I mean.) The experiment we made last year of distilling this oil in Spain, in the country districts where the plants flourish, was so promising, that this year we are going into it in a much larger manner. We hope this summer to produce at least 16 or 18 tons of Lavender Oil. This amount we want to double next year, and so gradually work up to a really big thing. But it needs a lot of thought and arrangement, stills and other 'plant' have to be sent out from this country, and men in the local districts in Spain have to be trained for the work. Mr. Macnaughton, a Scotchman, our resident partner in Valencia, is now in London, and we are deep in the affair daily. Yesterday I had a chat with him on the subject of a motor holiday in Spain, that is in the Interior of the country lying behind the Eastern border, that is the part of the country where we are working. He very strongly advised me not to think of it. He said that the roads are so bad, and the accommodation is so primitive, that it would only entail discomfort upon you and my wife. So I have dropped the idea. But what do you say to a couple of weeks with Rodolf and his car in Italy? I don't think June will be too late, and with the car we should see portions of the country which would be new even to that great world-traveller John H. Wrenn! Let me know what you think, and as soon as you can [give me] your dates of arrival in, and departure from, England. I will see about fixing up for the car.

The Spanish enterprise was precipitated by the partial failure of the French lavender crop in 1902. There was a rush to find alternatives and Spain was an obvious choice. The stills were portable and could be set up anywhere there was water, fuel and a good supply of wild plants. These were gathered from the hot and stony hillsides by peasant labour. Most of the production was from spike lavender which is a different species from true

49.  Distilling lavender oil in Spain, 1906

lavender (Lavendula spica rather than L. vera). Spike lavender has a more camphoraceous smell according to the experts: to an amateur it seems as if some rosemary were mixed with it. The plants are gathered in July and early August and mixed with water, are put into the stills, heated and the essential oil is distilled off to be collected. The whole affair was obviously a great success and extremely profitable. It must be from this enterprise that Wise made the fortune he later possessed. He would have had a comfortable salary as the cashier and chief clerk, but he had no stake in Rubecks. It seems certain that the essential oil manufacturing, both in Spain and later in England was a partnership between Wise and Otto Portman Rubeck, the son of the boss and ten years Wise's junior. Rubecks, the firm, stuck to dealing, but obviously dealt largely in the oils manufactured by Otto and Wise. They certainly advertised their Spanish oils widely and gave the impression that they were undercutting the market. Soon after Wise's letter, quoted above, he asks Wrenn to name three or four major American soap makers to sell the lavender oil to. In early 1907, the subject recurs:

> You will, I know, be glad to hear that our Spanish-Essential oil business is proving very successful indeed, far more successful so far than we had hoped. As a matter of fact, the lack of rain in the South of France during the early summer resulted in short supplies of oil from France, and the effect was high prices here. We sold all last year's output at 60% higher price than that upon which we had based our calculations. This, of course, considerably reduced the amount of capital remaining sunk in the business. Added to this, the oils themselves have given the highest possible satisfaction to consumers. The accounts for the past year have just been completed, and are pleasant to inspect. We have now decided to go into the thing on a far larger scale than we did last year. We are going to introduce steam power into three of the centres of production. As boilers, stills, and everything else have to be sent out from this country, it will mean that again this summer I shall be kept closely to it. But that the result will spell success is certain, and that will, I know, please my good friend.

Masquerade. Returnes  
together, Gentleman. Sick to...  

gone, enter  

Op. I know not, in...  
with his Portmantue,  
d robbe him : these by  
Then humane changes...  
ed and carryed off, then  
Dainty deuices in this...  
with their *Iauelins,*  
ttempt their persons, one  
es escapeth, a noyse of  
eir hornes within, as at  
te, then Enter  
e away the Satires, and  
rescued the Nimphes,  
ith them.  
more...with bright  
sent.  
In the...  
uention flowes  
ou shall taste other  
We change the Scene.  
An Iuy-bush, and oth...  
Ph. These cra...  
Scene  
Silence obscure.  

Op.  

Song  

Dich. *Swiftly, oh swiftly, I...*  
*What holds my wing...*  
*When euery Cloud...*  
*I heard my sister...*  
*They haue forsaken H...*  
*To attend anoth...*  
Queene, and  
Irene chaste Euen...  
Eu. Ir. *We*  
Diche, *haue stayd expect...*  
*Thou giu'st perfection to...*  
*And seale to this nights...*  
*Astrea shake the cold dew...*  
Eu. *Descend.*  
Ir. *Descend.*  
Eu. *Descend, and helpe...*  
*The Triumph of* Ioues *upp...*  
*And all the Deities tra...*  
C H  

*The Triumph of* Ioues *up...*  
*And all the Deities tran...*  
Eu. *Non gaze, and when...*  
*Tell what thou hast beheld...*  
Dich. *Never, till non...*  
*was poore Astrea blind,...*  
*That too much sight shoula...*  
*Am I in Earth or Heau...*

50. The missing leaf, stolen by Wise,  
returned to the play from which he took it

## 13

# BUYING UP 'THE PINES'

Wise's bibliographical reputation was rising along with his fortune. In 1901, he produced a specimen of a full scale catalogue of all his books, which he called the Ashley Library. In 1905–1908, a two volume edition of the same came out. This had no printed limitation but ironically, is much rarer than many of his printings with formal limitations. It is said that only twelve copies were produced and this may be somewhere near the truth. It is a most impressive production with numerous illustrations and detailed collations of many books described nowhere else. Its very inaccessibility acted like a candle flame to bibliographical moths who longed to possess a copy. Indeed, the third letter from Wrenn to Wise (as early as 1894!) is an appeal for information about the projected catalogue.

As the forgeries slackened off, Wise turned to theft in order to prime his book collecting pump. As well as collecting nineteenth century literature (where the forgeries were), Wrenn (and Wise as well) liked the seventeenth century, particularly plays. By the turn of the century, Wise was a respected figure at the British Museum, known as a generous donor of new discoveries in nineteenth century literature and a bibliographer of note, who was beginning to turn his attention to earlier centuries. He was probably accorded trusted status and allowed to keep books out on a reserved desk overnight: he could therefore have illegally taken volumes home. The British Museum collection of early plays is a famous one, and one of the glories of the national collection. From some fifty plays, Wise tore out about 300 leaves, using these stolen pages to perfect his own copies and these he sold to Wrenn and others. Most of the thefts seem to have taken place in the period 1901–1907 when he was selling so much to Wrenn. In one case the process can be timed. Nabbes *The Bride* 1640 was sold at auction (imperfect) in December 1902: in April 1903, Wise sold it to Wrenn, perfected with Museum leaves, as having come from a Mr Hartley, a mythical collector of plays ('very fine copies, with no blemish of any kind. . . . I had some difficulty to induce Mr. Hartley to part

51. Stolen leaves of plays from Wise's hoard

with these plays'). 'Making up' as such perfecting is called in the trade, was (and indeed is) common enough: but it should be avoided and the delights of making up are not generally reckoned to include stealing the raw material. Wise seems to have stolen in a pretty wholesale way – not just to perfect a particular copy, but as a general principle: on his death in 1937, he still had a packet of some eighty leaves remaining. But worse still (if possible) he exacted his toll from plays that Wrenn sent him to bind, substituting leaves from his own copy which were soiled or torn, for Wrenn's better ones. Wise seriously damaged important and historic books when he ripped the leaves out and showed wanton disregard for the very objects to which he had devoted his scholarly and collecting career: it is a relief to turn back to one of his other personae and the curious relationship of the two forgers.

'There is a good deal that I shall be glad of the chance to tell you; but I will defer it all till we meet', Forman to Wise 1901. 'Mr G. L. Craik has given me some interesting information: once more, truth is *very much* stranger than fiction', Wise to Forman undated *c.* 1900. Craik was a partner in Macmillan the publishers, and this cryptic note must refer to the discovery of a genuine *Carmen Saeculare* (Tennyson 1887), the position of which had been usurped, in the literary history of the book, by the forgers' own production. As Wise said to Wrenn 'This pamphlet which was suppressed, and held back, in consequence of the revision of the text, has been as much a puzzle to Messrs. Macmillan Co. as to myself, and it has taken some time to "see daylight" through it.' However, the daylight soon came streaming in and the genuine pamphlet was demoted to a second edition. Craik was a friend of Tennyson in his last years and intimately associated with the production of his final books. Wise's powerful and plausible manner had achieved a remarkable demotion.

The threat of a general exposure had receded and, after all, the actual forging (though not the selling) had stopped. But there were still uncomfortable moments. Messrs. E. T. Cook and Alexander Wedderburn, two devoted Ruskin disciples were engaged in publishing his great collected works in thirty-nine volumes. In Vols 12 and 18 (1903 and 1905) they clearly demonstrated that two of the Ruskin pamphlets were forgeries, and they express doubt about two others. However, these interesting discoveries

52. Theodore Watts-Dunton, an engraving, c. 1880

were in small type in the midst of the great set. Furthermore, Ruskin's critical reputation, and hence his collectability, was rapidly descending into the eclipse from which it was not to emerge for a generation. The remarkable detective work of Cook and Wedderburn must have caused Forman some sleepless nights: but there was no public reaction.

There were no more direct attacks on the forgeries though a good many knowledgeable people must have felt some unease at all those rows of pamphlets. One of them was the great bibliographer A. W. Pollard who wrote in 1907:

> Thus Mr. Wise, Mr. Buxton Forman, Mr. Gosse and others have done excellent work in bringing to light the stray printings of various English writers of the nineteenth century, though they have also all yielded to the temptation to create artificial rarities by obtaining leave to print various small pieces in private editions, an amusement which recalls some of the special-stamp issues of insignificant governments. If in this one direction a form of book-collecting which starts from the collector's own literary tastes may lead to doubtful results. . .

The situation was a bit like that obtaining before Piltdown Man was exposed. Quite a number of stray people in different places had their doubts, but no one put the doubters together or built up a generally convincing contra case. Piltdown Man remained for some forty years to vex the palaeontologists before he was exposed. So with the Forman–Wise forgeries, no one crystallized the doubts.

Wise's energy in the Edwardian decade seems boundless. There was yet another line he worked with great success. George Borrow, the gypsy writer and amateur polymath had died in 1881. His stepdaughter died in 1903 and left the manuscripts and papers she had inherited to a retired solicitor, one Smith, who was an amateur of gypsies. He sold all the material and the copyrights to Clement Shorter in 1904. Wise may well have advised on the purchase and was to make considerable use of it some ten years later. Meanwhile, Swinburne had died on 10 April 1909 and Theodore Watts-Dunton (aged 77) was left almost everything. Theodore it was, who had carried Swinburne off from his rackety life of drink and other strong meat, set him up in a suburban house and tamed him (castrated him would be a ruder way of putting it). He was trained as a lawyer and his practical abilities (e.g. dealing with potential blackmailers) were one of the reasons Swinburne valued him. Shaw describes how

> Henry Salt and I once took a walk with Theodore round Putney Heath, and lunched at The Pines afterwards. Theodore treated Swinburne exactly like a tutor encouraging and patronising a small boy. Also a little like the proprietor of a pet animal, coaxing it to exhibit its tricks. . . . Watts (I never picked up the Dunton) believed that his sonnets were the final perfection of poetry and his gipsy novels immortal; but he was a friendly man and a serviceable friend. . . . There was a ridiculous side to Theodore; but he was a real good man.

This was a summary with which not everyone would have agreed. The world's somewhat ribald attitude to Watts-Dunton was increased by his marriage aged 73 to Clara Reich (aged 29) in 1905. They had first met when she was a girl of 16 at boarding school; it was said by the uncharitable that Swinburne and Watts tossed up to see which of them would be the lucky man. Other complications over Swinburne's grave included his respectable family, especially his sister Isabel and his cousin Mrs Disney Leith who were possessive of his reputation. Wise lost no time in repairing to 'The Pines' and he picked his way among hate's cross currents with great skill. The course of the operation can be followed in a year's letters between Wise and Gosse. Drastically shortened, they still read rather like a dialogue:

> Wise: In the end he gave me the definite promise that if he sells, I am to buy the whole of the books and mss. in one lot. . . . The old chap is shockingly feeble and helpless, but amazingly *Wide awake!* [10 May 1909]
>
> Gosse: The news you give me – the whisper from "The Pines" – is quite exciting. I am rejoiced beyond measure to think you will get all the MSS. Hurrah. . . . You must come some day and look over my glorious set of S.'s letters. I have nearly 100. I suppose W. D. cannot make me disgorge them? I should destroy them all sooner than let him touch them. [10 May]
>
> Wise: I have sent W. D. this morning £236 for things bought yesterday, and I have appointments with him for tomorrow and next Sunday. He is *terribly* slow to deal with: brings out one item . . . a time, and talks over it for half an hour on end, with the idea of increasing my desire for it, and consequently my notion of price. I have utterly lost all respect and regard for him, as I have found him to *lie* to me consistently. To see an old man tottering on the brink of the

|          |  |
|----------|--|
| Gosse:   | grave, piling lie upon lie on the off-chance of squeezing an extra pound or two is pitiful in the extreme. [28 June] |

Gosse: You yourself are so scrupulously honourable in all your dealings that it has taken you long to discover what a rascal that old attorney is. But now you know it, have no mercy on him. Have you reflected on what his real relation to S. has been? It has been that of a hospital nurse, paid an accumulated salary of more than £20,000. And a liar! oh heavens what a liar! [28 June]

Wise: I went to Putney last evening, and bought a few more Mss. I got the old chap down a trifle for the single sheet poems, and bought them. He will not take less than £5 for a sonnet. He says he can sell all he has 'in several quarters' at this price (which he certainly can), and will not part with them at less. . . . I bought Swinburne's 1st copy of 1st ed. of Fitzgerald's "Omar Khayam", (bought for 1s out of Q's box in 1864), inscribed and signed by A. C. S. for £35, uncut in wrappers. This was a *bargain*. [30 June]

Gosse: It will not have escaped you that very few of these mss. are originals. They are copied out for the press, the copier being Swinburne himself. Consequently, their interest is a secondary one, for the movement of the poet's mind is not shown. Critically they are without interest: they are just curiosities. [30 June]

Wise: I spent the whole of yesterday afternoon and evening at the Pines, and this morning I am sending the old chap a cheque for £300, so you may guess I have got some treasures. As a matter of fact I have brought away some glorious treasures, all of which you shall see on Wednesday, when I will also tell you all I have seen and heard. Among others, I got the MS. of "Hertha"! This W. D. asked me to get bound for him in levant, in the same manner that I have my own bound. How *could* I let it remain there? But to get it I had to worry myself for hours, and it was like drawing a tooth blessed with a double allowance of fangs to get it out of him. But get it I did at last. He charged me £45 for it, and no doubt thought that in asking this price he was getting the last cent out of me. As a fact the MS. was *dead cheap*, for the poem stands in the front ranks of Swinburne's verse. I would have gone much higher rather than left it. [5 July]

On 10 July, Wise billed Wrenn £303 6s. for Swinburne manuscripts. In the same month a printing programme started; little unpublished pieces were put into pamphlets, the first few ostensibly under the aegis of Watts-Dunton, the later ones pure Wise. Gosse was soon involved in the (by no means simple) task of editing. The printed limitation notices range from seven to

thirty with most at twenty. The next letter deals particularly
with three pamphlets printed by Wise and Forman rather earlier, in 1890–93. Although they may be correctly dated, they
were piracies not authorized by Swinburne.

Wise:    Many thanks for the proof of "Twilight". I spent all last
evening over the MS. of this, and it now reads quite differently. Will send you revise next week. Bought some more
MSS. from your "Reptile" friend on Thursday, and am
going on Monday for more. He rather presses me to take the
autographed "Tombeau" at 12/12/– But I stuck to "No",
and told him "all or none". It ended looking very much like
"*all*". Now for some fun. He had got a copy of my S. Bibliography, and pointed out to me

> "Sonnets on Browning"
> "Grace Darling"
> and
> "Bulgarie"

"These are *damned* things: they are all 3 forgeries and piracies. I shall write to the Athenaeum and denounce them!"
I told him that to do so would do him much harm, as his
note would be replied to, and it would end by being shown
that he knew nothing about S's books at all.
That I could produce S's written permission for the
Browning Society to print the Death Sonnets, and also a
copy with presentation inscription to Christina Rossetti,
bought by me from Wm Rossetti after Christina's death.
That I could also produce *S's letter to myself* giving me
leave to print "Grace Darling", and a second letter thank-
ing me for copies of it.
"Oh yes" he said, "I remember, they are all right". As to
"Bulgarie", I said, the MS. was sent for publication to the
P.M.G., but held back from publication. Possibly the
P.M.G. people may have struck off a few copies before
returning the MS. to S. *That* would not be either "forgery"
or "piracy" – "Yes, I do remember something of the sort: I
think I won't trouble about them!" [10 July]

Wise:    What a wonderful fellow you are! This is the result of being
a Poet yourself: you see right into the poet's view. Now
that you have opened the window the whole thing is
clear. . . . I have made a fresh note out of your letter, and
shall give it to the printers on my way to 'Change this
afternoon. . . . I have bought some more Ballads, etc. from
him, so there will be more pamphlets. I shall see that you
get them all. He says he wants £5 a copy, but I'll make sure
of a copy for E. G. *free*. I only wish the old miser could know

it, and that I could see him receive the information. But it
would do too much harm. [19 July]

Gosse: The Swinburne Ms. has arrived, and I find that I shall have
no difficulty in solving all the queries. The old Fraud is
perfectly transparent, and when I get the proof, which I am
impatient to do, I shall go carefully through it, collating it
with the MS. . . . What a very interesting set these posthumous pieces are making! [19 August]

Wise: Here is new revise of "Portrait", and also *proof* and *revise* of
"Queen F." You will see I've used your words, but have not
given your name. I have allowed W-D's name to stand in the
one case; the other I have left anonymous. I am in a fix on
this score. If I give your name there'll be a scrap with W-D.
May I leave matters as they are for the present, and, later
on, when I complete the Swinburne Bibliography, wh. I
shall do shortly, I shall give the *full* story of these prints.
[21 August]

Gosse: I really do not wish you to give me any "credit" in the
prefaces to these interesting posthumous prints. It is really
better not to do so. As for me, it is the greatest possible
pleasure to help you, by deciphering and editing, to make
them as perfect as possible. [31 August]

Wise: I am about again, but hardly fit to be so – but affairs both
at Mark Lane and at Greenwich are very pressing, and have
to be attended to. [5 September]

Gosse: I have gone through "A Criminal Case" and have corrected
it. But I earnestly entreat you not to print it. It is the
flattest, dullest, most puerile fragment that it is possible
to conceive. It reveals Swinburne at his feeblest. [12 Sep-
tember]

Wise: I fully agree with what you say regarding the prose *Sketch*:
it had better remain in MS. W.-D. has sent me the MSS. of
the "The Sisters", "Lamb and Wither" and "Marston", all
of which I have accepted. I have paid him in all £2,154 up to
date, including your ms., 2 plays, and the things Wrenn had.
[14 September]

Gosse: I lose all power of speech when I think of the gluttony and
shamelessness of this old toad. But I think you are to blame,
a little, for encouraging him. Why do you go on feeding him
with money in this way? Surely the old MSS. which he
dribbles out to you cannot be worth half the money you so
generously give him. Left to himself, he would have made
hundreds where you have paid him thousands. I only do hope
that you will succeed, some day, in wiping the slime of T.
W.-D. off the pure marble of Swinburne's memory [6
October]

During all this, Wise was keeping up his other correspondences, including that with Wrenn. The latter wrote to him in October 1909, telling him that an American bookseller was offering Swinburne mss. obtained from 'The Pines' by an English bookseller, W. T. Spencer again. Wise professed to be staggered and had a long talk with Watts who defended himself vigorously: he could sell his own property to whomsoever he wished. The dialogue continues.

Wise: This has just come in from Wrenn. I feel too sick to say much. Despite all you have said about him (alas, how truly you spoke!) I trusted the old devil. He, W.-D. gave me his distinct word, that if I took everything he found as it came along, I should buy *all he had*. . . . I'm sorry for the feelings of the miserable old ghoul when he reads tomorrow m'g the letter I have just written him [21 October]

Gosse: The old creature at Putney seems to have got the better of you on all sides. I am sorry you have not been able to bring him to book, and I am sorry too, that you should immediately be paying him more money, and for imaginary advantages. [25 October]

Wise: You ask why I pay W.-D. for printing these tracts. I do so because I feel morally bound to do so. He has no legal right or power to stop me printing them privately. As I bought "unpublished poems" without executing any legal instrument reserving to him the copyright, I have full legal right to *publish* them, and to register the copyright against him. . . . But the old man accepted my word as being as good as my bond, and my word is sacred. I have never broken yet a promise I have once given. [27 October]

Gosse: Does the Asp of Putney spit forth any more venom? Or sit upon any more eggs? O that there should continue to breathe such a very wicked old man! [24 November]

Wise: I really think that 'A criminal Case' ought to be put into type, if only for this reason, – that unless the MS. be destroyed sooner or later it will be printed by *someone*. Hence I've had it set up, and here is a proof. I send it in case the spirit should move you to add a few words [12 December]

Gosse: I wish I could persuade you to destroy this utterly valueless fragment, which ceases before it begins, and is neither intelligible nor characteristic. I will have nothing to do with it, and I think its presence among the valuable and interesting posthumous pamphlets which you have brought out would be a calamity. [13 December]

Wise: I think you are right. I will have the types of that pamphlet disd. [15 December]

Wise: Would not the greedy old gent at Putney *curse* us if he knew

what we were printing – after his absurd (and legally futile)
letters in the press forbidding the printing of A.C.S.'s
letters? He can stop publication, but the law gives him no
power over private printing. [15 December, a second letter]

Gosse:  I suppose this really is the latest of the series? I shall feel
quite melancholy at the cessation of this excitement, which
has so pleasantly filled nearly nine months. I must thank
you again for your very great kindness in presenting me with
this most valuable and unique set of pamphlets: and for
bearing with all my criticisms and suggestions in so very
good-humoured a way. You are the kindest and most
patient of friends. I think posterity will be grateful to you
for having preserved so piously the last fragments of one of
the greatest poets of the nineteenth century, and one
whose posthumous works might easily have been lost, or
carelessly and unworthily produced. It is particularly
delightful to know that the originals are all safe in your
keeping, and preserved from danger of falling into unworthy
hands. What shall you be busy about next? I hope I shall be
allowed to share your interests whatever they are. [11 April
1910]

Wise did distribute the type of *A Criminal Case* (15 December
above) but only after printing the usual twenty copies, or so the
colophon claims. Buying manuscripts went on (on and off) until
Watts-Dunton's death in 1914 and pirating Swinburne pamphlets until 1920. All this new excitement made the now embar-
goed forgeries seem old hat. Wise still had cupboards of them but
they represented a past phase of his life. Like the successful
mafia man, he wanted to invest his ill-gotten gains in a more
legitimate business – such as printing Swinburne manuscripts.
What he should have done, was to have burnt the lot: what he
actually did was to sell Herbert Gorfin, most of his remaining
stock.

Gorfin left Rubecks in 1912 and started up as a bookseller on
his own in Charing Cross Road. He bought the library of T. B.
Smart, the bibliographer of Matthew Arnold. It may have been
Wise who steered the library to Gorfin and it probably was Wise
who encouraged Gorfin to full-time bookselling. Over the period
of 1909–12 Wise sold him about 900 copies of some twenty
different forgeries for about £400. The largest number of any
pamphlet was fifty-seven copies (perhaps near the entire print
run) of a late Kipling *White Horses*. Gorfin believed (he was not
very bright) or pretended to believe (he was not very scrupulous)

Wise's remainder story. Gorfin regarded this purchase as an immediate source of income and a nest egg for his old age: many second-hand booksellers keep a few things under the bed for this latter eventuality.

There are probably several connected reasons for Wise's remaindering operation, besides that already mentioned. One reason was that affairs at Rubecks were gathering pace. The Spanish distillation business had proved very successful. In about 1908, Wise and Otto Rubeck in partnership bought W. A. Smith & Co. Essential Oil Distillers of Greenwich. This explains the mention of Mark Lane and Greenwich in one of Wise's letters to Gosse quoted above. The new firm involved new responsibility in the running of a small factory. The second reason was that Wise was about to move, spending some of his Spanish gains. In 1910, he and his wife went uphill and bought a house in a fashionable part of Hampstead – 25 Heath Drive. This is a tranquil tree-lined street with substantial houses; No. 25 is a capacious house, now partitioned into flats. It is really quite near the Heath itself and only about a quarter of an hour's walk from the fashionable Leg of Mutton Pond and Jack Straw's Castle. All Wise's books were in boxes for several months, as he told Wrenn,

> Maple's men finally cleared out two days ago, and now I am securely in possession. The room is really a most delightful one, and you will certainly be pleased with it when you enjoy its welcome next summer. I am taking for myself also the Morning Room, and having this fitted with the book cases out of the old dining room. These I shall employ for "Collected Editions" and "Ana" ', reserving the Library for my Books – with a big "B"! [October 1910].

Wise was still selling steadily to Wrenn and they were projecting another joint continental jaunt. In a confiding mood Wise once told Gorfin, 'Wren is worth £1000 a year to me.' He also revealed that on one of their holidays, Wrenn agreed to pay all the expenses provided Wise did all the tipping, a European habit (then) which greatly irritated Wrenn. 'But mind you,' Wise said 'it wasn't cheap – having to pay all those tips!' Just as another bogus vendor was being lined up ('I have found Mr. Wallington an exceedingly agreeable and courteous individual; and the reverse of being greedy and grasping. The negotiation is a pleasant one.') Wrenn died, on 13 May 1911. This certainly closed a chapter for Wise, though his association with the Wrenn family was to continue. To finish off his domestic circumstances, we can add that his father had died in 1902. As reported to Wrenn

> we reached home at 9 o'clock in the evening, and just at midnight my dear father passed away. He had been an invalid for years, but his end here came quite suddenly at last. He went to bed – fell asleep – and never woke again. He was a quiet old fashioned Christian man, and death had no terrors for him. He was in his 75th year.

Well he was: but he died not in Hampstead but in Islington at 127 Devonshire Road and he died of drink. The proprieties were observed and he was buried with his first wife in Highgate cemetery. Another family skeleton is perhaps to be guessed at by the burial in the same tomb of one Amelia Groseman, a young lady of whom nothing more is known.

Three years later, Jeannie, Wise's second stepmother, remarried. George Wise, her second husband, was a cousin of her late husband and rather intriguingly was described as a retired publisher. Worn out by two difficult husbands, she died in February 1909. She left all her money to her brother in Aberdeen and just the family Bible and two portraits to her stepson Thomas. George Wise survived her by a bare nine months, dying of 'Exhaustion of chronic mania' in a home for down and outs in Kilburn. Wise had, in 1905, claimed an early Shelley supporter, Sir Thomas Wyse K.C.B. later British Minister at Athens, as his paternal grandfather's first cousin. Before fiercely condemning Wise for attempts to improve his rather sordid family background, we might ponder the pressures. The rigid class divisions of Victorian society bore particularly hard on those who rose through the ranks. When even Thomas Hardy, the undisputed doyen of English literature, could carefully build up a fictitious history of his past life and ancestry, how can we censure Wise?

# 14

# FORMAN AND HIS FAMILY

Minor sniping at the forgeries continued, but there was no mass attack. Dr A. W. Pollard wrote to thank Wise for a gift in 1909, 'These Swinburne pamphlets seem awfully jolly . . . they will be stamped and put in a cupboard in the Keeper's Room.' But buried in his *Encyclopaedia Britannica* article on bibliography published in 1910, Pollard restated with greater precision what he had first said in 1907.

> The type-facsimile forgeries are mostly of short pieces by Tennyson, George Eliot and A. C. Swinburne printed (or supposed to have been printed – for it is doubtful if some of these "forgeries" ever had any originals) for circulation among friends. These trifles should never be purchased without a written guarantee.

Pollard had cracked the essential point of Forman and Wise's creative forgeries. That there was a small informal circle who knew what was happening can be seen in another comment made six years later by Charles Fairfax Murray. C.F.M., artist, connoisseur, collector and friend of Morris and Ruskin, was a tough nut. He had quite a row with Wise over a Ruskin volume *Letters on Art and Literature* 1894 which was badly transcribed. He also knew Forman, who used him as an intermediary in the Paola Clairmont purchase. In March 1916, he wrote to an American collector,

> Equally spurious as to *date of printing* is the Chapel in Lyoness (or whatever it is called) [actually *Sir Galahad*] by Morris and reprinted from the ed. of 1858 by a speculator, it rests between two collectors of similar "varieties", either of whom are capable of the fraud. There was a copy of this in the Brayton Ives Collection. No doubt they were printed for sale in America after Morris became famous.

The Brayton Ives sale in New York in 1915, contained twenty-four forgeries, the largest group since the Lapham sale in 1908. There seems little doubt that Murray knew enough to have said Wise or Forman (though not, one notes, Wise and Forman) instead of 'two speculators'.

While Wise was centre stage, what was Forman doing? Wise had no children. Forman, as we have seen, had three: and he cherished them. Maurice, his father's favourite, settled in South Africa. After a five-year engagement at a distance, Lillian Braby went out and married him in 1897. Their first child – Laura and Harry's first grandchild – was born in 1898 (Clifford) and was followed by Maurice II (b. 1901) and Madeleine (b. 1907). Gwendolen (she to whom Orion Horne had left an Australian estate) married a Mr Roberts and he took her to Mexico. The climate did not agree with her and in 1904 Forman left at 48 hours' notice to bring her home. He was away some two months : it must have been expensive and inconvenient, but he did not hesitate for a moment. This seems to have marked the end of Gwendolen's marriage and there were no children. Forman wrote to W. M. Rossetti on 21 January 1904,

> What a mass of literary work you have been getting through since your retirement! It makes me quite envious to think of the superior wisdom of those who retire "while there is yet time". Here am I, within a year and a half of my "grand climacteric", entitled to retire today, if I like, not feeling very grand for purposes of regulated drudgery, & yet lacking the courage to say I will not do what the government want me to – stay & see them through the Rome Postal Congress, which, it now seems, may not be held till next year!

In 1902, and again in 1905, the Formans went on holiday to North Berwick to a house called St Christophers. This charming resort was then less built up than it is today and Forman liked it very much. At Christmas 1902, he sent Louis Vanuxern – a friend of whom we know nothing and would like to know more – a manuscript keepsake. He may have been following a tradition, since Maurice Bucke, the old Canadian friend, was asking Forman for 'the Vanuxern lines' as long ago as 1891. The keepsake comprises a verse retelling the St Christopher legend in terms which somewhat suggest that Forman had moderated his early agnosticism. He prefixed this with a verse preface, nostalgic for the Devon of his youth and the Scotland of his holiday. It is a piece of considerable biographical interest of which we have already quoted part (see p.14).

To Louis Vanuxern

Last autumn, Louis, up in the North,
We 'bode in a house on the Links of Forth.
St. Christopher gives the house its name –
The pilgrim-giant of monkish fame

Who forded the waters broad and long
And carried the Christ on his shoulder strong.

There many a day I spent in dreams
Of Devon's meadows & moors & streams;
But the talk of my folk was strange to my lips
As I watched the canny Scots & their ships;
My Nell & William & good Ned Bray
Seemed ever dimmer & more away;
Right little of livelihead I found
In the Sire & Maid of The Outward Bound;
And the woman asleep in her Widdicombe grave
– The poor dead Hannah whose tress I save –
And the Witch of the Copse with her dark romance
And George Gale's slayers and dear Mad Nance,
All strange on my sense their talk would fall
If ever they came to talk at all.

But at length I grew to love the Firth;
And strains in another key had birth;
And more & more they beset me there
As I roved abroad in the keen brisk air,
And noted the folk in their strenuous life,
Or gazed across to the Neuk of Fife;
For bathed in the sun, on the wind-swept grass,
I saw how the rack on the gale would pass
Adown the Firth & across its mouth
North east by east as it fled from the South.

And Louis, my friend, you need not look
In Christian story or monkish book
For the Christmas legend I send you here:
It was newly born the closing year;
On the light sea breeze it was carried about
And the blustering winds they blurted it out;
The wild-duck gaggled it up in the air,
And the sea-mews cried it above the lair
Of him who knew what they had to tell –
Of him, O Louis, who loves you well.

So he sucked it in as he lay & lay
At the edge of the North Sea day by day;
And he scrawled it wherever his hand might hap
To light on pencil & leaf or scrap.
And when to his home in the South he went
He bade one copy for your content
In script that readily may be read
A tale where fancy & truth are wed.

Forman wrote poetry all his life and even left his funeral instructions in verse. In its evocation of the poet's West Country past, one almost hears faint and far-off echoes of Hardy's *Wessex Heights*

> There's a Ghost at Yell'ham Bottom chiding loud
> at the fall of the night;
> There's a ghost in Froom-side Vale, thin-lipped and
> vague in a shroud of white

But the dates don't fit: and Forman hasn't Hardy's genius.

The Forman family had a tradition that in later life, Harry Buxton had 'boycotted' Wise. He could not have done that: but he may well have drawn apart somewhat. His ill health increased and was perhaps used as a means of evasion. He wrote to Wise in February 1904

> My "cold" is persistent especially nasal catarrh, for which I fre-
> quently use the pocket menthol inhaler you gave me when you were
> so bad. It is as good as ever & an excellent thing for temporary
> alleviation: I wonder how it manages to retain its virtue all these
> years. Of course I have been using stronger remedies too – salicylate
> of soda, menthol snuff, a wash-out affair for nose & pharynx, a benzoin
> comp. inhalation, & the Lord knows what

and again,

> Mrs Wise & you are so long-suffering in matters social that I have to
> take shame to my self and my weaknesses. At present I am in town
> actually; but we are technically doing what is known as living in the
> kitchen of a shut-up house; and as to going out of an evening – well,
> the two (or so) attempts I have made of necessity this summer have
> not startled me with their success. In truth I fancy I have made a
> little progress toward a sort of stable decrepitude – which is the best
> I can expect; but I dare not accept your kind offer to choose a day for
> the pleasure of an evening with you & Mr. Wrenn & Mr. Arnold. . . .I
> still go to the office, & take refuge *here* in hard mental work. I will
> write about bibliographical matters later. [Aug. 1904]

Forman had a dangerous operation (probably for prostate) in 1906 and in 1907, he retired from the Post Office after forty-seven years, to turn over a new leaf as he expressed it. He could not, however, turn Wise out. Forman saddled with Wise, suggests a man with perpetual toothache: sometimes the pain is imperceptible, sometimes it is agonizing – but it is always there. As well as the Oxford Standard Authors Edition of Keats which we have mentioned, Forman had several literary projects he could turn to in his retirement. He published *Letters of Edward*

*John Trelawny* with OUP in 1910: it is still the standard edition. Trelawny was the author of the partly fictional *Adventures of a younger son* 1831 and the man who ordered the boat in which Shelley drowned. Forman notes that the inspiration for the edition, was the bundle of Trelawny letters he bought from Paola Clairmont in Vienna.

> Fifteen, or it may be thirty, years ago, my son Maurice Buxton Forman had copied them all out for me. [In 1909] my son was once more under my roof after a long absence from England, and was working upon his Meredith books at the British Museum, where he was able to help me in certain researches.

Maurice was 37 in 1909 and a great Meredith enthusiast, as his father was not. He may have been the inspiration behind the *Jump-to-Glory Jane* forgery we have already mentioned. We have called this a forgery, but perhaps it is only a piracy: it may well be correctly dated. The term piracy is commonly used of publishers taking advantage of defective or non-existent copyright law and printing without paying the author or getting his consent. Wise and Forman's piracies were usually one degree worse than this, in that they did not announce their (or anyone else's) role as publishers and used an anonymous imprint which implied authorial permission. 'I do protest about these pamphlets coming out without any statment of what they are or whence they came' as Gosse once said to Wise. It is easy to see how tempting the next stage would be, which is to give false authority by adding a false imprint, or a false history by a false date.

Maurice's work on Meredith was preparatory to his bibliography but that was not to be published for some years. What he did produce, was *George Meredith, some early appreciations*, published by Chapman & Hall in 1909. This is a selection of reviews of Meredith, a pioneer venture in a genre which has recently become rather popular in academic circles. Four of these reviews were by James Thomson ('B.V.') better known as a despairing poet. Permission from the copyright holders was obtained for the book reprint. However, Maurice, probably aided and encouraged by his father, had the Thomson portion reprinted separately. It is a handsome little brochure of twenty-four leaves, the same setting of type as the book, but repaginated. It has the title *James Thomson ("B.V.") on George Meredith privately printed* 1909. It does have a printer's imprint (Clowes) but there is no indication who is responsible for publication. It has a limitation notice of fifty copies, and looks a typical little piece for the bibliophile market. However, in the same year appeared Meredith's *Twenty poems*, with the unrevealing imprint 'London, 1909'. It has a note printed on the half-title *The issue of this privately printed book consists of twenty-five numbered copies*. There is an anonymous bibliographical note explaining that the poems had been attributed on the basis of the office record of *Household Words*. There is no imprint, but the book was printed by Clowes. When he published his bibliography, Maurice gave no indication that anyone, let alone himself, was responsible for it. However, we know that Maurice (in 1943) owned the *Household Words* ledger and had inherited it from his father. Furthermore, Wise's copy is inscribed 'To my good friend Thomas J. Wise from M. Buxton Forman'. Meredith died in May 1909 so we do not have his indignant comment on the book as we have with *Jump-to-Glory:* there is little doubt that it is a piracy produced by Maurice Buxton Forman following in his father's footsteps.

In the same year, Maurice wrote to Wise reporting an unrecorded Tennyson, in terms which indicate he was putting on his father's mantle. Forman himself was working as hard as ever on literary matters and in 1911 appeared perhaps his greatest piece of transcription. This was the *Shelley Note Books*. Twenty-five notebooks were inherited by Sir Percy Shelley from his mother. By two different routes, twenty came to the Bodleian Library. The provenance of the other five notebooks is shown overleaf; and is a striking illustration of the American popularity of the romantic poets.

Bixby bought the three notebooks for £3,000: Wise had nearly succeeded in buying them before the sale for £1,000 as he told Wrenn ('three tiny note-books and ragged. They would almost go into one's waistcoat pocket. But they are vastly interesting relics'). Bixby allowed the Bibliophile Society of Boston to publish them (reserving 250 copies for himself). The introduction by Henry Harper, treasurer and one of the leading lights in the society explains that

> The plan of reproducing in facsimile the entire contents of the Note Books was first considered; but such a reproduction of the original MSS. would be no more interesting to the average reader or student than a Greek dictionary would be to one who could not read the

Four of the notebooks were sold to Richard Garnett,
and their subsequent provenance was:

| 1 Notebook | Miss V.E. Neale | John Spoor of Chicago sale 1939 | Library of Congress Washington |
|---|---|---|---|
| 3 Notebooks | Garnett sale 1906 | W. K. Bixby of St Louis sale 1916 | Huntington Library California |

The fifth Notebook was sold to the Rev Stopford A. Brooke,
and was split into two parts:

| One portion | Red Cross sale 1915? | Pierpont Morgan Library New York | |
|---|---|---|---|
| Remaining portion | Mrs T.W. Rolleston Brooke's daughter | Carl H. Pforzheimer Library New York | New York Public Library |

- - - - - - - - - - - - - - - - - - - - - - - - - - - - - - - - - - - - -

Provenance of five of the Notebooks sold by Sir Percy Shelley

Greek alphabet. The task of deciphering the contents of these Note Books seemed impossible; it could be accomplished only by one thoroughly familiar with Shelley's handwriting, and with an intimate acquaintance with practically his entire works, as well as a knowledge of his habits and characteristics, and the methods he employed in constructing his work. Shelley adopted no systematic order of paging in these books – sometimes he would write in the front, then in the back, then with the book bottom side up, and frequently he wrote up and down the pages lengthwise after having written across them – and never any too plainly.

Greek, Latin, Italian, Spanish and English are all mixed up together, and lines in one language often appear written directly or diagonally across other lines written in another language. In the work of transcription it was therefore impossible to proceed in an orderly manner from the beginning to the end of the books. Fragments of poems here and there all through the books had to be puzzled out and transcribed, and then fitted together with their related parts, wherever they might be found. To do this intelligently required a familiarity with Shelley's works almost equal to that of the ordinary individual with the English alphabet. Imagine one coming across a disconnected passage and, after disentangling it from a confused mass of crisscross lines, being able to identify it as the five hundred and ninety-first line of Prometheus Un-bound!

Harper was a partial witness but does not overstate the case. The three volumes of the *Shelley Note Books* are a triumph of Forman's patient and dedicated editing. He also contributed a light piece on *Belles-lettres in England in the twentieth century* to the Society's Year Book in 1911. This is a rapid round up of current literature, viz.

> Edmund Gosse does not now often enter the poetic lists, but per contra, he has given to us much charming and suggestive prose and, best of all, a truly admirable study of clashing temperaments in his biography, *Father and Son*, a book I am convinced posterity will value for its transparent truth and its vivid and deep spiritual interest. I may mention that the school kept by Plymouth Brethren to which he was sent as a "weekly boarder" is touched to the life: *crede experto*; for I, even I also, was educated at that school.

Forman's last book was *The life of Percy Bysshe Shelley by Thomas Medwin. A new edition printed from a copy copiously amended and extended by the author and left unpublished at his death*, OUP, 1913. This is again a most thorough piece of editorial work. It contains a charming dedication to Forman's elder brother. 'My dear Alfred, – My earliest recollections are of digging on the sands at Teignmouth. . .' which we have already quoted (see page 12). Despite the impeccable texts, both the *Shelley Note Books* and the Medwin have a reminder of the Mr Hyde side of Forman. This takes the form of a frontispiece portrait of Shelley which in Medwin is embellished with two lines of facsimile manuscript, very touching. It is in fact a copy of the Leonardo da Vinci head of Christ with slight alterations of hair and dress to bring it in line with Shelley. This confection was commissioned by Forman from one Alfred Soord, presumably in secret mockery of the whole Shelley cult. Perhaps Forman was waiting for an objection, after all he himself would have spotted it elsewhere very quickly: but none came. The fraud was not published until 1947.

# 15

## FORMAN'S DEATH

Meanwhile, Herbert Gorfin, erstwhile office boy, was a bookseller in Charing Cross Road. His first thirteen catalogues (1913–16: he was then called up) contain nearly 100 entries for the forgeries at prices ranging from £1/12s.6d. to £21. On the whole his prices were rather cheaper than Wise. No doubt Forman disapproved, as well he might.

> I have received your long letter and the Coleridge sheets and slips, – but I fear my catarrh is developing into influenza & will for days to come incapacitate me for examining proofs. I had hoped that things might take a turn that would enable me to give you a look-in & explain in few words some difficult matters. This perhaps may come off later, but *now* I am likelier to be in bed for days to come when I once get there – in an hour or two. So I hurry this off to beg you not on any account to proceed as you suggest about the Sonnets. I can give you excellent reasons; & am, as at this present, Yours sincerely H. Buxton Forman

he wrote to his collaborator in April 1913. One can speculate as to the impact of the surely significant conclusion of a letter between old friends: *as at this present,* Yours sincerely. Probably Wise was so pleased with his wholesaling that he was proposing to extend it to the Reading *Sonnets* which had come to be a star piece. Perhaps as a result of Forman's pleading, Gorfin was only allowed to sell it on commission (along with six Tennysons and a Thackeray). In December of the same year, Forman's Christmas letter to Wise included another conspiratorial passage.

> Certainly I have been suffering less pain & inconvenience: but I am still unable to get about much without more than enough of those articles. Still, I do not despair of dropping in on you and talking over many things that are better to talk about than write about.

Was he reproving Wise for a rash letter? It is notable that it is from Wise's pen that we have the only actual admission of forgery – the Pforzheimer document. And of the surviving letters between the conspirators, those from Forman (to Wise) outnumber those from Wise (to Forman) by about 4 to 1. There is no doubt Forman was much more wary and a more skilled clandestine operator.

By 1912, Wise's Swinburne printing had produced over thirty little pamphlets. Wise was very jealous of his rights in these texts. He had a furious row in 1910–14 with the Boston Bibliophile Society who reprinted some of them. It is notable how quickly Wise occupies the moral high ground. He wrote that they had

> printed a volume which is a disgrace to your Society . . . such a mix-up of hopelessly unsuitable material that it will only serve to make your Society a laughing-stock. The statement upon the title-page that the contents are from "unpublished MSS." is a LIE. . . . You certainly finally, after I had appealed to you repeatedly in vain did have my "permission" obtained by the highwayman from the traveller after he had got the poor devil in the dust, with a pistol at his throat.

The anger of the poacher turned gamekeeper is clearly evident; highwayman was exactly what Wise himself had been called over twenty years before by Dowden when he had no permission at all.

Meanwhile the Gosse–Wise letters in 1912 are full of interest. Here is a commodity dealer's view of the book market.

> When, some 25–30 years ago I was (to all intents and purposes) laughed at by Rossetti, Forman, and F. J. F.[urnivall] for paying £50 and £60 each for the Shelley "impossibles", I was quite content, – for I backed my own opinion. For those things I could now get £500 and £600 a piece. I do not say that the next 25–30 years are going to multiply the value of Swinburne's things by *ten*: Swinburne is not Shelley. But I do say that in my well-considered opinion the books and Mss. of Swinburne will never be worth less than they are at the present moment; but that they will, on the contrary, exhibit a steady and reasonable advance.

Gosse was just at this point writing his biography of Swinburne for the *Dictionary of National Biography*. Wise had noticed some supposed juvenilia in his bibliography published in 1897. These were verses published in *Fraser's Magazine* by A. C. S. in 1849–51 'I demand that you supply bibliographical references' wrote Gosse (2 August). 'The whole of these early verses were printed in Fraser and are all signed with the usual initials. I am with you in thinking that we are bound to accept them as Swinburne's – hence we are gathering them together', Wise replied (3 August). Wise's two booklets *The Arab Chief* and *Juvenilia* came out soon after in 1912. Gosse had his doubts ('I am unable to guess what induces you to attribute them to Swinburne') but put them in the *DNB*. 'He was, in fact, now writing verses, some of which his mother sent to *Fraser's Magazine* . . . but of this false start he was afterwards not pleased to be reminded.' Soon after they were in print, it became clear that something was wrong – one of the poems, for instance, was dated from the Carlton Club at a time when Swinburne would have been sixteen. There was an immediate hue and cry which resulted in grave embarrassment for Gosse and the discovery that the true author was Sir Anthony Coningham Sterling K.C.B., Brigade Major of the Highland Division in the Crimea. Gosse wrote a formal apology to *The Times*: Wise refused to sign it and somehow escaped the censure that was his due *and* he remained on cordial terms with Gosse. Poor old Gosse had already a reputation for inaccuracy which was increased. His mild and greatly understated hints about Swinburne's drinking, for instance, had already annoyed the family: now he had been handed to them on a plate. Wise emerged as a mediator between an hysterical Isabel Swinburne and Gosse, although it was he who had got Gosse into the mess in the first place: Mr Wise was clearly a serious loss to his country's diplomatic service.

Watts-Dunton died in June 1914 and there was a final clearing up at 'The Pines'. Wise bought little as he had already winnowed the chaff thoroughly. He sent a highly coloured account to Gosse.

> Was at the Pines all the mng. The place is a regular Hades, with those 3 women next door to fighting all the time. I expected trouble, but did not anticipate it would be carried on so openly or so shamelessly. Papers inscribed "This is mine, you dare to move it" etc. pinned on to half the articles in the house.
>
> "Mr Wise, do come upstairs and tell me about this"
> "Tom, you *dare* to go up, – you've come to help *me*"
> (When upstairs)
> "Tom put that book in your pocket and bring it down, it's mine – they've stolen it"
>
> Or:–
>
> "The executors are all on the side of these cats: if you won't protect me I must send for Douglas"
> "My father help me? I *hate* my father, the *damned German*"
> "No, my brother's a waster, he shall never come near me again"
> "How is my sister? You shall never see her again; she's a *beast*."
>
> In my opinion the lovely Clara ought to be sent to Hanwell. I bought

from her for £20 Tennyson's "Becket" given by A. T. to W.-D. I've
promised to spend the morning there tomorrow to sort out the
valuable books for them. On Friday they will go to Sotheby's. A nice
game to play over Swinburne's worldly goods!

She, Clara, declared that she had only 5/6 in the world, and could
get nothing from the Exrs. – which, if true, I fail to understand . . .
Mrs Mason has an unpublished MS. of Swinburne's but does not even
know whether it is prose or verse. Clara swears it is stolen, so Mrs. M.
rushed it off to the Bank to be held for her. When all is over I am to see
it. Several things which I know W.-D. had, and the resting place of
which I know, are gone. These women are evidently "pinching" things
against each other all round. [14 June]

In another letter, Wise meets Mr Taylor the lawyer and makes
tentative enquiries about copyright and his proposed printing of
more little pamphlets. He ends

Miss Watts is threatening to appeal to Chancery. W.-D.'s novel is in
type, but is not printed off. Lawyer says that it is technically published, and belongs to the estate. Miss Watts says it is *not* published
and is therefore an MS, and consequently is her sole property. [24
June]

By 1914 Wise's Swinburne printing had produced forty little
pamphlets. Finding these a pretty profitable racket and easy to
dispose of, he set to on Borrow. He had bought a quantity of
manuscripts from Shorter's purchase in 1904 and from these he
produced quite a crop of little pamphlets, forty-four in all, all but
two (1914) printed in 1913. Gosse helped him considerably when
he found out what was happening. Almost all the printings are
translations of popular stories and ballads. Gosse, with his literary
knowledge and fluency in Danish was able to identify the source of
the Borrovian borrowings and clarify the terrible muddle into
which Wise was drifting. When Wise's bibliography of Borrow
appeared, it might have been looked upon as an advertisement for
his private printings – like the Ashley lists – rather than a bibliography proper. By this time, Wise's output included bibliographies of Browning, Swinburne (both 1897), Tennyson (1908),
Coleridge (1913) and Borrow (1914). Soon to follow were Wordsworth (1916) and the Brontës (1917). All are more or less tarred
with Wise's own publications. We have considered all but the
Coleridge (three little pamphlets) and the Wordsworth. The
latter has one Wise pamphlet, one fake, and one curious item
which is neither. This is two leaves containing a Wordsworth

poem detached from the book they belong to and catalogued as a rare privately printed brochure. The object is genuine (a very imperfect book, in a way) but the description is phoney. It is another illustration of the complexities of deceit.

An undated letter from Wise to Forman, in an unpleasantly jovial style must come from about this time:

> My dear Harry Buxton F!
> Here's the bit of Borrow's first as promised. As soon as you are well enough come round & bring some more of the *E.B.B.* or *Mary to Claire* letters, & we'll make a "deal". I have a full set of the pamphlets & a nice representative series of the mss. & letters put aside for you. Ever yours, Tom Wise
>
> If you want a real fine Borrow ms or two, as you say, you had better bring a *real fine* Shelley letter with you!!!! One of the "good'uns"! – Now don't tell me I'm never greedy!

There is a slight feeling of the flick of a whip about this letter: one can understand Forman vainly wishing to boycott his partner.

Sydney Cockerell had not forgotten about the Morris forgeries and in March 1915 he wrote to Gosse in terms we can partly guess at from the latter's reply,

> Your caution about spurious 'first editions' is well-founded. I was very sceptical about the [Swinburne] *Dead love* of 1864. But I got a copy of it, and it has every appearance of being genuine; moreover it has been known for a great many years. I am unable to find any reason to doubt it. D.G. Rossetti's *Sister Helen* of 1857 is perfectly genuine. Watts-Dunton denied the authenticity of a private Swinburne pamphlet, until we discovered a letter from Swinburne himself acknowledging it! Merely negative evidence is very dangerous. I wonder if you are quite certain about the spuriousness of the *Sir Galahad* of 1858. I recollect seeing at Ford Maddox Brown's a copy of it, with an autograph inscription to him from W. Morris.

Gosse was well primed with Wise's lies but he obviously failed to convince Cockerell, as Gosse's second letter makes clear,

> Some day you will find time to give me another word about the Pre-raphaelite pamphlets, for you are in the first rank of bibliographers. . . . There are frauds of course:– the L[arge] P[aper] *Jason* [by Morris] is one, the Hotten *Siena* another. But there are not so many as the idle literary man supposes. Hallam Tennyson denounced the private issues of his Father, and it leaked out that the old man ordered them all in succession, for fell private purposes!

Gosse refers to an attempt by Tennyson's son to denounce Wise's fakes of his father: we have no other information about it, but Wise must have played the genuine private printings as evidence for the forged ones. He found that if you are sufficiently dogmatic and sufficiently eminent you can get away with quantities of lies and misstatements. The position is rather like that of a scientist who fakes his experimental results. If the results are reported in the proper form then they are taken as true. Only time and further work will show them up.

The last surviving letter between the two forgers is Wise to Forman in December 1916. Wise comments on his Wordsworth bibliography 'No. 30 pp 164 – 167. The statements made regarding the extant copies is quite correct. The bulk of those included in that little "remainder" which we divided were destroyed.' No. 30 is the forged *To the Queen* which was not jobbed off to Gorfin and is now seen to have been burnt by its publishers. Wise's unburnt stocks of all the other pamphlets were to come back and haunt him in his later years.

Forman had been ill for some time and he died on 15 June 1917, aged 74. He had left somewhat eerie funeral instructions in verse

> Let the prison'd litch-fire batten on the tissues,
> Leaving naught but ashes, clean and grey and pure;
> Gather, friends, the handful that from the furnace issues,
> Cushion them in crane-bill, and bear them to the Moor.
> Ashes of her poet, bear them to the one land,
> Take them up to Dartmoor and strow them in the Teign:
> Bid the river roll them, roll them through his own land,
> Rush them through the harbour and lose them in the Main!

He was cremated at Golders Green (where Wise was to follow him twenty years later) and his ashes were scattered in the Teign as he instructed.

The obituaries were respectful but somewhat distant. Gosse summed the matter up in a letter to Wise (June 1917) 'I see Buxton Forman is dead. I had not heard anything of him for years. I was never at any time intimate with him, and I confess there was something about him not quite sympathetic. He must have left interesting books and MSS.'

By his will, made in 1909, Forman gave instructions that 'The Buxton Forman collection of books manuscripts portraits and relics' should be separated from the other books and miscellanea and sold for the benefit of the estate. This may have been a coded instruction to the executors (his wife, a solicitor, and R.W. Hatswell his Post Office colleague and disciple) to weed out duplicates and multiple copies and compromising material. Maurice returned from South Africa and both he and T.J. Wise were much in evidence at the clearing up after the funeral. The probate valuation of the Buxton Forman collection proper was undertaken by Bernard Quaritch Ltd, the much respected firm of antiquarian booksellers. Mr Mudie of that firm, was short and stocky like Wise. One evening, after a hard day writing down, he came out of the library and put on his coat. To his surprise, he found in the pocket a book he did not remember, took it out and found a very valuable Shelley book, an annotated *Queen Mab*. Just at that moment out shot Wise and Mr Mudie discovered he had taken the wrong coat. 'Were you taking that home?' he asked Wise as they exchanged coats. 'Thought I'd look it over' Wise explained, flustered only for a moment. 'Quite forgot I had it.' He replaced it, chuckling genially.

The will was proved at the end of August for the sum of £27,000 – a substantial amount, say £675,000 in current values. The trustees were given considerable discretion as to how they should deal with the library: and rightly decided not to sell at once. There is a story in the family that Forman put by a mint sheet of every new issue of stamps while he had a senior position at the Post Office. This drawerful was not declared but sold by Laura for a considerable sum in cash, possibly to Healey & Wise. Stamp dealing had been a Wise sideline for many years. Gorfin remembered fetching parcels of stamps for him from Forman at the G.P.O. In 1922 he was to put some money into the firm of Edwin Healey & Co, stamp merchants in the city, and alter its name. Laura was left the house and all the other contents (including 'ordinary books... pictures prints statues musical instruments articles of vertu', etc.) and had a life interest in the estate. After this the estate was to be divided one-third to Gwendolen and one-sixth each to the two sons Eliot and Maurice. The remaining third was left to the trustees to invest for a rainy day. Maurice went back to his family and his job in South Africa and dust settled on the library at Marlborough Hill.

# 16

## WISE CARRIES ON

Meanwhile what of Wise? As early as 1912, Gosse wrote 'I do not know that I ever told you how pleased I was that you had freed yourself from the chain of business. You are so wise to do this betimes' (13 August). Buxton Forman had a better grasp of reality when he wrote in the same year 'May the first year of your retirement (*almost*) from business prove as great a success as your comparatively short career in the city.' (24 December). Probably Wise retired as cashier of Rubecks but kept on his interest in the firm of W.A. Smith.

The *Perfumery and essential oil record* carried market reports from its inception. To an outsider they have the hypnotic drone of someone else's jargon, to Wise they must have been meat and drink.

> Taking first the Sicilian essences, in the early days of the year lemon was firming in tendency . . . in March the improved tone of lemon oil, resulting largely from Government assurances as to the Camera, was well maintained . . . . In the succeeding month a speculative move to stop the ebb in prices was witnessed in a concerted effort among some producers to sell forward at a higher range, but although this was not completely successful, it imported more stability to the general market, and this was more or less maintained until the early autumn. New crop conditions meanwhile manifested themselves in a bullish character . . . . As regards bergamot oil, it was early noted that the pressing was proceeding slowly, and about the middle of the first month a demand sprang up at primary markets which gave a fillip to the situation, prices for shipment advancing 1s before the end of January, bringing 17s c.i.f. into effect, and even 17s 6d c.i.f. was named, with London spot called 17s . . . . Orange oil roused but little interest. [December 1910]

Some two years earlier, Wise had commented to Wrenn on the unexpected results of the Messina earthquake in Sicily.

> Messina and Reggio live largely – very largely – upon the preparation of Essential Oil of Lemon and Oil of Bergamot. Both these oils we handle largely, and usually carry a stock of some tons. During the last few months prices have been wasting, so we have only held a sufficient stock to cover our immediate contracts. Thus whilst the price of both oils has in a day more than doubled itself, our free stock of

each is an abnormally low one. Still, small as it is, it advanced in value nearly £300 at a bound.

In February 1911, bergamot oil seems to have dropped a little, but by October 1913, it was up to '24s to 25s or even 26s net'.

For many years, Wise had been immersing himself first hand in such market fluctuations. For some fifty years Rubecks were only wholesalers: Wise was probably the moving spirit behind the drive into manufacture. This can bring greater rewards but is also much more risky. In about 1913, W. A. Smith & Co. moved from Greenwich and took over a disused firewood factory in Clack Street Rotherhithe. Their perfume distillery was to remain in Rotherhithe until about 1930. During the difficult times of the First World War, with many imports disrupted, the factory was very useful to Rubecks but was also a considerable responsibility. Forgetting his earlier retirement, Wise wrote to Gosse in April 1914,

> I have just returned from Rotherhithe, where I had a worried day. The whole staff 'struck' on Wednesday, against the more or less oppressive (as they deemed it) attitude of the Manager, and I had to square things up. Fortunately I was successful as, by some curious freak of fate, I usually am! But what a quaint and contradictory attitude Fate assumes when moulding the destinies of her puppets! A more pugnacious and spit-fiery beast than myself never lived, and yet for twenty years past I have been constantly called upon to find a road that led to peace between Master and Man, and between firms who in the course of friendly rivalry have chanced to collide!

Probably Wise was drawn back by the difficulties of the times. In October 1914, Gosse wrote to him

> I mentioned the matter at the Admiralty last night, and Mr. Winston Churchill's secretary told me that nothing was further from the thoughts of the Government than to injure British shippers by delaying perishable cargoes belonging to them but shipped in German captures. He asked me whether, with regard to the cloves at Gibraltar, you had instantly made full application to The Admiralty Marshal, Royal Courts of Justice (whose telegraphic address is:– Admarsh, London)? . . . If you did apply to the Admiralty Marshall, and if any difficulty arose, I will with the greatest pleasure put the facts personally before Mr. Winston Churchill.

Later on, in April 1916, Rubecks seems to have been forbidden to export a consignment of cloves which had been quoted and accepted. Gosse's attempt to play Lord Emmot failed; as did a similar attempt in December 1916 to use Sir Henry Rew, head of the Contraband Dept and a great friend. It was difficulties like these that led in 1917 to the foundation of the *British Essence Manufacturers Association* to press for easing trade restrictions. Gosse's son, Captain Philip Gosse R.A.M.C. was at one stage rat officer to the British Second Army in France and was anxious to try the effects of different baits. His father succeeded in obtaining oil of rhodium from Wise, believed to be the last bottle in London, as Philip recounts in his charming book *Memoirs of a camp-follower* 1934. Another interesting story, that Rubecks cornered the market in vanillin during the war, seems to be a myth. The firm did, however, pay excess profits tax for several years so must have been pretty successful.

The market report in May 1918 suggests a recent surge after flat conditions (bergamot was quietly firm at 20*s*. to 21*s*., spot and c.i.f. prompt shipment 19*s*. to 19*s*.6*d*.). The public drug sale on 9 May had a number of items of perfumery interest (it will be recalled Rubecks were wholesale druggists before specializing in essential oils).

> The goods offered included two tins of ambergris, five cases of balsam of Peru, 45 cases of Japanese refined camphor, (slabs and ¼oz tablets) 40 cases of cassia oil, 214 cases of eucalyptus oil, 30 cases of menthol (in prize), 30 cases of Japanese "Suzak" mint oil (in prize), 16 cases of sandalwood oil (Australian), 40 bales of spike lavender flowers.

We would like to have a sight of some of these drug auction sale catalogues but we cannot find any: the whole commodity district was flattened by the Luftwaffe in 1942 and little survives. The only catalogue we have found is of a much earlier vintage: but we are assured by an old market hand that the catalogues he used to use were pretty similar.

Wise was still negotiating with Frank Taylor, the Watts-Dunton solicitor, and in June 1918, the latter commiserated with him that 'your factory was so badly damaged'; was there a fire? Wise finally bought the posthumous Swinburne copyrights from the executors and then resold them to William Heinemann. The economics of this operation are obscure, but it is unlikely that Wise lost. An informed later opinion on all his Swinburne transactions was that his total profit was something in the region of £10,000 (say £250,000 in current currency). Thus the continuing series of little pamphlets was punctuated by regu-

larly published Heinemann volumes viz. *Posthumous poems* 1917;
*Letters*, 2 vols 1918; and *Contemporaries of Shakespeare* 1919; and
there are seemingly endless letters between Gosse and Wise as
they discussed endless Swinburnian details. They were rather a
good pair, Wise supplying the raw material, the energy and the
eye for detail, Gosse supplying the literary knowledge and savoir-
faire. The letters tend to a sameness but occasionally Gosse's
well known irritability bursts into flame viz. 8 November 1917.

> Heinemann seems to be making a tremendous splash with Swin-
> burne. I hope he is not overdoing it. Keep your eye upon him.
> Meanwhile that over-advertised, self advertising Popish hag Mrs.
> Alice Meynell has sent out a most violent and poisonous manifesto
> against our poet.

Or again,

> Heinemann made a proposition to me that we should, for the
> selected Poems, translate all the Greek and Latin tags, and explain
> the meaning of the classical allusions. He actually cited the name *Pan*
> as an example!! I have indignantly refused. If people cannot find out
> for themselves who the great god Pan was, they are unfit to read
> Swinburne. Heinemann is in a state of fright that he will not be able
> to sell the Selection. You must deal with him. [May 1919]

In fact Gosse and Wise's selection of the poems, first published
in 1919, was the most popular of Heinemann's Swinburne
volumes and was reprinted at least five times. Wise bought
another batch of very jumbled Swinburne manuscripts in 1918
and yet more in 1920. He sent the unsorted boxes off to Gosse
who was able to make sense of the disarray and pull out the few
items worth printing.

Wise's bibliographies proceeded with Landor (1919, with S.
Wheeler), Swinburne, 2 vols 1919–20 and a five volume *Catalogue
of the library of the late John Wrenn*, Austin, Texas, 1920. The
imprint is explained by the fact that Wrenn's executors (his son
and son-in-law) were anxious to keep the library together. In
1918 they sold it for $250,000 (half the lowest estimate) to the
University of Texas who agreed to do so. The catalogue, compiled by Harold Wrenn (the son) from Wise's catalogue slips and
edited by Wise was not well received in the academic world and
some of Wise's more outrageous ascriptions came home to roost.

> Not only, however, is the material in the *Catalogue* ill-compiled, but
> even more deplorable, a large share of it is very doubtful if not quite

erroneous. Nearly every item bears the re-assuring statement 'the first edition'. An edition of Thomas May's *The Heire* dated 1633 for example, is so listed, whereas so common a reference-book as the *Dictionary of National Biography* mentions a quarto eleven years earlier .... The ascriptions of anonymous literature constitute, without question, the most unhappy feature of these five beautifully printed volumes .... Such a multiplicity of errors – for the present list is merely a selection of random examples – published under the editorship of an officer of the English Bibliographical Society, is rather shocking. The Preface contains an apology for misprints; but such mistakes as these cannot possibly have arisen from that source. Some of them are merely stupid blunders; but others, unfortunately, suggest an intentional desire to mislead and to make the items appear more important than in fact they are – a practice that is as needless as it is vicious, for the collection contains many books of great value. To accuse Mr. Wise of such a thing is unthinkable; but, unhappily, there are many booksellers sufficiently unscrupulous to raise the market value of a pamphlet by calling it a first edition or ascribing it to Defoe or to Pope or even to Mason – especially if they find their purchasers careless or ignorant enough to be uncritical. Apparently, neither the compiler of the catalogue nor the editor, either took the pains to verify these ascriptions, or had the knowledge to recognize the errors; and they seem merely to have copied down many of the ascriptions, learned notes and so forth from the sales catalogues out of which they had bought the books. Where these notes show knowledge, as they occasionally do, of bibliographical reference-books, it is, I judge, merely because the trade-catalogue happened to belong to a respectable house, and was rather carefully compiled. It is, on the whole, a melancholy reflection that these five volumes of Whatman hand-made paper, beautifully printed, in a limited edition, the results of twenty years' "earnest and discriminating" collecting, should, for scholarly purposes, contain, along with some really valuable data, an odd collection of items and notes from the miscellaneous catalogues of first-, second- and third-class book-dealers during the last generation.

A recent survey shows that some 17 per cent of the entries are 'completely inexcusable, or to put it more bluntly, deliberate frauds'. Wise mis-attributed the Wrenn books in a wholesale way and on the flimsiest evidence. When hostile reviews appeared, Wise shifted the blame on to the Wrenns, father and son.

Meanwhile, Forman's library was being sold, but this was not kept intact. In 1918, Clement Shorter, when on a visit to New York, told Mitchell Kennerley, President of the Anderson Galleries, the principal New York book auctioneers, that the Forman library was for sale. One of the stockholders in that business was John B. Stetson Jr; and Kennerley suggested to him that he might investigate the possibilities on his next trip to Europe. In December 1919, Stetson called on Shorter in London. Shorter took him to Wise, and Wise to 46 Marlborough Hill. After a perfunctory examination, Stetson bought the library for £16,000 without disclosing to the executors that he was acting for the Anderson Galleries, and indeed giving the impression he was a wealthy collector who would keep the library intact. Stetson at once sent the library to America where it was sold in three sales in 1920 for a total of about $180,000. The profit of about $100,000 (£20,000 in those days) was divided equally between Stetson and the Anderson Galleries. Probably there were minor pay-offs for Shorter and Wise: and despite all this, Wise remained on good terms with the Formans.

Forman's library was a most impressive affair. One reads the sale catalogue with wistful envy, and looks hard at any book bearing the Forman bookplate. This was engraved by Forman's one time friend and minor Pre-Raphaelite artist, William Bell Scott, who had provided illustrations for the early Forman editions of Keats and Shelley. It shows Forman in his library working on a transcription with a quill pen in his hand. Dominating the library is a bust of Shelley flanked by pictures of his birthplace and his tomb. The rather painful verse, typical of Forman, is rather hubristically modelled on Ben Jonson's poem commending the Droeshout portrait in the first folio Shakespeare.

> This figure that thou here seest put
> It was for gentle Shakespeare cut;
> Wherein the graver had a strife
> With Nature to out do the life . . .

> The figure that you here see put
> Was for H. Buxton Forman cut,
> Amid his household gods to bide
> And relics culled from far and wide.
> This book is his on whom you look;
> For Scott his graving tackle took
> And etched the man to watch therein,
> That none by guile the book might win.
> Then siste fur! of great and small
> The world holds books enough for all.
> Of roughly handling this beware,
> And put it in its place with care.

The books are a remarkable assemblage. One notices many complete (or nearly complete) collections with fine showings of Coventry Patmore, Gray, Peacock, Blake, Whitman, Kipling, Lander, Hawker of Morwenstow, Leigh Hunt, Felicia Hemans, Chatterton, Waller, Byron, W.S. Gilbert, H.G. Wells, W. J. Linton and William Godwin. All the authors in which he had a special interest are present in force with particular attention paid to runs of editions. Among the special items one might expect are: Shelley's *Queen Mab* extensively altered in manuscript; the poet's Sophocles; Leigh Hunt's *Foliage* presented to Keats; Fanny Brawne's copies of Keats's *Poems* 1817 and *Lamia* 1820, the latter inscribed. Less expected are a 'portion of the remains of Shelley, after his cremation: in a cardboard box' and Sir Timothy Shelley's gold watch.

There are some fine association copies, including: Fielding's Terence (English translation, 1598); Thackeray's *Night Thoughts* (by Young, 1790); Waller's Juvenal (English translation, 1660); Coleridge's *Orlando Furioso*; Thomas Gray's copy of a seventeenth century medical book; Tennyson's Petronius; John Locke's Journal (Harrison & Laslett 1605: not located); *Adam Bede* presented by George Eliot to Thackeray; and William Morris's copy of *Seven Lamps of Architecture*. Among the manuscripts are E.A. Poe's *The Spectacles*, Godwin's Will and account of his ordination, a Wilkie Collins short story, a scene from *Die Walküre* (Alfred Forman was Wagner's first English translator), Elizabeth Barrett Browning's sketch of an autobiography, four Blake letters and what was thought to be his poem *Genesis, The seven days of the created world* (it *is* in his hand but proves to be a transcription of Hayley's translation of Tasso).

Forman was not the great rebinder that Wise was and most books are in contemporary or original bindings. There is a Martyn's *Virgil* 1749 with colour printed plates in a signed (and therefore early) binding by Roger Payne, a Latin *Book of Common Prayer* 1727 in a fine contemporary binding which seems to be Christopher Smart's confirmation present 1735, coloured copies of Stedman's *Surinam* 1796 and Ayres' *Emblemata Amatoria* 1683 and a Cottonian binding on a Spanish book of 1810. This latter perhaps needs a little explanation: Southey's library was extensive but he could not afford conventional binding so he had his daughters paste coloured cotton prints over the original boards.

Southey's dreadful pun had made these charming chintz bindings well known and they are collected as attractive memorials of the library at Keswick. Wise bought one of the most appealing – Wordsworth's *Poems* 1807 – but had it rebound in apple green levant morocco by Riviere. Sometimes it is a mistake for book collectors to have too much money – or too little taste, come to that.

Forman had few early books, although he did have a first of Spenser's *Faerie Queen* 1590–96, a large quantity of sixteenth and seventeenth century poems in folio and quarto (which were slaughtered in a few lots) and the 1601 Pliny in English, presented to him by William Morris, Unexpected items include a Didot type specimen of 1819, a collection of books on Dante (with his brother Alfred he published *The Metre of Dante's Comedy* in 1874), an almost complete set of F. Anstey's works (including *Vice Versa* which deals with the misadventures of a Mincing Lane colonial broker), Darwin first editions, and what are said to be (but cannot be) twelve original copper plates for Blake's *Job* 'with a set of impressions pulled recently'. There are, of course, lots of his own publications, many in special copies variously annotated. He was always one for creating uniquity or rarity, cozening from his publishers copies uncut before binding or with unique cancels.

The sale itself was one of the first at which Dr Rosenbach the celebrated dealer began to establish that ascendancy in the auction room which was later to become so pronounced: he bought almost half the sale. He bought Harriet Shelley's last letter, the *Queen Mab* which Wise almost walked off with, and the one letter of Keats to Fanny Brawne which Forman still had. Christopher Morley, Dr Rosenbach's friend and court poet remembered the Wilde sonnet and turned another.

> *How about this lot?* said the auctioneer;
> *One hundred, may I say, just for a start?*
> Between the plum-red curtains, drawn apart,
> A written sheet was held . . . And strange to hear
> (Dealer, would I were steadfast as thou art)
> The cold quick bids. (*Against you in the rear!*)
> The crimson salon, in a glow more clear
> Burned bloodlike purple as the poet's heart.
>
> Song that outgrew the singer! Bitter Love

That broke the proud hot heart it held in thrall –
Poor script, where still those tragic passions move –
*Eight hundred bid: fair warning: the last call*:
The soul of Adonais, like a star . . .
*Sold for eight hundred dollars – Doctor R!*

Forman, remembering his hard tussle to preserve and publish would have approved this canonization.

Maurice Forman and Wise, who must have sorted out the 'Buxton Forman Collection' from all the other books at Marlborough Hill, made only two real mistakes. They included a packet of proof (3rd part, lot 1204 'Tennyson (Alfred Lord) The Building of the Idylls. By H. Buxton Forman') later to be published as the Pforzheimer document, which has some very indiscreet annotations. What else did they winnow out, one wonders? The second mistake was to sell five copies of George Eliot's *Agatha* '1869' all described as the rare first edition and all five folded uncut and unopened. Wise had sold nineteen copies to Gorfin in 1912 but the public display must have raised a few eyebrows. *Agatha* is an instance where Forman and Wise were copying an already existing book which is genuinely rare: at the time of the Forman sale only the one rare edition was supposed to exist. Those five copies must have stuck in someone's gullet and Wise's ingenious damage-limitation exercise was published in 1922. He claimed that

> *Agatha* was seen through the press upon behalf of the authoress by Mr. Buxton Forman. Of the first edition twenty copies only were printed. These, however, proved insufficient to meet the demands of friends who clamoured for them, and a second batch of fifty copies were ordered. But the types had already been distributed, and were set up afresh for the second printing. Mr. Forman claimed that these later copies were a "second issue of the first edition"; but as the types from which they were printed were re-set, they undoubtedly form a *second edition* of the poem. (Ashley Cat. Vol. 2)

Thus he took care of i) the undoubted real *Agatha*, ii) the attempted fake now called a contemporary second edition, and iii) the five copies of the second edition in the Forman sale. Just to complicate matters still further we may add that a second copy of the real thing was produced, probably in America, probably *c*.1920. This third separate edition is a fairly crude affair and a much worse copy of the original than Wise and Forman's attempt. It ranges with a similar fake of another Wise and

THE

Luckey Chance,

OR AN

ALDERMAN'S

Bargain.

A

COMEDY.

As it is Acted by their MAJESTY's
Servants.

Written by Mrs. A. Behn.

Thursday, be Printed, April 23. 1686. R. P.

LONDON,

Printed by R. H. for W. Canning, at his Shop in
Vine-Court, Middle-Temple, 1687.

53.  The raw material for the Ashley Library: a play in poor state, ready for restoration

Forman forgery: George Eliot's *Brother and Sister*, this time a creative forgery for which there is no original. There is absolutely no proof as to who produced these two rather poor quality pieces. There is, however, the possibility that it was the bookseller Max Harzof of the G.H. Baker Co. of New York, since he definitely did produce a similarly rather poor quality fake of another (unrelated) pamphlet, Vizetelly's *Extracts*. After this excursion, back to the high road.

In 1920, Maurice sold off some of the surplus books from Marlborough Hill. Quaritch bought a considerable quantity including many Villon society publications, a number of Forman's printings and about ten copies of Tennyson's *The new Timon* 1876. This latter is Richard Herne Shepherd's piracy, correctly dated, but Forman's printed additions on the title turn it from *Poems* to *The new Timon*. At the same time, Gorfin, partly through Wise, bought twelve copies of Swinburne's *Sequence of Sonnets* 1890, a piracy though probably correctly dated. Originally the conspirators described this as a potential great rarity (1896): it was one of the pamphlets denounced by Watts-Dunton (1909) so Wise may have felt he needed safer ground. In 1919 he fathered it on Forman who was supposed to have seen it through the press for Swinburne. This also, of course, cleared the sale: it was a natural remainder. What else, one wonders, was left in the cupboards at Marlborough Hill?

We have mentioned Wise's *Ashley Library*. This was his greatest bibliographical achievement, a complete catalogue of his books, with full descriptions and collations. The first two volumes were published in 1922 and volumes 3–4 the next year. This massive and still very useful book was to run to a final total of eleven volumes. Each volume had a preface by a different luminary. Those rounded up for the first four were Richard Curle, Augustine Birrell, John Drinkwater and (of course) Edmund Gosse. The edition was limited to 250 copies of which 50 were on special paper. This was a short enough limitation to cause quite a scramble for copies and it was the éclat associated with this book that finally set the seal on Wise's reputation as *the* bibliographical authority. Viewed with hindsight, some of the prefaces read rather oddly, none more so than John Drinkwater's. He observed

_____ The / Luckey Chance, /
On an / Alderman's / Bargain. / A
Comedy. / As it is Acted by their
Majesty's / Servants. / Written by
Mrs. A. Behn. / This may be Printed,
April 23. 1686. R. P. / London, /
Printed by R. H. for W. Canning,
at his Shop in / Vine-Court, Middle-
Temple. 1687

Collation:— Quarto, pp. xii + 70;
consisting of Title-page (with
blank reverse) pp. i-ii; The
Epistle Dedicatory pp. iii - v;
Preface pp. vi - ix; Prologue pp.
x - xi; List of Actor's Names p. xii;
Text of the Comedy pp. 1 - 69;

54. Wise's manuscript draft cataloguing of a play

———— The / Luckey Chance, / Or An / Alderman's / Bargain. / A / Comedy. / As it is Acted by their Majesty's / Servants. / Written by Mʳˢ· A. Behn. / This may be Printed, April 23. 1686. R.P. / London, / Printed by R. H. for W. Canning, at his Shop in / Vine-Court, Middle-Temple. 1687.

Collation : Quarto, pp. xii+69+ii; consisting of Title-page, as above (with blank reverse), *pp. i—ii; The Epiftle Dedicatory " To the Right Honourable Laurence, Lord Hyde, Earl of Rochefter, one of his Majefty's moft Honourable Privy Council, Lord High Treafurer of England, and Knight of the Noble Order of the Garter"* pp. iii—v; *Preface* pp. vi—ix; *Prologue Spoken by Mr. Jevon* pp. x—xi; List of *Actor's [sic] Names,* with *The Scene London* at foot, p. xii; and Text of the *Comedy* pp. 1—69; followed by two unnumbered pages carrying the *Epilogue Written by a Perfon of Quality, fpoken by Mr. Betterton.* The reverse of the last page is blank. Upon page ii, between the end of the Epilogue and the word *Finis,* is an advertisement of Mrs. Behn's novel *La Montre, or The Lover's Watch.* There are no head-lines, the pages being numbered centrally between round brackets. The signatures are A (4 leaves), *a* (2 leaves), and B to K (9 sheets, each 4 leaves). The book was issued without a half-title.

The *First Edition.* Bound in red levant morocco by Riviere, with gilt edges. The leaves measure 8½ × 6⅜ inches.

———————————————————————————————————

## 55.  The printed version

I could tell of many an engaging little packet of duplicates and such things, that have had their very satisfactory uses, but that might embarrass Mr. Wise. But I do know that when you have seen the shelves of his library, you have not seen all. I doubt whether anybody has.

Trial volumes for the Ashley Library were printed by Clays, as was all Wise's work up to 1922: but the Ashley catalogue itself was printed in Edinburgh. In 1911, Clays had moved from Bread Street Hill in the city, to Brunswick Street in Southwark, over the river. Many of their records were destroyed then. In 1921, the Brunswick Street works was sold and all printing transferred to Bungay; many more records were destroyed but not quite all. This upheaval caused Wise, after nearly forty years, to transfer to the Dunedin press in Edinburgh, who were to print all his future books.

Maurice kept in touch with Wise and he followed his father in working for the Post Office and doing literary work in his spare time. In 1919–24, he produced three pamphlets of Meredith's letters to different correspondents. Each is limited to thirty copies and they follow Wise's Swinburnes and Borrows: though as they were produced in Cape Town or Pretoria they do not look much like them. In 1922–24 his standard bibliography of George Meredith appeared: it was published by the Bibliographical Society (of London).

Wise's rise in bibliographical circles now began in earnest and he became president of the Bibliographical Society, 1922–24. This is the London Bibliographical Society, its seniority shown by the lack of any geographic qualifier. He was a popular president though he somehow succeeded in evading the presidential address he should have delivered.

Conrad was yet another author with whom Wise was involved. He chatted him up to such an extent that he could practically dictate presentation inscriptions or annotations, some of which being very bibliographical read very oddly: the voice is Jacob's voice, but the hands are the hands of Esau. Conrad had published in periodicals a number of minor pieces which had never been collected or reprinted. Wise did not risk creative forgery: he paid Conrad for the right to reprint them and produced twenty-one little pamphlets in the familiar mould. The second tranche have the imprint as 'printed for the author' or 'for Joseph Conrad', but this is Wise just the same; the authorial imprint was better for business. As usual he topped things off with a bibliography in 1920, with a revised edition in 1921. He made several excursions into print as the Conrad expert, one (*Bookman's Journal* 7 January 1921) being headed 'More frauds of the book forger'. Gosse reviewed the bibliography in his regular *Sunday Times* column.

> It is a tribute to the popularity of Mr. Conrad that he has not escaped the ingenuity of the forger. In detecting the wiles of this class of deceiver, Mr. Wise knows no rival. He is the terror of all fraudulent booksellers, and "fakes" are to him what rats are to a terrier. I am not sure that it is not to take the pleasing mania of book collecting too seriously when we hunt the faker to his hole, and smoke him out of it.

In the same year, the *Bookman's Journal* carried a laudatory account of the Ashley Library, one of many journalistic impressions of its riches. Another appeared in 1923 (*Boston Evening Transcript* 5 May) 'The Treasures of a London Collector'

> A single handsome room in his house up at Hampstead on the north edge of London contains what Mr. Edmund Gosse has called "the finest private library in the kingdom" . . . Mr Wise has always had a flair for the best and rarest things that the last five centuries of

English printing yields: for the kind of books that possess intrinsic value or exceptional rarity or association: and for the manuscripts and proofs of authors who are either immortal or deserve to be. He had specialized in our early plays and masques in the restoration drama; in the early poems and issues of our greatest poets from Spenser and Shakespeare to Tennyson and Swinburne: in manuscripts and letters as well and all those desirable things that make the staple of the best connoisseurship in book-land. He has made himself an expert bibliographer and has presided over the labors of our best societies in this field; and his private printings of choice unpublished things in his collection are accounted rarities to be proud of in the library of other men.

In 1923, Wise wrote an innocuous introduction to W. Harris Arnold's posthumous *Ventures in Book collecting*. However, in Vol. 4 of the Ashley catalogue published in the same year, he pointed out that Keats and Shelley signatures reproduced in *Ventures* are both forgeries, probably by Thomas Powell. He appeared again under the banner of the forger fighter in the *Bookman's Journal* in May 1924 when he denounced forgeries of *Adonais* and *Hellas* derived from his own Shelley society reprints: 'among the persons who have fallen victim to the fraud are two of the foremost and most widely experienced antiquarian booksellers in London.' His reputation rising all the time, Wise was elected honorary fellow of Worcester College Oxford (1924) and honorary M.A. of Oxford University (1926). These honours were initially due to the friendship of C.H. Wilkinson, Dean of Worcester, and may perhaps have been suggested by speculation as to the ultimate fate of the Ashley Library. Wise was on easy unbuttoned terms with Wilkinson (who was a great book collector) and he wrote to Francis Needham, another Oxford figure, in 1924

> As to the disposal of my library – the question occasions me such concern . . . I certainly think that Oxford would be a fitting resting place for them, and after the kindness I have been given at Worcester College, my heart has been drawn to that city . . . I also am aware that though they have only cost me barely £40,000, their value today is at least three times that sum. All of which makes me very careful in deciding upon their ultimate disposal.

56. Bill for Wise's purchase of a very rare Wordsworth,
together with his cancelled cheque in payment

# WISE IN RETIREMENT

Maurice Forman followed his father as a book collector, bibliographer, editor and forger: but his achievements were on a smaller scale. His major book collection was of the works of Eden Phillpotts, the West Country novelist, and he assembled a virtually complete roster, together with some manuscripts. He commissioned a bookplate from his wife's niece, Dorothea Braby, a professional wood-engraver who did a good deal of book illustration. Her plate shows a quill pen and an arum lily conjoined across an open book with a map of Africa resting on it and the Southern Cross above. On the book is a quotation from Keats 'so I may do the deed/That my own soul has to itself decreed'. Dorothea has recorded what a charming and impressive man her uncle was and how 'he walked everywhere – even from St. John's Wood to Kensington – a fact unthinkable to this legless generation. If he was constrained to patronise a public vehicle he would nonetheless get off one or two stops before his destination so as to get some walking!'

As a bibliographer we have mentioned his Meredith: a bibliography of Eden Phillpotts was aborted as someone else got there first. As an editor, his time was yet to come. As a forger, he produced his one undoubted effort in 1925. This was a single leaf Lewis Carroll acrostic poem set with the date of composition at the bottom to be taken as the date of printing. He sold one at the Anderson Galleries in 1925. In 1926, he wrote to Morris Parrish, a noted American collector of the great Victorian writers, commenting, 'The only copy I have heard of on the market was sold at the Anderson Galleries last year for $27.50 – a good price and one that I should not refuse for mine.' When his daughter sold the final residue of the family library nearly fifty years later, it had nine copies of this rare piece (shades of Gorfin). However, it did not carry conviction and the standard bibliography published in 1931 (not by Forman) calls it a modern reprint c.1910–20.

Meanwhile, Wise had produced another four Ashley Library volumes (Vol. 5 1924; Vols 6–7 1925; Vol. 8 1926) and also *A*

To. T. J. Wise Esq. M.A.
for the Ashley Library.
with Sincere Greeting
for the part he has play'd
in the creation of this
Library, and in memory
of his Long friendship with
Lord Brotherton, and above all,
the encouragement, advice,
and constant care he has
Lavished on his younger friend
and companion, The Librarian.

J. Alex Symington.

Oct: 1936.

1. of 25. Copies printed on
Art-Paper.

57. Inscription from Symington to Wise
in a copy of the Brotherton catalogue

*Shelley Library* 1924 and *A Swinburne Library* 1925. These latter were simply reprinted sections from Ashley, pasted up in a different form with a few corrections. The *TLS* review of the latter contains a just assessment

> his "Swinburne Library" contains a good deal of dross, and not a little garbage. But as a horde it is unique. "The Pines" and the character of its inmates – for it seems there was nothing Swinburne would not keep and nothing Watts-Dunton would not sell – provided Mr. Wise with such an opportunity as perhaps no collector ever had before. In these pages we see how he took it; watching and waiting and striking, immensely resourceful and infinitely patient, like some beneficent bird of prey.

The reviewer also picks out Wise's account of the discovery of a remainder of *The Devil's Due* as an example of his skill in delineating the character of Watts-Dunton: skilful yes, but a fictitious remainder and a partly fictitious character. Wise and Gosse's joint stranglehold on Swinburne studies finally produced the collected edition which was for years looming in the background of the negotiations with Heinemann. This was the Bonchurch Edition of Swinburne in twenty volumes, 1925–27. Percipient readers could deduce that Wise's treatment of the Swinburne manuscripts had made the editorial work much harder. The final volume of Bonchurch is a revision of Wise's bibliography of 1919–20.

One of Wise's numerous friends was Frederick Page, author of a book on Coventry Patmore and editor, often anonymously, of a number of others. He worked for the Oxford University Press; publishers of the *Dictionary of National Biography*. Perhaps Wise's most piquant achievement was, aided by Page, to write the biography of Forman in that august reference book; the volume came out in 1927.

Another of Wise's acquaintances was Alexander Symington, civil servant and part-time bookseller in Leeds; in 1923, by dint of toadying to Lord Brotherton, he was appointed his librarian. Lord Brotherton, urged on by the vivacious Dorothy Ratcliffe, who had married his nephew, began seriously to collect books in 1922. By 1926, the collection was becoming important and, while still private property, had tentatively been promised to the nascent University of Leeds. Wise and Symington were old acquaintances (a letter of 1928 speaks of forty years of friend-

23, COVENTRY STREET,
PICCADILLY,
LONDON, W.

*Nov 27* 1899

T. J. Wise Esq.

# Bought of

**ROBSON & CO.,**
DEALERS IN RARE BOOKS,
MANUSCRIPTS, DRAWINGS, &c.

Nov 25 Lot 1393 Sotheby's (The Falcon)          52 .
                    10%                              5 4 .
                                               £57 4 .

£99
hence £57.4
Robson & Co
pr Jefferson
With Thanks

With Compts

---

1393  Tennyson (Lord) The Falcon, FIRST EDITION, *original wrappers,*
      *uncut*                              *printed for the author,* 1879     Robson
      \*\*\* Fine copy of the exceedingly rare private issue.

---

58.  Wise creates a record by buying a forgery at an inflated price

59.  A catalogue cutting from the Sotheby sale at which
the book was bought

ship) and their joint association had a considerable effect on the library. Of course a regulation quantity of forgeries was supplied. By this time, Wise must have been running short and a number seem to be really his second copies and to have his bookplate. One of them, Tennyson's *The Falcon* is such a copy. Inserted in it is a bookseller's bill showing it was purchased at Sothebys for £52 in 1899 for Wise. This was the first appearance of the forgery: it could only have come from Wise: he was therefore buying it against his own reserve to create a price. The Brotherton group of fakes look as if prepared for sale many years before. Doubtless the approach of a new Maecenas whose buying was done by one of his own satellites caused Wise to unbelt.

More important for the library, however, was a change of emphasis from fine individual items to collections, particularly of letters and manuscripts. Just such an opportunity was approaching. Sir Edmund Gosse died on 16 May 1928. Wise was, of course, at once drawn into the aftermath. The books were comparatively easy and a sale at Sothebys was quickly arranged. Wise was in charge of the details and Charles des Graz of Sothebys consulted him anxiously about strengthening part of the sale. 'Sothebys tell me you are in charge of the disposition of Edmund Gosse's library' wrote a potential borrower. The letters and papers were more difficult. Wise suggested that they be sold to Lord Brotherton for £1,000. The offer was eagerly accepted on both sides – 'the word "Archives" has caught on at 17 Hanover Terrace. I go there from about 4.30 to 7 two or three times a week' Wise reported to Symington. Harrods sent six cases of papers and documents to Lord Brotherton and followed this up with three more cases a bit later. However, one of these was Wise's own. Originally the Gosse family had given him back the letters he had written to Gosse. On reflection, he decided to give them to the archive, perhaps remembering Gosse's letter to him in December 1913 'You and I will certainly go down to posterity hand in hand. We must be remembered or forgotten together.' He suggested to Symington that he might like to edit the Gosse–Wise letters 'when I follow Gosse across the River'. He followed up his letters to Gosse with much more of his own archives: mostly recent letters and carefully sorted, no doubt: but a generous gesture.

The situation in Leeds was confused: the library was swelling but its final destination was not settled. Despite the semi-official nature of the library, no records were kept and Symington seems to have been allowed *carte blanche* by Lord Brotherton. How far Wise and Symington took advantage of this it is impossible to say. On one occasion Wise swapped some of his numerous Swinburne manuscripts for a fine copy of *Wuthering Heights* 3 vols 1847, a celebrated rarity in good condition. This accounts for the incongruous appearance of a handsome morocco case lettered 'Brotherton Collection' in the Ashley Library. In June 1930 it was announced that the library would be given to the University, but the deed was not formalized. Lord Brotherton died four months later. The officials were on tenterhooks until his two residuary legatees presented the library and it was installed in a grand and spacious new building in 1936. It is still there: one of the nicest academic libraries in the country. The official account demurely states that Symington's period in the University's employ was not a success, and Dr Richard Otter, the University Librarian, took charge of the collection in 1938. The University Vice Chancellor's private diary supplies more lively details. 12 October 1930

> Saw T.J. Wise who told me he had had much talk with E. Brotherton about the gift of the Library to the University. His influence was certainly important & always on the side of the University; said he had helped E.B. to prepare his speech for the laying of the foundation stone in June; I did not tell him that I had written the speech.

7 November 1930

> S[ymington] tried to see E. B. during his illness to get him to sign documents ensuring that he [S.] would be curator etc. S. is a treacherous disloyal man ... they will have the collection properly catalogued by an expert with the accounts paid. S. has apparently taken off certain valuable books to his own house, & became rather uneasy when told he must return them. I have had some rather damaging information about his misdoings when assisting the Librarian of the City Library, from which he apparently took and sold to his father in Harrogate certain pamphlets belonging to the City Library. He is a dangerous man to entrust with a valuable collection.

17 November 1930

> In the afternoon went to call on T.J. Wise in Hampstead to talk over the Brotherton collection. Rather garrulous man, but very alert & full of memories. Said he had been largely responsible for finding the purchases of E. Brotherton.... Mrs Wise also thinks Symington

quite honest and trustworthy ... [she] rather treats her old husband as a bore & as a much younger woman would treat a husband who had disappointed her expectations.

Symington, when he could not get life tenure, tried to divert the books from the University. He was sacked in 1938 because he was found to be charging research students for the use of the library. Local folklore suggests there was an exciting confrontation with Symington being set up while the officials listened behind a curtain; they then sprang out and sacked the librarian when he had asked for his fee. The consequence of this was that the library has no record at all of any acquisition before 1938: probably Symington kept what there was at home for his own purposes. The Wise letters to Gosse mostly (but not entirely) remain at Leeds. But the rest of Wise's papers were abstracted by Symington and (after Wise's death) were sold to line his own pockets. The largest block went to Rutgers University, New Jersey: others were sold elsewhere, some as late as the 1950s.

Wise and Symington were also associated together in editing the *Shakespeare Head Brontë* 19 vols 1931–38 modelled on the Bonchurch edition of Swinburne. Wise's misattribution and wholesale distribution of the Brontë manuscripts had made the editor's job very difficult and the project almost died on its feet until revived by C.W. Hatfield. As it was, the projected twentieth volume of bibliography never appeared. This pursuit of Symington has taken us rather a long way: we must retrace our steps to 1927.

In that year, Wise was elected a member of the Roxburghe Club. This is the most patrician and exclusive book collecting club in existence. It was founded in 1812 and has always consisted of a few dedicated book collectors and many members of the peerage (many of whom had or have extremely fine libraries). In 1927 they were most anxious to protect themselves against the trade. Sydney Cockerell gently grilled Wise on the subject – was it possible he had ever sold or made money out of his pamphlet printings? Oh no, said Wise 'no man has ever regarded his books in a less mercenary manner than I have throughout my active life' – his last and greatest whopper. Cockerell obviously did not associate him with the Forman whom he had challenged about forged Morris so many years ago and he was one of his sponsors for the club: the other was Lord Kenyon. Not surprisingly Wise seems to have had some difficulties. He wrote to Cockerell in August 1928,

> I fear that at the last Roxburghe Club dinner I must have shocked you by my strange get-up. The simple fact is, I was late and changed in a hurry, and in my haste snatched up a morning coat instead of a dress coat. This to my horror I noticed when I arrived at the Ritz – too late to do anything.

There is also the suggestion from Cockerell that Wise compile a volume of letters for his Roxburghe book – in due course each member is expected to print a book for presentation to his fellow members. Wise never did so.

For a self-made merchant brought up in the back streets of Islington, the Roxburghe Club was a really remarkable achievement. From this time on, Wise's letters often refer to his ill health (he was approaching 70). For instance, a letter of 1 January 1927 to one of his greatest friends A. E. Newton

> I've been too ill to write. I have been ill since early in last July, & for four weeks had a serious operation ("short circuit" for duodenal ulcer) hanging over me. But this I have escaped, and the X Rays satisfied my own doctor & Lord Dawson that the real cause of the trouble is a ventral hernia, coupled with an abdominal adhesion.

He then turns to other matters.

> I think Shorter's estate will prove to be about £50,000 net, or perhaps a bit more; & as his wife has means of her own beside, the sale of the books is not a serious matter. As a fact there will not be many of any importance for sale at all. The Ms. of "The Return of the Native" is to go to Trinity College, Dublin, together with a collection of suitable books to be selected by me, to form a small library in memory of his first wife. Then Mrs. Shorter will retain a large quantity of books to fill up the shelves of the library. . . . As you know, Shorter was never a "collector" in the proper sense of the term. He accumulated a lot of books it is true, but these for the greater part were the tools of a working journalist. He very seldom bought a scarce book, and when he did, he usually sold it again. His Dr. Johnson books also, will go to Sotheby's. Among these are a few nice pieces. His last Hardys (apart from the big Ms.) & Brontes, & Borrows he sold last summer. I miss the poor old fellow terribly. Since 1885 we have been chums, & since about 1895 we have lunched together every Thursday.

As Wise's health declined, his correspondence grew greatly. He had blossomed into such an authority that, as one of his correspondents said 'A total stranger must apologise for addressing you but a collector of your fame has almost ceased to be a private individual.' It must be said that, to a large extent, his fame became him well. He was extraordinarily generous about helping scholars and never seems to have turned down a request for access to his books or copies of his manuscripts. The latter was not only inconvenient and could damage the manuscripts but also reduced their commercial value. As Wise was keenly aware, a manuscript, particularly by an important author, is held to be worth much less if fully published: yet he never flinched from arranging typed copies, photographs or rotographs (a sort of primitive photocopy). The chorus of praise includes letters of thanks from W.W. Greg, J.H. Griffin ('Honestly I feel quite touched by your munificence'), C.K. Hyder, Leslie Hotson, T.L. Hood ('How staunch a sponsor you have been to me'), Ernest Rhys, G.C. Williamson (enquiries about Balm of Gilead also), H.F. Brett-Smith, Gordon Wordsworth, Violet Hunt ('Dear Tom, you are kind'), E.H. Coleridge, Gordon Haigh, J.H. Ingram, R.W. Chapman, Percy Simpson, D. Nichol Smith, Newman Ivey White, and G.A. Aitken. All of these are collectors or scholars of substance with serious queries answered. The other side of the moon is represented by letters asking for the best general book on Tennyson (Ali Mehmet of Bucharest), the gift of a complete Shelley (G. Knowles), advice on book-buying on an income of £1 a month and details of a supposed variant of the fourth issue of Canto IV of *Childe Harold* (a gentleman from Bootle); also offers of a visiting card of Ibsen, a portrait of Shelley ('unquestionably spurious. It looks like that of some nice well behaved choir boy' Wise commented), or an Armenian Evangelistary.

Another penalty of fame was of course Sydney Cockerell: after describing some Fitzwilliam gifts he continues 'Now can you dip into your lucky bag and sent us something equally exciting? Why not Shelley's Ode to the West Wind? We have but one poor scrap of Shelley. Do not be out-done' (29 June 1933). Wise was called in to help a gentleman who had bought a lot of books from W.T. Spencer. He cannily got Sothebys to comment: we cannot resist quoting one item from the damning report that Charles des Graz sent in.

> Tristram Shandy 1760–67. This book is in the unusual condition of being unduly complete. It has half titles in all volumes, whereas, in fact, volumes 1,2,3,7, and 8 were issued without half titles. The

correct ones in your copy, i.e. those in volumes 4,5,6, and 9 appear to be from another and shorter copy. Where the incorrect ones came from I really can't say.

The post bag also included letters from:

Leicester Harmsworth: Cordial, enquiring about Wise's health, particularly his eyes.

Frederick J. Higginbottom: advice about his book, published in 1924 as *The vivid life. A journalist's career*. Another Higginbottom (H.E.) occasionally helped Wise in his bibliographical researches and went on a visit to Cambridge with Wrenn. They were Mrs Wise's uncles, and F.J. sends 'love to Lulu'

Ernest Uriah Maggs, a slightly sinister letter (26 March 1930) 'My dear uncle, We have a client who is worrying us very much about a copy of Mrs. Brownings sonnets from the Portuguese. We are wondering whether perhaps you know of a friend who has a copy and might be willing to part with it.' The 'uncle' is a long maintained pleasantry but how much did he guess? and how often had the friend obliged?

Clara Watts-Dunton: 'Dear Tom', he was still on amicable terms with her.

Philip Gosse

Mrs Thomas Hardy

A.E. Newton: 'For God's sake take care of yourself, there are only a few of us left'.

Stephen Crane

Bret Harte

G.B. Shaw: 'it is only in proof as yet . . . when it reaches the stage of a tiny edition for rehearsal purposes I shall be better supplied, *and so shall you.*'

William Andrews Clark

Maurice Buxton Forman.

The two latter are particularly interesting. Mr Clark was a major collector as is shown by the library in Los Angeles which now bears his name. He had just published an elaborate edition of

30 July '923.

My dear Wise,

I've been away the last few days and am delighted on my return to find the Bibliographical Society copy of your Catalogue awaiting me here. Gosse's Introduction really does not exaggerate your services. You stand out as the One Provident Man who has been buying and buying the right things. when richer men, who belong to a much more distinguished

60. Letter from A. W. Pollard, the celebrated bibliographer, to Wise

society than the Bib. Soc. claims to be". Either didn't buy at all or bought what there was little need of buying. If the bibliographical history of our modern literature can ultimately be written elsewhere than in the United States, it will be due to you.

Sincerely yours,

A.W. Pollard.

60.  *concluded*

*Sonnets from the Portuguese* which included a facsimile of the Reading edition. Wise was sent one and responded

> What would Mrs. Browning have said, if she had ever dreamed of the magnificent form which would one day be given to her beautiful sonnets. But, as you will no doubt remember she more than once confesses in her letters that the best lovers of her books were Americans. [February 1928]

At this time Wise had his arm in a sling with an acute attack of neuritis and many of his letters including this last are dictated to Mrs Wise. A later letter (1 December 1932) to Clark's librarian details more ill health.

> On July 21, just as we were leaving home for our summer holiday, luggage all packed ready to be put on the car, I met with a serious accident injuring my hips & left shoulder. I spent 11 weeks in bed, during the first of which I could not even turn myself over. I am now just beginning to hobble about out of doors, helped by a stick in one hand, & holding the arm of the nurse with the other. But the chief trouble now is the shock to my nervous system, & the doctors warn me that it will be several months yet before my nerves are steady again. Hence my inability to properly arrange my thoughts, or to write letters, – those of any importance I cannot even dictate. So let your kind heart forgive all faults!

Maurice Forman seems to have been starting up a correspondence after a considerable lapse. He had been continuing with his minor private printing. In 1927–29 one pamphlet was about George Meredith, the other two printed letters (by Shaw and Browning) to or about his aunt Alma Murray in her great days as an actress. All three were printed by the Dunedin Press in Edinburgh, a firm he shared with Wise. His letters to Wise in 1928 give a good deal of family gossip

> I have just finished carving twenty pounds of solid beef to be made into sandwiches for a Sunday school picnic my son Jack [the nickname of Maurice II] is running tomorrow. It doesn't sound like my family does it? But it is a fact that as a scout master, a Sunday school teacher, and general leader of young people my younger son is quite distinguished in Pretoria – And so that I may feel worthy of some of the reflected glory I have devoted the best part of an evening to carving beef! "He carv'd some beef exactly to suit my appetite, as if I had been measured for it" – Keats in the long journal letter of Sept. 1819, which is in the Pierpont Morgan library. A glorious letter terribly mangled in the Speed version! Mama tells me you are dealing with Sir Edmund Gosse's books. Who next will leave you this job!

In less than ten years Maurice was to perform it for Wise in melancholy circumstances. He comments on Wise's bad health – 'one damn thing after another'. He was engaged in the family tradition of Keats scholarship and was revising his father's last edition of the letters, which comprised two volumes of the five of the 'Complete Edition' of 1900–1901. This was to be published in 1931 though he had completed work – adding ten more letters – in 1928. Partly in relation to the work on this, he reflects 'The older I get (57 this month) the more I regret my long exile, knowing all the time that it is wrong to do so.'

The correspondence continued: in 1931 Maurice writes 'Mother was very pleased to see you again. Her report of your condition might have been better. I think she is herself so splendid at 90 that she expects us boys to be robust – forgetting that we are really "old boys".' His sister Gwendolen had died in 1930 and his elder brother Eliot died in 1931: he had gone bankrupt and taken to drink.

Maurice was about to retire: his valedictory notice in the South African *Postal and Telegraph Herald* was published in January 1932.

> Mr. M. Buxton Forman, Assistant Secretary Posts and Telegraphs, retired on 10th December, after nearly 38 years' service. With remarkable unanimity – and no matter whether the main reference was one of approval or disapproval – everyone described him as "a gentleman". Gentle and retiring in disposition and sharing the characteristics of a family noted alike for its Post Office and literary connections, the fierce struggles which have sometimes been fought for place and precedence in the department hierarchy found no protagonist in him.

He settled affairs in South Africa and by 26 April 1932 he was writing to Wise not from Pretoria but from the family home at 46 Marlborough Hill. Like many expatriates, he could not really decide which country he liked best. His publication of little pamphlets continued: *John Keats and his family, a series of portraits* 100 copies, 1933, *John Keats. letters of Joseph Severn to H. Buxton Forman*, 50 copies, 1933 and *John Ruskin on John Keats*, 30 copies, 1934. This last is a rather odd production, printing two letters of Ruskin advising a Mr Harris not to buy Keats's love letters, in rather wild terms ('Isabella's brothers are nothing better than the murderers in Macbeth – or the children in the wood – and girls who grow basil out of their lovers' heads are not characters, but maniacs'). The originals of these letters have never surfaced and it may be that they were invented by Forman senior as a literary joke – similar perhaps to his Shelley portrait.

Wise was getting older and more venerated than ever. There were no children and speculation about the fate of the Ashley Library had certainly increased. He said nothing publicly and might possibly have had a knighthood in return for a gift to the British Museum. But his second will, drawn up in 1926 in the aftermath of the general strike, states,

> In my previous will I had bequeathed to the Trustees of the British Museum a number of printed books of rarity and value which are not to be found upon the shelves of the National Library at Bloomsbury or are only represented by inferior copies and I desire to express the extreme regret I feel at not including such a bequest in this my last will but the high death duties and inflated income tax will so greatly reduce the net value of my estate that I feel I am not justified in carrying out my former wish. I have at all times over a period of more than forty years experienced so much courtesy and kindness from the various leading officials at the Museum that the decision at which I have reluctantly arrived has caused me profound disappointment and has only been made after prolonged and earnest consideration. I have therefore directed that my library of printed books, manuscripts and autograph letters is to be sold.

The crusty old capitalist speaks, taking a political revenge on the defenceless British Museum. In 1928 he did, as a very minor sop, bequeath the copyrights in his bibliographies to the Bibliographical Society.

The Ashley Library ground on, producing Vol. 9 in 1927 and Vol. 10 in 1930. Apart from offshoots of this (e.g. *A Landor Library* 1928) Wise's bibliographical work came to a halt with *Two lake poets* (Wordsworth and Coleridge) 1927 and Byron, 2 vols 1932–33. This latter has an interesting reminiscence in the preface to volume 1 where he tells of his early collecting of Byron and Shelley. He had his collections bound in half blue morocco (Byron) and half red (Shelley) by 'William Fullford, a combined printer, bookbinder and stationer whose establishment was situated at the foot of Pentonville Hill, near Kings Cross Station'. He soon sold these early experiments but they several times came back to haunt him: he replaced them by uncut copies in original bindings. Wise could hardly scale any other peaks among the cognoscenti: but his fame among the public in general was increasing all the time. It seems he could not resist the publicity, rather as if he were promoting a product that could then be sold in large quantities.

So we have 'Mr T.J. Wise's world-famous library' (*The Bazaar* 14 December 1929)

> Great collectors, like great poets, are born, not made. Mr. Thomas J. Wise, whose private library, within its range (and a great range it is!) is probably the finest in the world, was under the spell of books and bookmen even in his boyhood. I have been told that, as a child he would walk a long way from his home of an evening to the Chelsea Embankment on the shadowy hope of seeing the great Thomas Carlyle taking his evening stroll.

and 'A treasure-house of books' (*The Strand* August 1930)

> E.V. Lucas has called Mr. Thomas J. Wise's house in Hampstead "a devilish difficult place to find on a foggy night". In one way, perhaps, it is just as well. Foggy nights are favourable for burglary. And though Mr. Wise himself probably does not care a straw about the market value of his books, I have heard this put at sums ranging between a quarter and half a million pounds sterling.

and finally 'A wonderful library a talk with Mr. Thomas J. Wise' (*John O'London's Weekly* 28 March 1931)

> In an unpretentious house in a quiet tree-lined road at Hampstead reposes one of the most remarkable libraries in the world. It is known as the Ashley Library, and has been accumulated during a lifetime of painstaking research and unflagging enthusiasm by the eminent bibliographer, Mr. Thomas J. Wise . . . . The library is a big square room, a peaceful sanctuary from the ceaseless flux of the world without. Glossy walnut panelling, glass fronted bookcases hide its walls. Here are two comfortable settees, there a writing desk. A broad window looks out on to a trim garden. Here is the arm chair in which Conrad used to sit, there the famous bust of Browning carved by his son, which formerly stood in the poet's own home. "My wife and I spend most of our evenings here" says Mr. Wise. "She on that settee and I on this one. Here we read and talk after dinner." He is the retired business man among his books, his sole hobby.

The interview reveals also that when Wise is sure that a book or manuscript submitted to him is a fake, he tears it up and challenges the owner to sue him for damage to property; that he acquires books only as a service to scholarship and because he wishes to read them; that the library, now overflowing into five rooms is not insured against fire or theft; that the present slump in the first edition market is a slump only in the trash; and finally that he has made provisions that the library will not be dispersed after his death but continue to serve the research student. Wise reminds one a little of his own characterization of W.T. Spencer made many years before to Wrenn as one who never speaks the truth save by accident or under great provocation. However, Wise's market views were generally very sound.

During the thirties, the book market exhibited the same boom and bust as the stock market. Speculation in books rose to a fever pitch in 1928–9, only to relapse with the stock market in 1930. Wise's letters during this gyration are full of good sense. As an experienced commodity dealer, he was used to such fluctuations and he correctly predicted the end of the boom. What was not so widely known was that he was always ready to sell bits of the Ashley Library – if the price was right. 'The reasons for the temporary depression in value of these two books would occupy too much space to detail here: suffice it to say that they have merely responded as all articles of commerce must, to the inevitable law of supply and demand', he wrote in 1894. And in 1929 in a letter to Richard Curle, the writer and bibliographer, who was then acting as his American agent, he wrote:

> In a few days I will try and send you some further letters of Shaw, &c. It is not worth while, I think, to send you my ordinary Shaw books worth about £5 or so each; but if you look into Vols V & VIII of the Ashley Catalogue you will see what I possess. Three of the excessively rare 'Trial Books', The Dark Lady of the Sonnets, Great Catherine and Overruled are not signed by G.B.S. so they might go. But I would not part with them unless I got a really large price for them, for I don't fancy that these really rare things of Shaw will go down in price, as the ordinary books most certainly will. For instance I quite expect in a year to be able to replace 'Plays Pleasant & Unpleasant' for about one third of the £50 or so you will get for it. So you might tell me what you would get for the 3 pieces mentioned above: and also what prices for one or two of those with inscriptions to Vallentin described in Vol V of Ashley Cat.

Another financial point which Wise thoroughly appreciated was made to the Maggs brothers, when he was reported to have said 'he was a collector not a dealer hence there were no business taxes and auditing of accounts to run away with the profits, all of which could be ploughed back into building up his collection with no questions asked'.

However, Wise's great house was built on sand. And the rain descended, and the floods came, and the winds blew, and beat upon that house; and it fell; and great was the fall of it.

61. Wise's bookplate

# THE EXPOSURE

The terrible two-handed engine that brought about Wise's downfall was driven by two young booksellers, Graham Pollard and John Carter. Graham Pollard was born in 1903: he came of a distinguished academic family and spent some time reacting against it. At Oxford, he claimed to have beaten Evelyn Waugh for the half blue at spitting (target at ten feet). He held party card No. 1 of the Young Communist League of Great Britain; he edited the magazine of the University Labour Club; and in one of a series of murals by Oliver Messel, Pollard was represented in a punt accompanied by a load of bombs. He spent much time in bookshops and while he was at Oxford C.H. Wilkinson brought T.J. Wise to see his collection. It included one of only three known copies of George Crabbe's first book *Inebriety*, Ipswich, 1775, which Pollard had bought for two guineas. It has a note in Crabbe's hand but lacks the title page: Wise's only comment was to reprove Pollard for buying imperfect books. After coming down, he bought a share in Birrell and Garnett's bookshop, soon to move to Soho, and settled into a rather bohemian life as an antiquarian (or perhaps second-hand) bookseller. Pollard's regime was to work late into the night, sleep late, lunch at Chez Victor, and arrive at the shop at about 2.30 p.m. He had various political irons in the fire: he edited *The Distributive Worker* (which is what booksellers are) for the Communist Party and had a hand in redesigning the *Daily Worker*. He was beginning to acquire that knowledge of obscure parts of book trade history and economics (he insisted on the second) for which he would become famous in bibliographical circles. He also had various academic projects in hand, proceeding at his usual ruminative pace, one of which led him into collaboration with John Carter.

John Carter was born in 1905 at Eton into a family who had many connections there but not much money. Jake – as he was called – went to Eton and Kings on scholarships and obtained a double first in Classics. He was always an elegant figure with an eyeglass and a patrician look about him: it was perhaps rather a surprise that he opted to join Scribners bookshop rather than the diplomatic service. He quickly rejuvenated their moribund antiquarian department with new ideas and his excellent taste. He had a determined intelligence and in those days took little on trust. He began to consider the case of the Reading *Sonnets*, his initial curiosity stimulated by that same Mudie of Quaritchs who had worked on Forman's probate valuation. 'It's a book we don't much care for', Mudie replied when pressed for a copy of the *Sonnets*. Not another word would he say and Carter began to wonder why. A.E. Housman had been an inspiration to Carter at Cambridge and the pupil adopted some of the master's critical acumen and lack of respect for tradition. Housman's characteristic paper *The Application of thought to textual criticism* ends thus: 'Knowledge is good, method is good, but one thing beyond all others is necessary; and that is to have a head, not a pumpkin, on your shoulders, and brains, not pudding in your head.' Carter and Pollard amply qualified.

The former began some preliminary investigations into the accepted history of the Reading *Sonnets* which seemed to lead to disquieting conclusions. Pollard had been reading up Ruskin in preparation for a bibliography; he had ploughed through Cook and Wedderburn's thirty-nine volumes and duly noted the two fakes that they had unmasked. Carter and Pollard were on gossiping terms as most antiquarian booksellers are in their small world. They met at a bookseller's party early in 1931 and the Reading *Sonnets* and the Ruskin fakes were aired in the same conversation. It had not escaped notice in the trade that Gorfin's infrequent catalogues (he issued his last, No. 38, in 1930) always contained long runs of nineteenth century pamphlets. Someone else mentioned this, fished his catalogue 38 out of the waste paper basket and gave it to Pollard. It was the first intimation that Browning and Ruskin were not isolated fakes but a group to which the catalogue provided a rough and ready guide. Several recent sales at Hodgsons with long runs of the pamphlets also added to the list. Carter and Pollard soon agreed a collaboration and set to work.

Carter's file on the Reading *Sonnets* grew and grew and looked more and more convincing. There was no presentation copy (privately printed books tend to have a higher level of inscription than those published commercially); no copy in Browning's library; no copy in an old binding; no copy with any signature inscription or mark of provenance before about 1900; and the account of the history of the book given by Gosse was contradicted by Browning's own letters. This was all very well: but it was negative evidence. Pollard's researches into the history of the book trade were able, after hours of research, to provide some positive evidence. After sifting through many obscure technical manuals he was able to chart the chemical history of nineteenth century paper more fully than had been done before. There was no copy of the *Sonnets* in any public collection in England and the enquirers could hardly go to Heath Drive and ask for a paper sample. They obtained their tiny piece from Flora Livingston, of the Widener Library, 'I have had the courage to trim off a little slip of paper from the bottom of a badly folded leaf of the Sonnets. It will never show, and if it does no one will know the who or the why' she wrote (6 April 1933). She was not a friend of Mr Wise, having clashed with him over several bibliographical points.

Chemical analysis of the paper showed that it contained an unmistakably significant proportion of chemical wood pulp. Since, however, this constituent was never used in England until 1874, it followed that the Reading *Sonnets* could not have been printed before that date. It was absolutely impossible that the book could have been printed in 1847. Once the forgery group was investigated as a whole, several other cracks appeared in its façade: wrong texts, wrong publishers' addresses, illustrative blocks copied when the originals could have been used, and so on. Armed with the growing dossiers, Pollard and Carter confronted Gorfin. They were able to realize, after a few minutes' conversation, that Gorfin was not himself the forger and (probably) did not know what he was selling. He confirmed that he was the consigner of the recent sales at Hodgsons which had contained runs of the pamphlets: and he astonished Carter and Pollard by stating that he had bought the whole lot from Thomas James Wise. What was more, he could prove it. He had a small notebook with jottings of purchases and a linen bag with his cheque book stubs from 1909–12, some twenty years before. From these could be constructed and proved the astonishing quantities of the pamphlets which Wise had sold. The fact that Gorfin had kept the evidence for so long is remarkable: few part-time booksellers can be bothered to keep twenty-year-old cheque stubs. Perhaps

A close examination of the type used for the composition reveals two characteristic sorts which are of some significance in yᵉ enquiry.

There is a l.c. rom f̅. I have distorted the false kern as indicated but in the original (wh. is printed in about 10 point) it is quite clearly visible.

Secondly the query mark to the fount is not as expected, I.e.

not ? but ?

In other respects the fount is an ordinary slightly condensed modern. Now these two sorts ought to enable a positive identification of the fount to be made, whether S. B & Cᵒ Caslon or whose; and it is possible that a local directory giving anno 1846 or 7 lists of

62.   Part of a letter from Stanley Morison
to Graham Pollard, about the Reading Sonnets

in his heart of hearts he did have doubts about the propriety of
the whole affair. The Gorfin revelation gave a new focus to the
enquiry. Carter had already written to Wise asking about the
Reading *Sonnets* (19 December 1932) and this sighting shot had
elicited a letter parading only the familiar history of the book.

Pollard knew a great deal about the history of type, that is,
the printed letters used in books since the invention of printing
in the fifteenth century. But almost all of the historical material available to him dealt with the aesthetics rather than the
economics of type design: it obviously had little or nothing to
say about the undistinguished nineteenth century typefaces in
which the forgeries were printed. The Reading *Sonnets* was the
key piece, but, as we have seen, was not available to the
enquirers. Pollard asked Stanley Morison, the great typographer
who was due to visit New York, to look at the Pierpont Morgan
copy. He wrote to Pollard pointing out two special features of
the type, firstly a kernless 'f' and secondly an alien question
mark.

> I may be all wrong but I have not noticed the broken backed f as early
> as 1850 and if I had been asked I should have said that it was evolved
> in order to prevent broken kerns occurring on high speed presses of
> which there cd. have been few in Reading or anywhere else in 1847.
> [January 1932]

Pollard plunged into typographical history at the St Bride
Printing Library, off Fleet Street; the best collection on the
subject in the world.

A kerned letter is one in which a portion of the face of the
letter extends beyond its body, e.g. the overhanging top on an
'f'. This thin projection, the kern, is both exposed and fragile.
When composing machines for setting type came into use in the
second half of the nineteenth century, it often broke off. This
inconvenience created a natural demand for a kernless type. Graham examined some 170 nineteenth century specimen books and
could find no kernless types before 1880 and a rapid increase in
them after that date. This is a general argument and is, in fact,
not entirely correct though it sufficed at the time. The kernless
'f' and 'j' were a special feature of the Reading *Sonnets* type. The
other was the alien question mark which clearly did not belong
to the fount. The enquirers now had Wise in their sights and
were able to find the Reading *Sonnets* fount with both the

special peculiarities in a legitimate Wise production which had
the imprint of Richard Clay and Sons. Everything now clicked
into place. The matrices from which the type was cast were
supplied by P.M. Shanks & Co; cast by Richard Clay and called
their Long Primer No. 3. In about 1877, they altered the 'f' and
'j' to eliminate the kerns and about the same time they lost or
broke the proper matrix for the question mark. They cast round
for an alternative and came up with the question mark from the
predecessor of Long Primer No. 3, Miller and Richard's Long
Primer No. 28. The introduction of this mixed fount can be
dated to the month by *Macmillan's Magazine*, also printed by
Clays. There it was first used in April 1877.

Other printers used the Shanks type: but the particular mixture used in the Reading *Sonnets* with kernless 'f' and 'j' and an
alien question mark was only used by Richard Clay. The enquirers
remarked of this special hybrid type that it was apparently in
use as early as 1842 and as late as 1893, and at such widely
divergent places as London, Manchester, Kendal, Reading, Edinburgh, Woolwich and Cambridge, Massachusetts. Not only had
they proved another sixteen pamphlets to be misdated and
therefore forged, they had also nailed the original printer of the
fakes. The firm of Clays admitted that this evidence proved they
had printed the things: but they had pulped most of their
records and had no documentary evidence for whom they were
printed. The evidence from paper and from type was extended,
but remained the same in principle. The enquirers had come up
with a list of some fifty pamphlets which could be condemned on
one count or another and were clearly a homogeneous group. By
this time they thought Wise was the culprit but could not
prove it. Pollard wrote to Wise suggesting a meeting, which
took place in October 1933. As he went into Wise's study to
confer with the great collector, surrounded by his famous
library, Mrs Wise warned him 'You must not excite him'. But
everything Pollard said was exciting and Wise's colour got higher
and higher. Mrs Wise, behind his back, made desperate signals to
go easy, but Pollard remorselessly continued. When he reached
the crucial subject of typefaces, Wise began to shout incoher-
ently. The interview was over. The enquirers did submit a list of
pamphlets for details of provenance, but it was never filled in.

Pollard had taken care to say nothing of Gorfin. Wise panicked and immediately sought his aid. Their relationship had distanced almost to nothing since the days before the First World War when Wise had encouraged him in Charing Cross Road. Gorfin was rather a nominal bookseller, working during the day as a greengrocer's assistant and latterly as clerk to a corn factor. Wise did not know where to find him and sent urgent letters to old addresses, even dispatching Mrs Wise in a hired car to run him to earth. What followed is best described in Gorfin's own words.

On or about the 13th October 1933 I received a letter from Mr Wise, dated 12–10–33, inviting me to call on him on Tuesday the 17th instant, an appointment altered by a subsequent wire (10a.m. 16–10–33) to an invitation to lunch. This appointment I kept, and was informed by Mr Wise that trouble had arisen respecting some of the pamphlets that I had bought from him: that he had had a visit from a Mr Pollard on October 14th: that a number of these pamphlets were stated by Mr Pollard to be fakes, and that it was my indiscreet marketing of them in numbers that had led to an investigation being made as to their origin, and to the assertion that they were spurious. He suggested that something would have to be done and proposed that I should agree to the destruction of all the copies still retained by me, and that, "as they are now mere waste-paper", he should compensate me for their loss to the extent of £25 or £30, and that I should make the statement that I had had them from Mr H. Buxton Forman (not from Mr Wise, as was in fact the case), and that he (Mr Wise) and H. Buxton Forman's son (H.B.F. being then dead) would substantiate the statement in question. This I at once definitely declined to do. I had intended telling Mr Wise at this interview that I had been in touch with Mr Pollard and Mr Carter, but Mr Wise was in such an excited state, and I was so shocked by his changed appearance and evident condition of ill-health that I considered it better to defer doing so. I therefore wrote on October 18th to Mrs Wise, giving her the full facts of the case, explaining that I had been in communication with Mr Pollard, explaining also how I came to be in communication with him, finally leaving it to her to "convey the information to him as and when you think best". At our interview on the 17th I had told Mr Wise that whilst definitely declining to agree to his proposal, I regarded it as necessary to take time to consider my position. Mr Wise asked me to let him know what I had decided by 4.30 o'clock on Thursday, October 19th, when I was again to call upon him at 25 Heath Drive. However, I had so definitely decided that his proposition was impossible and considered that no good could come of further discussion on the line proposed, that I wired on the morning of the 19th as follows:– (10.15 a.m. Thursday "Impossible agree HBF proposal. Herbert" To this wire I received one in reply:– (11.52 Hampstead) "Wire received anyhow we expect you to tea" To this I again wired:– "Position impossible seeking independent advice do not expect me to tea Herbert." On Friday morning I received the following wire, handed in at Hampstead at 10.5 a.m.:– "Mr Wise cannot travel please come today your reputation and pocket perfectly safe Mr Wise has already stated that the goods were bought from Forman and sold to Gorfin." To this I wired a reply:– "Wire received arriving 3.30 to 4 o'clock, Herbert." At this interview Mr Wise adopted at first an extremely spacious attitude. It was so unfortunate that we had seen so little of one another these late years. Why was it, &c. If we can once get over the present little difficulty there was no reason whatever why we should not again do good business together. He would be quite willing on his part to pay me back whatever sum it was I had originally paid him for the pamphlets, £400 wasn't it, and as I seemed not to like the idea that I should say I purchased them from H.B.F., that little difficulty could be surmounted by our agreeing that, although I actually paid him (Mr Wise) for the various items, it was fully understood all the time that he was acting as the agent of Mr Forman in the matter, and that the pamphlets were actually coming to me from Mr F. though through Mr W. This again I objected to. I informed Mr Wise that I had purchased all the pamphlets from him direct, that I had accepted his statement regarding their origin, viz. that they had been found in sheets upon the demolition of a publisher's warehouse and that he (Mr Wise) purchased the sheets in bulk: that I had always regarded them as perfectly genuine and that I would subscribe to nothing but the plain unvarnished truth respecting them or my acquisition of them. The potential value of the property, I continued, was something like £2000, had they been genuine – as I had every reason to believe them to be when I bought them from him that I was now fully convinced in my own mind that the author of their existence was none other than himself, and that I considered I had been disgracefully treated in the matter. Mrs Wise was present at this interview, had indeed been at this and upon previous occasions. She suggested that perhaps Mr Wise could give me books of a value to satisfy me, to which I replied that I did not want books but considered myself entitled to the value of the property which his (Mr Wise's) action had destroyed. To this Mr Wise replied he had not £2000 nor in fact even £200, and then made a remark to the effect that "he could of course get young Forman to sell some of these – waving his hand towards the cases – but it did not seem as though it were any good paying me anything at all, seeing that the pamphlets were now just so much waste paper", to which opinion Mrs Wise agreed, and Mrs Wise then left the room. Mr Wise then made a remark about blackmail whereupon I indignantly rose to leave, protesting against so outrageous a suggestion. We had some further conversation and I took my leave, as there seemed to be "no object in discussing the matter further". Mr Wise then asked me whether I was going away to "stir up further mud". I again protested that "the mud was all of his making and had been stirred up by him", and I left. Mrs Wise met me in the hall and followed me out to the gate, despite the unpleasant weather. Her last words to me were, "You will come, Herbert, if I want you?"

After taking legal advice I wrote on October 29th as follows:– Dear Mr Wise, Anent our conversation of last Friday week, the 20th inst., and your proposal that, in consideration of my destroying the whole of the forged pamphlets remaining in my possession, you would compensate me in the sum of £400. I have carefully considered the matter and am prepared to accept your proposal. It would of course be understood that I am not expected to state that I purchased the pamphlets from Mr H.B. Forman and that you undertake, as you agreed to do, to accept responsibility for any claim that may be brought against me by former purchasers. Although such a settlement as this takes no account of the serious damage to my reputation that must result and has indeed already shown itself, I am anxious to be clear of the whole very unpleasant business. Yours very sincerely, Herbert E. Gorfin. I next received a letter from Mrs. Wise, written on behalf of her husband, in which he agreed to pay me £400 as compensation, and arranging that I should call on "Wednesday or Thursday next" (Nov. 8th or 9th). At this interview it was arranged that I should deliver the pamphlets to Mr Wise's solicitor, Mr Gedge of Messrs Gedge Fiske & Co., 10 Norfolk Street W.C.2. The pamphlets were duly delivered and cheque received. At a subsequent date I received a letter from Messrs Gedge Fiske & Co. as follows:– (11th November 1933) Dear Mr Gorfin, I write as arranged to inform you that the whole of the pamphlets which you left with me have been torn up in my presence. Yours truly, (Signed) John A Gedge.

Carter described the affair from the enquirers' point of view.

Wise bethought him of Gorfin, with whom he had been out of touch for a decade or more, and invited him to tea. He did not know that Gorfin had "come clean" to us, and he broke the news, as he supposed, that there was "some talk going on about some wrong things" among the pamphlets of which he had sold Gorfin so large a number twenty years before. He suggested that it would be best for all concerned if he took back whatever Gorfin had left "at their market value," which he estimated at a total of £25. Gorfin did not dare tell Wise that we had already taken down his evidence, but he had enough sense to say he would think over Wise's offer. He came straight to my office, and he was still sweating slightly: Wise was an extremely formidable character, and although Gorfin was free, white and fifty-five, in that choleric presence he was again the subservient office boy. We advised him to write the truth to Wise if he did not, as he insisted, dare to tell him to his face.

He did so, and the result was electric. A series of telegrams summoned him "immediately" to 25 Heath Drive, where Wise offered to repay his whole original investment (£400, sixteen times the previous day's offer) in the now worthless pamphlets, on one condition: that Gorfin would endorse his intended statement that they had all come from Harry Buxton Forman, editor of Shelley and Keats, and a notable book-collector of Wise's period, who died in 1917. Gorfin declined to support this story, which he then heard for the first time, and again left, promising to consider Wise's revised offer. We advised him to accept it, accompanying his acceptance with a specific repudiation of the Buxton Forman story, which seemed to him (and to us) to be an alibi for which Wise needed any support he could beg, borrow, or in this case buy; and we recommended that he get a lawyer to draft the letter. He did so; and he got the £400 in exchange for his stock of the pamphlets.

Wise also mobilized his influential friends and an informal defence committee was set up in Oxford. This was headed by (Sir) Humphrey Milford but the active member was Frederick Page, an old friend of Wise whom we have already met. He took it as a matter of course that the enquirers' left wing conspiracy would soon be shown up. He put his research assistant onto the job of hunting up contemporary evidence for the Reading *Sonnets*. His first doubts began when Wise insisted that it was a waste of time to look for contemporary evidence: he should attack the enquirers' evidence from paper and type. As filtered through Wise himself, this was not easy to do and Mr Page did not understand the force of the technical arguments.

Maurice Buxton Forman was still living in his father's old house at 46 Marlborough Hill. His mother had died in 1932 aged 92 and Maurice was settling into life in England. Wise got in touch with him and told him the balloon was about to go up. By a mixture of bullying, blackmail and old friendship, he readied Maurice on his side for the coming campaign. In January 1933 Wise altered his will. He freed his wife from trustees and gave her financial freedom of action. He also directed that his library should be offered in the first instance to the British Museum at a price to be fixed by Mrs Wise in consultation with solicitors and trustees. This greatly increased the probability of the library passing to the nation at a favourable price. In the autumn of 1933, Wise went to see Clays, specifically Cecil Clay the managing director. He had by now digested the technical evidence provided by the enquirers, made his own enquiries within the firm, and come to his own conclusions. Wise left his wife in the waiting room and went off with Cecil Clay to the boardroom. Wise: 'Can't you say you had nothing to do with these things?' Clay: 'How can I when you know we printed them for you. Aren't you rather giving yourself away?' The interview came to an abrupt end. Wise was still not well – after all he had his 74th birthday on 7 October – and in November he injured his head in another fall.

Meanwhile the enquirers completed and polished their book; an initial draft was headed 'Wise-cracking'. At the same time Wise's influential friends went to work. The book was to be published by Constable in England and Scribners in America. The directors of Constable were approached by all sorts of influential people who warned them in the friendliest but weightiest possible way against putting any trust in those wild young men. Carter was much more of an establishment figure than Pollard. He was borne off to numerous lunches with the great and the good. 'I always wondered when he came back', Pollard used to say, 'whether he had ratted on me: but he never did.'

The book Carter and Pollard wrote had a studiously modest title: *An enquiry into the nature of certain nineteenth century pamphlets*. It is a title which harks back to Malone's great exposé of the eighteenth century forgeries of William Henry Ireland viz. *An inquiry into the authenticity of certain miscellaneous papers* 1796. The tradition was continued by James Boaden, *An inquiry into the authenticity of various pictures and prints, offered to the public as portraits of Shakespeare* 1824; N. Hamilton, *An inquiry into the genuineness of the manuscript corrections in Mr. J. Payne Collier annotated Shakespeare* 1860; and (to leapfrog a moment) Nicolas Barker, *The Butterfly books. An enquiry into the nature of certain twentieth century pamphlets* 1987. These last two demolish the forgeries of John Payne Collier and Frederick Prokosch. In Carter and Pollard's *Enquiry* all the trails seemed to lead to Wise's door: but not unnaturally he refused any explanation to the enquirers. They could not name him as the forger because there was no absolute proof: but their indictment was damaging.

Mr. Wise, by his credulity, by his vanity in his own possessions, by his dogmatism, by abuse of his eminence in the bibliographical world, has dealt a blow to the prestige of an honourable science, the repercussions of which will be long and widely felt ... like the thirteenth stroke of a faulty clock, which discredits the hours which have gone before, the spuriousness of these books must inevitably cast aspersions on many similar books which are, in fact, genuine. If these, so plausible, so well-established, are forgeries, what can we trust? If Mr. Wise, one of the most eminent bibliographers of our time, can be so extensively wrong, who can we be sure is right? In the whole history of bookcollecting, there has been no such wholesale and successful perpetration of fraud as that which we owe to this anonymous forger. It has been converted into an equally unparalleled blow to the bibliography and literary criticism of the Victorian period by the shocking negligence of Mr. Wise.

# WISE AT BAY

Two letters from America give some idea of the general reaction. A.E. Newton, the well known writer of popular books on book collecting wrote to Carter 'the man who seems to be involved is almost a National figure. He is now old, and I am told very infirm. I urge you in the name of humanity not to make his last days more agonising than they must inevitably be', while another prominent collector W.H.T. Howe wrote to both

> The opinion has been unanimously expressed to me from dealers and people who speak with more or less authority in regard to rare books that you gentlemen will have a pretty uphill road in America establishing your claims. Mr. Thomas J. Wise stands very high in America as he does in England both for his scholarly integrity and for his ability as a bibliographer.

Not surprisingly the publishers worried about the possibility of a libel suit and they submitted the book to J.P.R. Lyell, a lawyer who was also a well known book collector. He concluded that the whole book was libellous but Wise would probably not sue. Nevertheless he suggested that as a precaution, Gorfin's evidence should be sworn before a lawyer: and so it was. His two statements covered first his original purchases from Wise and second Wise's attempts to suborn Gorfin after Pollard's visit. With everything, it seemed, nicely buttoned up, Carter and Pollard awaited publication with growing excitement, spiced with apprehension. Although their book had been discussed in a small bibliographical circle, there were few leaks. The first that most people knew of the affair was a vast letter in the *Times Literary Supplement* 24 May 1934. This was an attempt to blunt the effect of the *Enquiry* in advance – though signed by Wise, it was drafted by Frederick Page, and typed by his assistant.

> Sir, – The suggestion has been pressed upon me that this book, with an imprint "Reading [Not for Publication]" is an impostor, not printed until many years after 1847, I possess two copies, and they are described in my catalogue as being the first, privately printed, edition of "The Sonnets from the Portuguese." The hitherto accepted story is that the Book was committed to the press by Mary Russell Mitford, who lived close to Reading.

The claim that the book is an impostor is supported by two contentions: (1) that it is printed on wood-pulp paper and that this did not come into general use in England before 1880; (2) that in the type used for its printing are two characters, a lower-case "f" and an interrogation mark, specially cast for a certain firm of printers and not made till the eighties. I shall comment upon these two arguments later. In the meantime it must be admitted that they would never have been put forward but for the absence of any reference to the 1847 book in the printed correspondence of Robert and E.B. Browning, and in the correspondence of Miss Mitford, so far as it has yet been published. A very great deal still exists in manuscript only; I hope this may all be examined. It has further to be admitted that no reference to the 1847 book appeared during the lifetime of Robert Browning. The first printed mention of it was by Edmund Gosse in an introduction to an edition of the "Sonnets from the Portuguese" published by Messrs. Dent at the end of 1894. The introduction wʌs reprinted as the first article in his "Critical Kit-Kats," 1896. In reprinting it he wrote: –

"Robert Browning laid upon me as a duty the publication of what I have written. What is here found, in matters of fact, regarding the Sonnets of his Wife comes with the authority and is presented at the desire of Browning."

Since then, until last year, Gosse's account has been generally accepted and widely repeated. One detail, indeed, and a very important one, was contradicted by Miss Lilian Whiting on the authority of Browning's son. Gosse's version was that the manuscripts of the Sonnets were put into Browning's pocket by his wife, coming up behind his back one morning after breakfast, at Pisa, early in 1847. This would be compatible with their being printed later in that year at Reading. Miss Lilian Whiting, with the authority aforementioned, said that it was not till 1849, and at Bagni di Lucca, that Browning saw them. I maintained in my "Browning Library," 1929 (pp. 84–5), that Browning's son was confusing two different manuscripts of the Sonnets.

But last year there was printed an edition of Browning's letters mainly from originals in my possession, and the reviewer in your issue of September 28, 1933, was able to quote a passage, then first printed, from Browning's letter to Leigh Hunt, October 6, 1857, which supports Miss Whiting's contention, and constitutes a real difficulty in the acceptance of the 1847 book. Browning writes: "I never suspected the existence of these "Sonnets from the Portuguese" till three years after they were written: they were shown to me at this very place (Bagni di Lucca) eight years ago." We should therefore be bound to accept 1849 as the year in which Browning first saw the Sonnets, were it not that Browning was notoriously inaccurate when speaking of his wife's works. Gosse's story is based on a statement made by Browning himself eight years before his

death "to a friend, with the understanding that at some future
date, after his own decease, the story might be more widely told." In
1881 Browning was telling and partly dictating to Gosse the story of
his life, and this story, up to and not beyond Browning's marriage on
September 12, 1846, was printed by Gosse in the *Century Magazine*,
December, 1881, and reprinted in his book, "Robert Browning: Per-
sonalia," in 1890. The friend, then, to whom Browning made the
statement alluded to was almost certainly Gosse himself, and the
discrepancy between 1847 and 1849 is easily to be explained as a lapse
of memory on his part or even on Browning's.

But Gosse (in 1894 and 1896) went on to say that E.B.B. was
persuaded by her husband to permit Miss Mitford to pass the
Sonnets for press, although she absolutely declined to accede to Miss
Mitford's suggestion that they should appear in one of the Annuals,
and accordingly a small volume was printed, entitled "Sonnets. By
E.B.B. Reading: [Not for publication.] 1847," a small octavo of 47
pages.

Again it is clear what happened. With the 1847 book in front of
him, the genuineness of which he had no reason to suspect, and the
date 1847 in his mind, Gosse confused the inclusion of the Sonnets in
"Poems," 1850, with the presumed privately printed book of 1847.

I may be driven to the conclusion that the 1847 book is not
authentic, but I will consider another alternative first, the possibility that some time in 1846 or 1847 Mrs. Browning sent the Sonnets
in manuscript to Miss Mitford, who was to get them privately
printed so that Mrs. Browning might surprise her husband with
them shortly after their marriage. This would be compatible with a
passage in her letter to him of July 22, 1846:

"You shall see some day at Pisa what I will not show you now. Does
not Solomon say that 'there is a time to read what is written.' "

Now suppose the Sonnets to have been printed through Miss Mitford's agency in 1847, how are we to account for the suppression of
the privately printed book. Browning himself may have accounted for
it without knowing that he was doing so, in that letter to Leigh
Hunt, where he goes on "they [the Sonnets in manuscript] were
shown to me . . . in consequence of some word of mine, just as they
had been suppressed through some mistaken word." He would have
been shown the Sonnets in manuscript (at least five transcripts were
made by Mrs. Browning) because the printed books remained in Miss
Mitford's hands, to be kept till asked for.

If the book was indeed printed in Reading in 1847 it was, as Mr.
W.J. Roberts said in his "Mary Russell Mitford," 1913, probably
printed by Miss Mitford's excellent friend, "Mr. [George] Lovejoy,
our great Reading bookseller" whom, in 1849, she called "my excellent coadjutor." This is a clue which it may be well to follow up.

All this is only an hypothesis. I will now consider the theory of
unauthorized printing.

With whom could this have originated? One name must be cleared out of the way at once: a name which would never have been brought into the matter but for a mistake of my own. In the introduction to "A Browning Library", 1929, writing forty-three years after the event, I told the story of a visit to W.C. Bennett in 1886, and said that I acquired my two copies of the 1847 book from him; and earlier than this, in the first volume of my Ashley Catalogue, 1922, I said that my copies came to me from W.C. Bennett. What I actually brought away with me was his own sonnets, "My Sonnets," privately printed at Greenwich in 1843. The confusion of two such books may seem incredible, even after thirty-six years. It is to be explained by the subjects of our conversation: his friendship with Mary Russell Mitford, our common interest in the Brownings, Mrs. Browning's association with Miss Mitford and the presence among his poems of two sonnets, one on Robert and the other on E.B. Browning, and the mention of both of them in yet another sonnet. In size and outward appearance the two books are almost identical.

My two copies came to me not from W.C. Bennett but from Harry Buxton Forman. From whom did he obtain them? Neither I nor his son Mr. Maurice Buxton Forman can tell with any certainty, but how he may have obtained them I hope his son will be able to ascertain from an examination of his father's correspondence.

I now come to the technical arguments from paper and print. The contention is that paper from wood-pulp did not come into general use in England until 1880. The Oxford English Dictionary, s.v. "Pulp," supplies me with the following quotation from *Fraser's Magazine*, November, 1862: "It is only necessary to put the wood into one end of the machine, and take out at the other the pulp ready for being converted into paper." I have been told that a patent was taken out for it in 1853. But this was probably for a new or improved process of manufacture. Paper made from wood-pulp had been used for book-printing as far back as 1801, and such paper must have been in use from that date onwards, its employment rapidly increasing after 1853, when the perfected process of manufacture was patented. I have had a portion of one of the leaves of the 1847 book chemically analysed, and it proved to be a mixture of wood-pulp and rag.

The notes of interrogation in the 1847 book are the very familiar form of a "pothanger" with a dot underneath, very much like an inverted italic i, not the more usual human-ear-and-earring. I see no difference between those in the 1847 book, those in Douglas Jerrold's, "Comedies and Dramas,' 1854, those in the Tauchnitz edition of Rossetti, printed in Leipzig in 1873, and those in a volume in Cassell's National Library, printed by Cassells in 1887. Further search would doubtless reveal many other examples, but I will leave further exposition of this and the lower-case f to those who have a more microscopic eye than I can boast of.

The technical points about paper and type show that Wise had not absorbed Pollard's arguments. The really striking point about this letter, however, is the abandonment of Bennett as the source of the forgery. This was because, while Wise was blundering about looking for help, Sydney Cockerell was drawn in. He was a connection of the Bennett family and warned Wise that unless W.C. Bennett was taken out of the firing line, he would be in trouble. Wise obediently chopped him out but at the cost of total loss of reputation. Consider his account in his *Browning Library* 1929 with the retraction printed above:

> Dr. Bennett, who was an elderly bachelor, and lived in rooms some-where in Camberwell, told me of his friendship with Miss Mitford, also that he possessed copies of the privately printed *Sonnets* which he had received from her hands. Ultimately he invited me to visit his home to inspect these and other literary treasures. Hence one after-noon, after 'Change, I called at the office in Queen Victoria Street where he was employed as an accountant, and accompanied him home to Camberwell. I remember that the meal awaiting us was "high tea", and that it consisted of hot buttered toast and sausages. After his landlady had cleared the table, letters and books were brought out, among them the much longed-for *Sonnets*. One of the copies was in an old and broken half-calf binding, with the edges fortunately left untrimmed. But it had inserted the manuscript of the additional Sonnet, *Future and Past*, which had been sent by Mrs. Browning to Miss Mitford to complete the series of forty-four. I bought the tiny booklet for £25, and carried it home rejoicing. I also purchased one of the unbound copies. It formed the nucleus of the matchless 'association volume' described at length on pages 85 to 88 of the present catalogue. Shortly afterwards Dr. Bennett sold the remaining copies. They were bought by Harry Buxton Forman, Robert Alfred Potts, Sir Edmund Gosse, the Rev. Stopford A. Brooke, John Morgan of Aberdeen, Mr. Walter Brindley Slater, and other friends to whom I carried the good news. Dr. Bennett received £10 for each. All were uncut and without wrappers, but traces of pale buff paper remained upon the spine of each, which told that wrappers had once been there. The reason why the wrappers had been removed could not be explained by Dr. Bennett, who assured us that the pamphlets were in this condition when they came to him from Three-Mile Cross, Miss Mitford's home near Reading. Some years afterwards Sir Edmund Gosse sold his copy for £50. It went, I believe, to Charles B. Foote of New York, Stopford Brooke also sold his copy, to a London bookseller, for £40.
>
> Among the many interesting letters Dr. Bennett shewed me was one he had received from Alfred Lord Tennyson. It includes a small pen and ink drawing illustrating the text. Such an example is unique

in Tennyson's correspondence. I coveted that letter as Ahab coveted the vineyard of Naboth, and upon many subsequent occasions made fruitless efforts to obtain it. Bennett was a man of modest means. The price of the little document would have been serviceable to him, and he was frequently tempted to sell it. But in the end patriotism prevailed over cupidity. He presented the letter to the British Museum.

Dr. Bennett has long been dead, and most of the friends who in my early days were associated with me in admiration of Browning and in love of his books have also passed away. I am one of the few persons still living, and I believe the sole remaining man, who broke bread at Browning's table.

One of those duped by Wise was Richard Jennings and he produced (as 'Richard Gullible') an irresistible parody both of the original account and of the retraction.

The Boskage, Kensington.
My Dear Sir,
I hear that you desire to print the sonnet by E.B.B. I communicated to you some months back. I have no objection, so long as only a very small number of copies be circulated amongst the great poetess's remaining admirers. I suggest a rigidly limited issue of 25 copies, of which 853 be assigned to myself.

I hear also that you would like to make a covetable collection by inclusion of the unknown poem I acquired during one of the early eighties of the last century. I am tolerably sure that this monologue, recognisably in the vein of Robert Browning (though signed, if signed it may be called, with his initials only), is indeed his. But before you judge I had better reveal to you the circumstances of its acquisition.

I had agreed, one memorable evening, to dine with my dear old friend, Clem Stunter, whom you may remember as the author of *Banjo Ditties* and *Odes for Bargees*. Clem, I well remember, lived on the banks of Thames Reach near Rotherhithe. So, immediately after the opening of the pork shops in Whitechapel Highway, I picked up Clem not far from Clink Street and we made our way merrily enough – for the gin palaces were then not closed at fixed hours – to my old friend's neat villa down Wapping Stairs. After a savoury meal of tripe and onions, washed down with a mug of double Bass, I saw Mrs. Clem, who was bending over the washer, taking something out of her hair. "Curl papers, mother?" said my dear old pal laughingly. And in high good humour his faithful wife untwisted from her head this very poem which I now transcribe – after who knows how many years? – for you. "Why, Clem," I remember saying, "this may be Browning." "It might be blacking for all I care," he jovially answered, and added: "How much?" He had no bank account, hadn't Clem; so, placing a sovereign on the kitchen dresser – we were of course on the gold standard in those days – I came away the proud possessor of what I am convinced is an unpublishable poem by the Mark Tapley of English verse. To me I confess it is obscure. But so was Browning. Do with it as you will.

Yours very untruly, Richard Gullible

And the burlesque retraction was

Since I communicated the poem to Mr. Carter I have become increasingly uncertain whether I did, in fact or fiction, receive this most interesting copy of verses from the late Mr. Stunter. More and more vividly, as I sit thinking of it, it comes over me that all I bought of my good friend Clem, in those days or nights, was a limited issue – an issue limited to, I think he told me, to 10,500 copies – of my dear pal's lively volume *Crumpets for Crimps*. This was a sizeable tome illustrated with colour plates by my aged Chum's "Old Dutch" as he used to call her. It was (I remember) bound in tarpaulin with a cover design of sprats being chased by a whale. I had much difficulty in squeezing the volume into the capacious pocket of my Macfarlane, as I made my way home to tell my fellow-collectors the good news. From whom then – you may ask – did I receive the poem by R.B.? It was (if an old man's memory may be trusted) from a friend of a friend of the late Sir Edmund Gosse's friend of the Poet. His name escapes me. But in those jolly days we were all friends together.

It was as if two junior clerks in a stockbrokers had proved (well, virtually proved) that the Governor of the Bank of England was uttering forged five pound notes.

Meanwhile, the next TLS carried two further letters, one from Graham Pollard defending the technical side and the other from Maurice Buxton Forman:

Sir, I was glad to read Mr. Wise's letter in *The Times Literary Supplement* of the 24th instant, because it gives me an opportunity of confessing a sin of omission, which I feel sure he will forgive, and also of confirming a statement he now makes.

When "A Browning Library" reached me in South Africa in 1929 all my unofficial time was occupied with John Keats and his letters, and on its arrival it went straight on to my shelves to be cut open and read at a later date. That date was a few days ago. Had I read the preface when the book reached me I should certainly have stumbled at the statement that the Reading "Sonnets" came direct to Mr. Wise from Dr. Bennett; and I probably should have enjoyed writing to him and asking whether he had not made a mistake in attributing the source of his two copies to Miss Mitford's old friend instead of to an old friend of his own, my father, to wit, who was an acquaintance of Dr. Bennett. I believe that Sir Edmund Gosse had a copy of the little book before my father purchased the bulk of the remainder, and that Mr. Wise had both his copies from him in the course of one of their many exchanges. I cannot be sure, but I have good reason to think that the additional sonnet, "Future and Past," also came to Mr. Wise from my father, to whom it had come with the mass of Mrs. Browning's letters and manuscripts left to him by Richard Henry Horne.

Of three copies I found in this house when I went through the "Buxton Forman Collection" in 1919 one belonged to my mother and was sold privately, one was in the library, and the third my mother gave to me. It is still in my possession, where it will remain, whatever bibliographers and booksellers may like to call it.

This is a broken backed affair, which reads a little like the notes extorted from kidnap victims.

The *Enquiry* was published on 2 July 1934 and caused a sensation. The *Daily Herald* ran a headline story 'Faked first edition sensation' and even a poster 'Famous books denounced as forgeries'. They also sent a reporter down to Hastings and received the only public explanation Wise ever gave (apart from the TLS letters).

From our special correspondent. Hastings. Friday.
Mr. Thomas J. Wise is recuperating here after a long illness. This is what he said during an interview I had with him tonight: "A large proportion of the books which they condemn are genuine. Those that are wrong were apparently printed in the middle and late eighties of last century. At that time I was a young man in the twenties hunting for books and seeking for knowledge about them. These things were accepted as genuine at that time by such men as Buxton Forman, Sir Edmund Gosse, William Rossetti, Dr. Garnett, of the British Museum, The Rev. Stopford Brooks, and others. If these men of age and experience accepted them as genuine, why should I their junior, suppose them to be spurious? From the late seventies until the end of the century Buxton Forman had habit of buying and 'salting down,' as he called it, small remainder of books, pamphlets and autographs of authors whose works he believed in. In later life he disposed of these largely by way of exchange. A considerable number of them were handed by him to me in exchange for manuscripts and letters of the Brontes Swinburne, Rosetti, Borrow, George Elliot. He also used to give me these pamphlets, together with others, in payment of his subscriptions to the Shelleys Society, debts, etc. I was the secretary of the society. They were disposed of through the medium of Mr. Gorfin (who is absolved by the authors of all connections with the forgeries). That is how they passed through my hands to Gorfin who opened a shop in the Charing Cross-road. He asked me if Forman would let him have the pamphlets. Forman said he could have them all and I passed them over. I was the only vehicle. [sic] I was the messenger lad who took the goods for delivery. They

were planted on Forman and not on me. For the last two years I have
heard subterranean rumours and remarks. One day Pollard (one of the
authors of the book) wrote to me saying they had found some things
that were wrong. Would they, he asked, allow him to come and see
me as I was the only one who could give information.

My nurse wrote and fixed an appointment. Mr. Pollard called and
told me that they had found some wrong things, particularly Mrs.
Browning's Sonnet. I replied that I was very interested in this and
said that I would be pleased to aid and assist them in any way I
could. I asked him to tell me what they knew and said that I would
add to it if I could.

He instantly said, 'No, we don't want any help, but we would like
to know when and from whom you purchased your own copies of
certain pamphlets,' a list of which he produced.

I replied that to tell him off-hand where and when I purchased the
pamphlets, which cost a few shillings each between 30 and 50 years
ago was an impossibility because the copies I had in my library were
frequently not the copies I received from Buxton Forman. The next
day he sent me a typed list of about 30 or more pamphlets and
requested that I should fill in the source from which my copies came.
This I should have done had I not heard just at that moment
rumours of what was going on. My own opinion is that the things
that really are wrong were produced by Richards Herne Shepherd.
[sic]"

On 12 July, Wise's second TLS letter appeared and embedded in
it was another letter from Maurice, who was jumping through
Wise's hoops with a subservience few could understand.

Sir, – I have glanced hastily through the pages of the book dealing
with the above subject, which has just reached my hands, and I lose
no time in writing to explain my position with regard to the pamphlets of which the authenticity is challenged. With the single exception of Swinburne's "Ballad of Bulgarie" (which was printed by me in
conjunction with Sir Edmund Gosse as described in my Swinburne
Bibliography) and "The Devil's Due," which I purchased from
Watts-Dunton, under circumstances also detailed in the Bibliography, I never "held stock" of any one of the condemned or questioned
pamphlets. A short while ago, upon hearing certain vague rumours, I
wrote to Mr. Maurice Buxton Forman asking him for any information he could give me regarding his father's store of manuscripts
and pamphlets. In reply I received the following letter, which he has
now given me permission to print:–

46, Marlborough Hill, St. John's Wood, N.W.8.
Dear Mr. Wise,
It is quite well known to you that during his early middle life my
father was in the habit of buying, whenever he had the opportunity

of doing so, small parcels or remainders of books, pamphlets, manuscripts, and autograph letters with the idea of "salting them down,"
as he termed it, and later on making use of them as exchange for
other things he wanted. I know that you yourself had quite a number
of them from him in this manner, and that he did exchange with the
booksellers. He had a nose like a terrier for "finds," and he had luck
too; look at his wonderful good fortune in discovering the remainder
of "Laon and Cythna," getting the Keats love-letters, and many
Shelley things (you know the story of *Oedipus* for half-a-crown and
"Blake's Poetical Sketches" for 4d.!).

His inheritance of the books, manuscripts and papers of "Orion"
Horne brought him an extraordinary assortment, more than he knew
for there were boxes of it still unsorted when he died. He was always
hoping to repeat his Keats and Shelley luck and find something *Big*,
and I don't think he neglected any likely clue that he struck.

In speaking of lacunae in his collection he would say, "Well, it will
turn up some day" – and you know how right he was from your own
experience! I wonder whether Herne Shepherd, and possibly others,
knowing how keen he was, manufactured small pamphlets with the
sole object of planting them on him? It is not a nice thought, but it
seems to me by no means improbable. The cost of printing them
would not be much, and the few pounds obtained from my father and
others would have been ample reward.

I wish I could recall all the people my father acquired such things
from. The names that stand out in my mind are Paola Clairmont,
Fanny Brawne's children, Leigh Hunt's sons, Mrs. Cheltham
(Hunt's daughter), R.A.M. Stevenson, Charles Baxter, Townshend
Mayer, A.H. Japp, Miss Bird, Dr. W.C. Bennett, Fairfax Murray,
Mr. Chatto, Frank Kerslake, R.H. Shepherd, Herbert (Bookseller of
Goswell Road), O. Walford, Hutt of McMillans and some other
Hutts, William Rossetti, the Rev. Wm. Fulford, Alexander Strahan,
Kegan Paul, Bertram Dobell; no doubt there were others whose
names I do not remember. If you can put me in mind of any I shall be
glad.

I went to South Africa in 1894 and up to that time was living in
my father's house and had the run of the library, and naturally I saw
quite a number of the things he bought, but unfortunately I cannot
remember definitely from whom each came. I may be able to trace
some records among the large quantity of correspondence left by him
at his death; but some of it, as you know, went to America owing to
his habit of clipping letters and sometimes paid cheques into his
treasures.

I had almost forgotten William Morris. I think I told you some
time ago that I found in a cupboard a batch of remainders he got
from the offices of the *Commonweal* and *Justice*. He frequently called
at the former when Morris was editing the paper, saw Morris, and
often brought away a handful of pamphlets, and occasionally some

good stories. With the material he used when he was writing "The Books of William Morris" I came upon some quite nice things.

Many of his Morris things such as "Love is Enough," "Sir Galahad," "Alfred Linnel's Death Song," and some of the Socialist pamphlets were presentation copies inscribed to him by Morris, but of these, alas! I only found one.

I have just thought of another. I am certain that his proof copy of "Sister Helen" was given to him by Watts-Dunton, and I believe he had some other Rossetti things from the Rev. Wm. Fulford as well as from dear old W.M.R. I know that W.M.R. sold a good many of his brother's drawings, etc., and that Fairfax Murray, whom nobody seemed to like, came into the picture for a time.

I am afraid I have been rather long-winded, but I type as I think, and my typing is not very expert!

Yours very sincerely, (Signed) M. Buxton Forman.

Mr. Forman made it a practice to use his store of "remainders" to exchange for books or manuscripts. During the thirty years or so following 1886 I was constantly making exchanges with him, "Swops" as he styled them, and he invariably gave me a packet of pamphlets in payment of the annual subscription of £21 towards the debt of the Shelley Society resulting from the loss caused by the heavy cost of the performance of *Hellas*, which he and other members of the Council, of whom I was one, undertook to pay off. At first I disposed of these myself, but afterwards I handed them to Mr. Gorfin, in whom I had full confidence, to sell upon commission. About the end of 1909 Mr. Gorfin informed me that he intended to leave his employment and establish himself as a bookseller. Naturally I did all I could to assist him. Among other things, I asked Forman to let me have for him a selection from his store of pamphlets. From April, 1909, until about the end of 1912 I was purchasing from Watts-Dunton a considerable quantity of manuscripts, books and autograph letters preserved at The Pines, and following our usual custom a selection of these passed to Forman. Hence when I begged him to let me have a portion of his "Stock" for Mr. Gorfin he readily agreed, adding that as he had retired from business life he would be glad to clear out the lot. The proposal to have all "remainders" in his own hands pleased Mr. Gorfin; and in consequence I obtained the pamphlets from Forman in batches as he found time to make them up, and sold them to Mr. Gorfin, who promptly paid for them. These payments cleared the amounts due from Forman to me for the Swinburne manuscripts. I have no recollection of just what these parcels contained, but I am quite satisfied with Mr. Gorfin's account of them. Needless to say, every item handled by Forman had been dealt with by him in perfect good faith: in equal good faith they were accepted by me; and in equal good faith they were purchased by Mr. Gorfin.

> When I have read the book with the care and attention it deserves I shall doubtless have something to say regarding its contents.

The next issue of the TLS carried a letter from Gorfin denying that Wise had ever before suggested Forman as the origin for the pamphlet stocks. Wise's defences were long, rambling and unconvincing. At the time, informed opinion was shocked by Wise shifting the blame on to Forman himself: and baffled by the way Maurice Forman was helping him. As we have seen, blaming Forman for the forgeries had a certain truth – at least the conception was his. Wise attempted a more studied defence in an article prepared for *The American book collector*. This adds little to the letters printed above, though one does feel oneself to be swimming in a sea of words. If Wise had been taken to law, doubtless his able Q.C. would have reckoned on providing so much evidence that the jury drowned in it. Wise suggested that his stocks of pamphlets came to him from Forman after he had written his bibliographies and he then at once sold them off to Gorfin and that he never held stocks in his life. Apropos the sales by Rubecks he remarked that 'My associates in business were business-men and rare books are marketable commodities.' The whole statement has a very threadbare air and was hastily withdrawn before publication.

Carter and Pollard were anxious to extract more information from Wise and were trying a fairly ruthless finesse which did not, in the event, succeed. They met Page and told him that if Wise went on blaming Forman *without offering any evidence* then they would publish evidence of Wise's attempt to suborn Gorfin. The distinction of the italics was lost both on Page and on Wise. Page wrote to Wise a letter of understandable emotion, resigning as adviser, and returned all his past gifts of bibliographies. Wise withdrew the American statement and retreated into silence. The public controversy ended in August when a letter from Mrs Wise stated that Wise

> as a result of a nervous breakdown more than two years ago arising from overwork, and the long and painful illness which followed, is utterly unfit to carry on any public correspondence or controversy, and his doctor has strictly forbidden him to do so.

# 20

## WISE'S DEATH

The *Enquiry* threw a very large stone into the placid waters of the book collecting world and some of the ripples took time to die down. The members of the Roxburghe Club were naturally very agitated ('Wise must be made to talk before it is too late. He is an old and ill man and no time should be lost' Lord Rutland to Viscount Mersey) and he was cautiously approached. His first line was 'To say what I know now, and what I knew forty years ago, would involve the introduction of the names of gentlemen of position, one of whom is, I believe, still alive. This I could not possibly do'. To another member Wise seems to have hinted that he might leave the Ashley Library to the nation if he were kindly treated.

On 26 November 1934, Wise finally wrote to Lord Aldenham in surprisingly revealing terms.

> The so-called "Enquiry" is no enquiry at all. It is a grossly exaggerated and entirely one-sided mixture of facts and suppositions. Of the pamphlets mentioned in it, a very large proportion are genuine; they seem to have been introduced into the book mainly to increase the apparent number. Had they all been "planted" by one man, or had they all appeared within a short time, suspicion would certainly be awakened. But this they did not do. They crept into the market singly and silently over a period of about 12 years or more . . . . Once one of any of these pieces, genuine or spurious made its appearance, Forman started upon its trail, and nearly always succeeded in acquiring what he believed to be the remainder of each. With one exception I was the youngest of the circle of book-loving and book-collecting friends. Forman was my senior by 17 years, others were older still. The pamphlets, most of which were cheap trifles whose values were measured in shillings were accepted as genuine by everyone concerned.

Wise was not going to give up, and in this statement we probably catch authentic echoes of a defence prepared with Forman many years ago. He denies that he printed the pamphlets but seems to know a great deal about their distribution. As Lord Crawford observed to Lord Aldenham, 'while it may have been foolish or imprudent to make these reproductions, it was their circulation & sale in the auction rooms which was most culpable.'

Finally on 10 December, Sir Frederic Kenyon and Cockerell visited Wise and persuaded him to resign on the grounds of ill health. Wise wrote to Cockerell on 12 December giving yet more information.

> The pamphlets mostly crept into circulation almost unnoticed & had it not been for Forman's habits of acquisition, they would never have made themselves very apparent. Unlike Maggs, who when 30 or more years later they bought the bulk of the copies of the pamphlets printed by Conrad, Shorter & Mrs. Hardy, had a wide outlet for them among their customers, Forman was forced very largely to pass his stock through a far more restricted outlet than he ever anticipated would be the case.

This comes pretty close to an admission: it is tantalizing to reflect on what Wise could have told if he had fully confessed. This point was in the forefront of Carter and Pollard's minds: they wanted more information. And, lurking in an American library, was the Pforzheimer document, the one frank admission of forgery that might have produced a general confession.

The only published defence of Wise was a naive booklet by the American bookseller Gabriel Wells, *The Carter–Pollard Disclosures* 1934. This had one intriguing effect. It drew attention to a lot sold in the Forman sale in 1920 viz. his manuscript of *The building of the Idylls*. His attention drawn to this, W.A. Jackson, librarian to Carl H. Pforzheimer, carefully read the packet of manuscript and proof, unexamined since the Forman sale. To his astonishment, he found that clinching rejoinder by Wise to Forman. 'We print "Last Tournament" in 1896 and want "someone to think" it was printed in 1871! *The moral position is exactly the same!*'

Carl Pforzheimer showed this to Carter on 28 March 1935 under conditions of secrecy. Here at last, the enquirers thought, is what we need to open the whole can of worms. With this in hand we can find out all that Wise knows, all we have failed to discover, all that there is to discover. They were correct in thinking that there was a lot more than was in their book, but they were incorrect in thinking that they would be allowed to use this startling piece of evidence. For reasons that remain mysterious, Mr Pforzheimer sat on his document for ten years and by the time it was published, Wise was seven years dead. Its potential leverage on the one man left alive who *knew*, was never used.

Wise retired into his shell and the enquirers had no way to prise him out. It was noted, by those who still visited Heath Drive, that Maurice was often in attendance. One thing Wise did not lack was courage. He pressed on with the eleventh and final volume of the Ashley Library which appeared in 1936. It was dedicated to Mrs Wise and had a charming portrait of her as a frontispiece. On p. 52, fully catalogued 'Demy octavo, pp. xii + 400 Uncut in the original ruby-red cloth boards, with gilt top, lettered in gold across the back' is Carter and Pollard's *Enquiry*. It has the note 'For an able comment on the contents of this book see *The Carter–Pollard Disclosures* by Gabriel Wells, 1934.' The *Enquiry* itself, when eagerly sought in the Ashley Library, turns out to be almost virgin and unannotated. Wise died on 13 May 1937 aged 77. It is said that on his death bed when urged to confess, he said 'It's all too complicated to go into now' and expired. He was cremated at Golders Green on 15 May at a service attended by many friends and acquaintances from the world of bibliography.

*The Times* obituary was by far the best and most informative.

> The financing of the Ashley library was achieved partly by skilful selling of duplicates, partly by designing and stocking the libraries of rich collector–aspirants, partly by shrewd copyright speculations . . . . Now that these pamphlets were shown to be spurious and manufactured many years after the dates on their title pages, it became obvious that Wise had been more completely deceived than any bibliographer of his experience had a right to be. Many people in the book world were not satisfied that this was just a case of Jove having nodded . . . . In person, Wise was of a short medium height with a fresh complexion, a large forehead, a rather intractable mouth, and eyes at once shrewd and guarded. His manner tended to the abrupt: he was often aloof from themes of general conversation, but always showed himself acute and tenacious as to all that concerned his beloved books.

Several people laid quite determined siege to those beloved books including Dr Rosenbach who telegraphed for the lot. However, Mrs Wise, under the terms of the will, had considerable discretion. The will, shorn of details, provided that two-thirds of the estate went to Louie and one-third to Wise's brother, Herbert Athol, and his family. The executors were

63.  The first two books which Wise collected,
the foundation of the Ashley Library

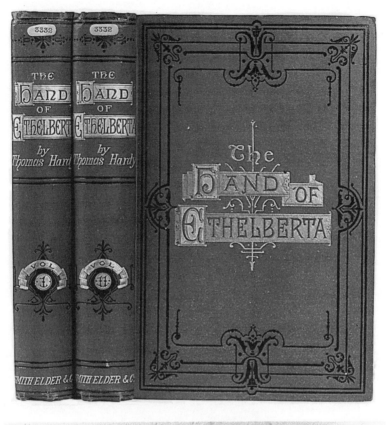

64.  A fine copy of an early Hardy novel,
with an inscription, from Wise's Ashley Library

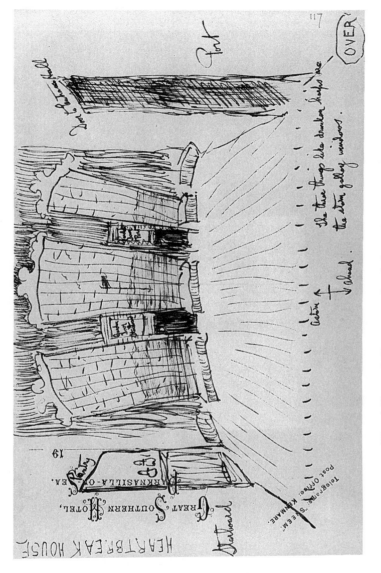

65.   A Bernard Shaw stage sketch from the Ashley Library

Davos
# PRINTING OFFICE.
*Managed by*
**SAMUEL LLOYD OSBOUREN & Co.**
The Chalet.

*1882*

Dear Weg,
[? 9 Nov. 1881]

If you are taking ~~Dear Weg~~ young folks,
for God's Sake Twig the
it is incredible ~~editorial style~~; we are all left Panting *in*

*the* REAR. twig. O twig it. His
name is Clinton; I should say the most
melodious proseminer now alive; it's like
buttermilk and blacking; it sings and hums
away in that last sheet, like a great old Kettle
full of bilge water. you Know: none of
us could do it, boy. see no 571, last
page: an article, called "Sir Claude the Conqueror"; and
~~with~~ read it aloud in your best rythmic
tones; mon cher, c'est épatant.

the story in question, by the by, was a last
chance given to its drunken author: not Villiers,
— that was a nom de plume — but Viles, brother to

66.   A Robert Louis Stevenson letter, from the Ashley Library

Wise's oldest friend, Walter Brindley Slater, A.E. Treacher, Wise's accountant, and H.E. Higginbottom, Mrs Wise's uncle. They were asked to offer the library 'in the first instance to the Trustees of the British Museum at a price to be fixed by my said wife after consultation with my Executors and Solicitors'.

The estate came to £138,000 excluding the library so there was considerable room to manoeuvre. Also Mrs Wise was anxious to save some of her husband's reputation by a heritage deal, which was rapidly arranged: the British Museum agreed to purchase it at a price of £66,000, payable over ten years, though this was not to be publicly announced. The news leaked out in August – 'Exposed faker of books will have memorial at British Museum' was the *Daily Express* headline – and there was an official statement in September. When the British Museum came to make the practical arrangements for removal, they found things were not quite as straightforward as they expected. The B.M. officials, including the young Howard Nixon, went up to Heath Drive and found that Maurice was in charge of the removal. This was done in weekly instalments, and Howard recalled how Maurice would always indicate carefully which books were 'ready' while he would then go on to work on the next bay of shelves.

This censorship should not have been allowed: when the Ashley books were formally accessioned, it was found that more than 200 items were missing. Some were forgeries, removed by Maurice, others were expensive items Wise had not been able to resist selling. The most spectacular of these latter was a copy of an 1814 Dante which had belonged to Keats. It has his sonnet *A Dream after reading Dante's Episode of Paolo and Francesca* on the flyleaf and is inscribed to Fanny Brawne. Maurice presumably also sifted through letters and destroyed any that were compromising: more than one of his father's letters to Wise, for instance, was cut up to remove certain passages. This clearing up and censorship explains why a number of unbound pamphlets in the Ashley Library appear in envelopes titled in Maurice's hand. To visit the Ashley Library now, is a hard task. The books sit rather uneasily in standard grey metal shelving within a locked cage. They are no longer in the bookcases that Mrs Wise gave with the collection which have been thrown away (when dismantled, their mahogany was found to be the thinnest veneer over plain deal). The oriental lamp, the framed prints and the comfortable sofas are no more. Also lacking is the great showman himself, and in his absence the books look rather unconvincing. If he were present he could not pull the manuscript of one of Elizabeth Barrett Browning's sonnets out of his fake *Sonnets* because it has been taken away and bound into one of twenty-four composite volumes of loose manuscripts, and put in another department. Neither could he produce Swinburne's flagellation manuscript (a favourite showpiece of his) since that has been exiled too.

There are eight bookcases placed back to back to give about 160 shelves. The first impression is surprise that the collection is not larger: the second is surprise at the amount of morocco. The early plays are fine but thin: all are rebound, as (to be fair) was the current convention. Contemporaneously they were so thin that they were almost always bound in composite volumes in calf or perhaps vellum. But collectors and museums do not like such volumes, the grouping being inconvenient to them. With eighteenth century books, the excuses for rebinding are less and one expects more contemporary bindings. Here the Ashley books are particularly disappointing. Most are either rebound or in rough contemporary condition: at the date Wise was collecting, better copies would not have been too difficult to acquire. We have retold Wise's story that his first two books were Shelley's *Cenci* 1819 and Moore's *Epicurean* 1827: they may be said to epitomize the collection. Well, the *Cenci* is rebound: the Moore is not, but it is a nasty copy in boards, with an ugly reback, worn sides and a clipped label. From the nineteenth century books it is clear that Wise threw away his dust wrappers, another infraction of the current code. All in all, there is a slight feeling of paradise lost about the Ashley Library. Despite this carping, there is no doubt that it was a significant capital investment and, if sold, would have made many times what the Museum paid for it.

Mrs Wise had the letters of condolence on Tom's death bound up in a handsome morocco volume. She and Maurice then destroyed all the recent correspondence. The earlier material up to about 1932 had all been sent off by Wise to Symington to join Gosse's letters at Lord Brotherton's library. But as we have seen, they were not destined to get there. Maurice was interviewed by the enquirers (rather a formidable pair) and as Pollard

67.   The sale catalogue of the contents of Wise's home

was to say later, reference to his father's reputation seemed to drive him to the brink of tears. Having propped Wise up and supported Mrs Wise, there was no going back. He now had to live a lie. He must have turned with relief to renewed literary work. *His* first edition of the Keats letters appeared in 1931 and revised editions in 1935, 1947 and 1952. In 1937, he edited a collection of Charles Brown's bits and pieces (he was perhaps Keats's best friend) and contributed an elegant foreword to his friend Edgecombe's book *The letters of Fanny Brawne to John Keats*. Edgecombe was curator of Keats House to which Forman senior had made important gifts: Maurice was to continue the family tradition. However, his most serious work was the Hampstead edition of Keats, a complete edition in eight volumes published in New York in 1938–39. On the titles, Maurice coupled his name with that of his father: it was a fitting memorial to the family tradition.

Louie Wise survived her husband by only two years, dying in 1939. Her will makes various minor bequests 'to Mrs Arundall Esdaile the diamond brooch formerly belonging to Mrs E. Barrett Browning' and sums of money to her gardener and her two maids. The bulk of the money was left to the families of her husband's brothers Henry Dauncey and Herbert Athol Wise. The estate was valued for probate at £64,000, perhaps some £20,000 or £30,000 less than might have been expected allowing for a two-third share of her husband's estate. This might be explained by the fall in property and stock values in a country on the brink of war. Possibly connected with this shortfall is her clause releasing and forgiving any money owing from Arthur Treacher (Wise's accountant) and Otto (Portman) Rubeck, Wise's late business partner. The final clearing up included a house sale at 25 Heath Drive in July 1939. One lot was 'a parcel of 17th and 18th century plays, pamphlets by John Dryden and others'. It included the final residue of Wise's workshop for making up plays and of at least 102 leaves we think were present, over 80 relate to known Wise thefts, some from the British Museum. This side of his villainy was not then known and Pollard, who was at the sale, let the lot go away for a mere £1/5s. to another bookseller. Two months later war was declared.

Maurice was very patriotic and determined to remain in England, though he now yearned for South Africa. He gave many of his father's manuscripts for salvage and still did a little genteel dealing. In 1941 he sold a particular set of four Swinburne forgeries (they were not exposed until 1948) to Simon Nowell-Smith, and gave him a copy of the *Two Poems* remainder. Nowell-Smith was struck by his gentleness, charm and evident probity.

> He was a nice honourable honest man, when I knew him (in the war), with a weight of his father's guilt on his shoulders, longing to get back to South Africa, away from it all – and endlessly delayed after the war by passport and travel restrictions. I did not see then, though I do now, the significance of his remarking, when he had given me a pamphlet (genuine) from a cupboard full of pamphlets and I had innocently asked how he came by it, "I don't have to tell you that."

He finally cleared up Marlborough Hill, gave many books to Keats House, sold more to a bookseller, and took his final selection back to South Africa, where he was to die in 1953. As the war came to an end, Carter and Pollard took up their research again. Their attempt to obtain badly needed clarification from Maurice failed. His final melancholy reflection was 'this horrible business has always been in my mind, and I have wondered how I might possibly clear my father's name.' Further work, by the original enquirers and others was to slam this door firmly shut. We end with a splendid piece of prose by one of the original team. Mr Pforzheimer, it may be remembered, had refused to publish Wise's confession until ten years after its discovery and seven years after Wise's death. He invited Carter to contribute a postscript to the book in which it was finally printed. However, when the book appeared in 1945 this was omitted. Here it is:

> By the courtesy of Mr. Pforzheimer the papers here reproduced were shown to the writer in March, 1935, with the stipulation that the contents remained unpublishable pending their owner's decision. That decision has now been made, and no one will greet it with warmer applause than one who has been constantly advocating it for ten years.
>
> It may perhaps be suggested, by some who read these papers for the first time, that the withholding of evidence in so grave a matter as the responsibility for a fraud has not only obscured the face of truth and handicapped the progress of scholarship, but has even denied to innocent purchasers of the forgeries the grounds for legal action against their perpetrator, who lived for more than two years after the discovery of this decisive evidence. It may also possibly be maintained that publication of these papers during Wise's lifetime would inevitably have elicited from him, if not a full confession, at

least some statement which would have thrown a more sustained light (now lost forever) on the forgeries affair in general and particularly on the relationship between Wise and Forman – so important and, on the present evidence, so nebulous.

Propositions such as these, however, ignore one cardinal principle: that a man has a right to do what he likes with what he owns. These papers are Mr. Pforzheimer's legal property, and his obligations to the rest of the world in respect of them – to scholarship, to literary history, to bibliographers, to book-collectors – have therefore been throughout a matter solely and entirely for his own judgment. That his scruples about publication have seemed in general to benefit Wise rather than those who, both in England and America, have been investigating Wise's operations, is not, therefore, a matter for discussion. They, like other interested persons all over the world, will be duly grateful, as they read these fascinating and significant documents, that Mr. Pforzheimer has (in his own words) "at length decided to consent to their publication".

# EPILOGUE: THE FORGERIES IN CONTEXT

Forman and Wise are not the only fish in the sea. There are many other types of forgery even in the restricted world of books and manuscripts. There are plenty of books that one might pick up and say 'That's a fake' but there are plenty of different possibilities to account for this epithet. Successful forgers hope to remain anonymous and some succeed. A quick examination of other types of forged books may set our two forgers in context.

The commonest kind of forgery is that of making good an imperfect volume. The portion made good ranges from a letter or two of text where a tear has been repaired, to whole sections of the book, title pages, plates, maps, or text leaves. In general, and as might be expected, the more that is supplied, the more likely it is to be detected. The trick (if you are a forger) is not to excite suspicion. If one systematically examined every volume – just as if one automatically assumed everyone one met was a crook – then it would take too long and make ordinary social intercourse too laborious. But once one has noted, more or less mechanically, that (say) the book was in fine clean state in a Riviere binding of 1900, or Mr X's stockbroker was Messrs Y., then suspicion is aroused and the detection is much more likely.

Riviere was a firm with wonderfully skilled workmen. For some thirty or forty years, say 1880–1920, a constant stream of cripples – that is books in some way defective – must have passed through its shop to emerge in gleaming new gilt morocco with all the hurts made good – titles supplied in facsimile, imperfects imperceptibly married to make one perfect – wormholes filled in, tears repaired and the whole book washed to uniform whiteness. Riviere was so good at it that his name pallet on a binding acts nowadays as a warning signal to look more closely at the contents of his morocco. The interesting point is that it is only when such a volume is described as what it is not, that it becomes a forgery. The same book may be described chez Messrs A. as 'a fine copy in blue morocco gilt by Riviere' or chez Mr B. as 'title repaired and the lower portion made good in pen facsimile, a washed copy in blue morocco gilt by Riviere'. So the same book may be genuine or fake depending on how it is described. The intention to deceive is supposed to be the acid test of forgery. This is, however, not really satisfactory. Did Riviere intend to deceive in 1900 when the book was perfected? We can hardly tell: he probably carried out his customers' instructions and may have guessed at an intention to deceive: we can hardly accuse him of forgery on such hypothetical grounds.

Forgery then, is perhaps in the eye of the beholder, a book may be a potential fake but not actually so until it is misdescribed. After all the same plant can be a weed in one border and a flower in another. Besides the laborious technique of pen and ink, print itself can be used to copy print. This is, of course, not much use for partial facsimile but can be deceptive for whole leaves and very deceptive for whole books. As T. J. Wise said when reprinting *Pauline* 'there is a sentiment attaching to the very form in which a book of this description first appeared which is entirely wanting if the same work is perused in another dress.'

The mischief comes when the cherished object is passed off as the original. The facsimile may have been produced with quite innocent intent, but it has the potential to be a fake. Many famous and expensive books have been reproduced as facsimiles or deceptive copies – Walton's *Angler*, Fitzgerald's *Rubáiyát*, Shelley's *Rosalind and Helen*, the Columbus letter, Gray's *Elegy* and so on. If the facsimile is on old paper and carefully doctored to simulate age and provenance it can be most deceptive.

The Columbus letter is a celebrated rarity printing Columbus's letter to his sponsors, the King and Queen of Portugal on his discovery of America (actually Watling Island in the West Indies). It was first published in 1493 and was several times reprinted in different languages. As can be imagined, it has long been a celebrated item of Americana: holding it in his hand, the collector, even if (as is probable) he cannot read it, imagines himself back to medieval Europe and the discovery of a new continent. But suppose the *frisson* is supplied by a forgery? It is a modest looking object, a mere four leaves, and has often been forged. In 1891 the library of General Brayton Ives was sold in New York. His Columbus letter was sold for $4,300, a really tremendous sum. It was returned as a fake and the General sued the London firm who had sold it to him. The jury ignored all the expert witnesses and declared the letter genuine in the belief (apparently) that this decision would help the General to recover his money! Very recently another fake Columbus passed through the hands of no less than three reputable booksellers, even starring in a prestigious London bookfair. It was bowled out by the library who finally purchased it as yet another fake. The crucial test with such suspicious items is comparison with an original – if you can find one. However much care is taken, the production of an absolutely exact copy is so difficult that a discrepancy of ink, paper or type is inevitable, even if undetectable. If the copy were absolutely exact in every detail . . . then it would be genuine.

The fake of the Freeman's Oath that recently surfaced was a printed fake, but with the striking and important difference that there was no original with which to compare it. It was in fact a creative forgery in the mode invented by Harry Buxton Forman. The forger, one Mark Hofmann, supplied a known (because documented) piece of printing of which no copy actually survives. He was filling a gap in the historical record just as the Piltdown forgery supplied a gap in the records of fossil man. It has been known for several centuries that probably the first piece of printing produced in North America was the Freeman's Oath, a sort of prototype saluting the flag. The text was known, the printer was known, the type and paper of his other printings were known – but no Freeman's Oath. This duly surfaced as recently as 1984 with a provenance showing it had been bought in a New York book store for $25 and a price tag of $1,500,000. The case for the oath collapsed when Mark Hofmann, the discoverer, proved to have forged various Mormon documents and to have murdered to cover his tracks; he finally blew himself up with his own bomb. The world of old books is not used to conducting business in this fashion. Hofmann's forgeries were now thoroughly examined and exposed, and he himself confessed how he had produced them. This was just as well, since the quality of his work had already deceived more than one examination. As T.J. Wise said in 1918 'The whole thing proves once more that, easy as it appears to fabricate reprints of rare books, it is in actual practice absolutely impossible to do so in such a manner that detection cannot follow the result.'

Book collectors want the original and there are various other ways in which books can be manipulated to provide something that is not the original. Colour plate books and atlases are very attractive: one opens the volume to see a map with a gilt and coloured cartouche of Neptune and Tritons, an early view of one's home town surrounded by green fields, a scarlet poppy, a red and green parrot, white boats on a blue sea. Such attractive books are often broken up and the plates sold separately and framed. The fact that the demand for decorative prints exceeds the ready supply means a) that prices for the books shoot up, and b) that modern colouring is often used to make good the short-fall. It is often applied not only to plain copies of books that *are* found with contemporary colour but also to books which were never issued coloured in the first place. This sometimes has bizarre results as when the descriptive text of a flower book decisively contradicts the colours now borne by the flowers in the illustrations. There must be hundreds of thousands of nine-teenth century steel engravings sold with the impressive note 'genuine engraving' or such like. Well, yes they are: but the colouring was added last week. But like most matters of type, the world is not black and white but shades of grey.

John Gould, a celebrated nineteenth century ornithologist who produced a massive series of forty-one colour plate bird volumes, provides an example. After his death in 1881, the firm of Sotherans bought the entire stock – lithographic stones, coloured plates, plain plates, text, and the colourists' patterns used to copy from the colourists. They even completed *The Birds of New Guinea* left unfinished at Gould's death. Naturally enough they supplied Goulds to all who wanted them, colouring plates according to demand just as Gould himself had done. This went on and on: what was entirely acceptable in 1890 became by 1980 a rather more doubtful practice, especially when the modern colouring was not acknowledged – though it was in unbroken tradition from Gould himself and the original pattern plates were used. Some ten years ago there was a public discus-sion of the matter: and Sotherans now clearly state which plates have modern colouring. But is colouring of 1890 fake? or 1920? or 1960?: where is the line to be drawn?

Book bindings are another fruitful source of fakes and semi fakes. Book collectors want original condition: quite so; but how about an extremely skilful and almost invisible repair to an old binding? Like the Riviere facsimile work, this is acceptable as long as correctly described. Complete recreations in period style rarely carry conviction though they are often very nice. But certain Parisian binders still have the eighteenth century tools of their forebears, and can do uncannily good work in pastiche of earlier bindings. Some of the juggling that goes on is a bit like repairing old furniture; endpapers may be supplied, a boring book in an exciting binding swapped to give an exciting book in an exciting binding (a book in a binding that originally did not belong to it is called a *remboitage*), clasps or patches of leather may be copied and made good. It is only a fake if all this is not correctly described.

More serious, and incapable of innocent explanation, is the addition to honest contemporary bindings of the crest or coat of arms of princes or prelates or other notables who never owned them. Prince Grimaldi in the sixteenth century and Madame de Pompadour in the eighteenth have suffered particularly from these unauthorized additions to the canon. Bookplates too can falsify the history of a volume and where there is a plentiful supply of minor books from a major library the bookplates tend to migrate from the dull books really owned by a celebrity to more interesting ones he never saw. David Garrick's copy of (let us say) the eighteenth edition of Johnson's *Dictionary* is not going to raise a collector's blood pressure much: but David Garrick's copy of the fourth folio Shakespeare is a different matter – particularly if it owes its provenance to the *Dictionary*. Loving inscriptions by the author have been known to migrate from book to book, though the careful paper matching necessary is difficult to achieve. Inscriptions lead on to manuscripts.

Manuscript forgeries are a wide sargasso sea of troubles for the unsuspecting and (sometimes) even for those on red alert. They range from simple copies of known inscriptions to complete fabrications. In the former category a good example is the pass 'granted to Mr. Ryerson, with his negro man, Dick, to pass and repass the picket at Ramapo. Geo. Washington'. This was copied so many times that it has been suggested that Mr Ryerson and Dick constituted the first important traffic jam in American history. The copyist (originally) was Robert Spring (1813–76) a forger who specialized in Washington. He is now a minor celebrity in his own right and genuine fake Spring Washingtons are worth more than fakes of the same, which is as it should be.

Manuscript forgeries have a long legal history. In 1514, the abbot of St Peter's in Gloucester won a court case on the strength of an original charter of Henry I which was, in fact written one hundred years after Henry's death: and there are a number of similar cases, some involving the manipulation of the seals which were supposed to be an extra safeguard. But again, as often with forgery, the verdict is not quite clear cut. The monks may have copied an important charter as a matter of course and, as long as the wording was correct attached no importance to the particular copy submitted.

In another case, however, there is no ambiguity. In 1368, the abbot of Bruern was trying to establish his right to maintain a gallows at Eastleach Turville: he used in evidence a Charter of Richard I granting this privilege at Fyfield (very necessary no doubt) but with Fiflehida erased and Estlech substituted. Many of the later forgeries of literary and historical figures forge not only the handwriting but also the content: they are both physical and literary forgeries.

So it is clear that Wise and Forman stand not alone but in a long tradition. The best known of their predecessors are literary forgers. Thomas Chatterton with his chest of old poetic manuscripts, William Henry Ireland who, as Shakespeare, got his *Vortigern* on to the stage (and hissed off it), and John Payne Collier who could not resist filling blank spaces in Shakespeare's biography. Apart from a few lines of preface, Forman and Wise were not literary forgers. Forman's brilliant ideas of creative forgery may not, originally, have been anything of the sort. He may have dabbled in printing *Galatea Secunda* to please an ageing friend and poet. After all, Horne had composed the piece in Melbourne in 1859. It is only when the germ of the idea was expanded and enlarged, when the books were sold for gain and wrongly described, that forgery is in question.

Does it matter? Is there not much to be said for Bernard Shaw's view that the whole thing was a joke? Did not the rich collectors richly deserve to be humbugged? Well, perhaps they did. But those who supplied them were acting illegally. They were defrauding the buyers but also defrauding the authors, who had a legal right and a moral right to the words they wrote. Some certainly objected to having their juvenile pieces brought before the world again; almost all would object to having the history of their writings falsified. But it is in the effect on the two forgers themselves that one can most clearly see the consequences of a wrong choice. Forman was a genuine admirer of Browning and Swinburne and a competent critic of their poetry. He had a more intimate association with William Morris whom he greatly admired. Yet because of his forgeries Forman's writings are a muddied spring and his insights and enthusiasms go to waste. Even in his published writings one can see him wrestling with his conscience. What he suffered privately can only be guessed at. Some sombre hints appear in his correspondence with Wise who might be thought of as the old man of the sea, with Forman as Sinbad, the legs knotted round his neck. It is a measure of how many things in life turn out to be appropriate that Wise, who did not know the prick of conscience, was exposed before he died. 'I am an old man with the crematorium facing me' he began his defence and his last three years of life were miserable indeed. His final words were an admission that the fraud was too complicated to describe on his death bed. The creative forgeries and the methods which Carter and Pollard used to unravel them, have now become part of the common fabric of bibliography. The two forgers have thus achieved a certain left-handed immortality. 'For man walketh in a vain shadow, and disquieteth himself in vain: he heapeth up riches and cannot tell who shall gather them.'

# NOTES

In 1983, Nicolas Barker and I published a second edition of Carter and Pollard's *Enquiry*, together with another volume of sequel. The present book adds nothing to the technical evidence published in 1983, where all references to such material should be sought: in some cases, I have quoted sections verbatim without acknowledgement. What the present book attempts, is to re-arrange the material in chronological sequence and this has involved some differences of interpretation. I have not given detailed references for the new biographical material where I have felt the sources – census returns, rate books, local director-ies, poll books, and standard editions of letters – are reasonably obvious.

I have given what seems to me the most reasonable interpre-tation of what happened and the notes will supply such further information as there is. However, it should be clear that in many cases, there can be no certainty and my descriptions of the course of the conspiracy should be taken as my view of what *probably* happened. In particular, the account given of the chron-ology of the appearance of the different forgeries is bound to be incorrect in detail, although I believe it gives a reasonable general outline of the publication programme.

*Prologue*
Details of Lord Crewe are taken more or less verbatim, from J. Pope-Hennessy *Lord Crewe* 1955. Christopher Dobson was kind enough to confirm the guest list from the Roxburghe Club records.

*Chapter 1: Forman's childhood*
Some family detail from W. Courthorpe Forman 'Alfred Forman' 1926, an unpublished typescript. General detail on naval sur-geons from J. Keevil and others *Medicine and the navy 1200–1900*, 4 vols, 1957–63. The P.R.O. in ADM.105 has fascinating detail for the period, a little of which I have used. Details of the *John Brewer* in P.R.O. BT98/370. General details of Teignmouth from

H.J. Trump *Teignmouth*, 1986. On Keats's visit see D.E. Robinson 'Notes on the Antecedents of John Keats: The Maritime Hypothesis', *Keats–Shelley Journal*, Vol. 34, 1985. B.F. Cresswell *Teignmouth* 1901 was the first to identify Keats Cottage and she quotes Harry Buxton Forman. It is clear, however, from letters in Keats House, that he thought 'the matter is one of theory' and he never made the identification himself. I have partly quoted Dorothy Hewitt's biography here. The Teignmouth museum has a single volume of *Teignmouth Post*, which provides the Formans' addresses in 1849–50. Brunel attempted to propel his trains using a vacuum tube, but the technology was way behind the idea and the scheme was an ignominious failure. However, according to its latest historian (P. Kay *Rails along the Sea Wall* 1990) 'it came very near to being a permanent success'. I should like to thank Mrs Dot Butler of the West Country Studies Library in Exeter for considerable help with the Devon details.

*Chapter 2: Forman at the Post Office*
For general background, H. Robinson *Carrying British Mails Overseas* 1964 and M.J. Daunton *Royal Mail, The Post Office since 1840* 1985. The quotation to illustrate the Hicks painting is from G.A. Sala *Twice Round the Clock* 1859. The Post Office Records issue a number of most helpful guides from which it is not difficult to see where to look for Harry Buxton Forman. The quotation on the Post Office Janissary comes from the official report published in 1883 and his description of the 1887 mission in a letter to R.M. Bucke, further details of whom will be given in a later chapter. The quotations from official correspondence are mostly from POST 48/229 and POST 48/313 in the Post Office Records. Details of the different Post Office buildings are conveniently given in Post Office Records *HS No. 9 Headquarters of the General Post Office since 1635*, duplicated 1968. Forman's retirement speech is printed in *St. Martin's-le-Grand*, October 1907.

*Chapter 3: Forman in London*
On Bucke, see A. Lozynsky *Richard Maurice Bucke, medical mystic* 1977 and S.E.D. Short *Victorian lunacy* 1986. Forman's letters to Bucke are in the University of Western Ontario library and

Ed Phelps was most helpful in arranging a complete set of pho-
tostats. These letters provide almost all the domestic detail of
Forman's life, see M.A. Jameson *Richard Maurice Bucke, A catalogue* 1978. The 'recent historian' is Short on p.109. A particularly good short summary of Comte can be found in Robert
Gittings *Young Thomas Hardy* 1975. Charles Lewes's 'recent
biographer' is K. Adams *Those of us who loved her*, 1980. For
information on the Selle family, I must particularly thank Diana
Howard of the Central Reference Library, Richmond. Indeed I
began to wish that all my characters had lived in Richmond. The
description of St John's Wood is more or less verbatim from
Pevsner. No. 38 was renumbered as 46 in about 1878. There are
two biographies of Horne; A. Blainey *The Farthing Poet* 1968 and
C. Pearl *Always Morning* 1961, the latter, though less scholarly,
giving a much better impression of the poet. Both of these need
to be supplemented by the material sold from the estate of
Harry Buxton Forman's granddaughter (Sothebys 24/25 July
1972, lots 448–460).

*Chapter 4: Keats and Shelley*
The two books I found most helpful on the historiography of
Keats and Shelley after their deaths are J. Richardson *The ever-
lasting spell* 1963 and S. Norman *Flight of the Skylark* 1954. The
best account of Forman's Shelley purchase is in K.N. Cameron
*Shelley and his Circle*, Vol. II, 1961 pp.910–12. A certain amount
about the Villon Society can be found in T. Wright *The Life of
John Payne* 1919. Severn's letter to Forman can be found in John
Keats *Letters of Joseph Severn to H. Buxton Forman* 1933. A letter
at Keats House which I consulted too late to incorporate in the
text, throws further light on the Dilke enigma.

> The conduct of Sir C. Dilke appears most singular . . . . I think he
> must have a twist in his temper, like his grandfather, who for some
> time was my Guardian, and once in a fit of ill humour injured my
> interests rather seriously, and what was still more galling to me, and
> never to be forgotten, his sneering observations on the nervous
> irritability of my poor brother. [Fanny Llanos to Forman 29 June
> 1879]

The quotation from the same correspondence but from Forman,
comes from the same source. The librarian at Keats House,
Hampstead was very helpful in giving me access to a considerable

quantity of Forman material, not all of which I was able to consult as carefully as I would have wished.

*Chapter 5: Wise's childhood*
Further details of Wise's grandfather can be found in J. Culme *The Directory of Gold & Silversmiths*, Vol. I 1987, p.69 (under Butler). Mr P.J. Willis of Gravesend Reference Library was very helpful with local details. The estate agent quoted (and again later on) is A. Cox *The Landlord's and Tenant's guide* 1853. No. 52 Wrotham Road has been renumbered as No. 95. The staff of Islington Central Library were helpful with local details and also sold me a copy of a remarkably detailed book E. A. Willats *Streets with a story: The Book of Islington* 1988, which was extremely helpful and also P. Zwart *Islington: A History and Guide* 1973. The business reminiscences quoted, come from H. Macdonald, 'A merchant looks back', contained in I. Norrie *The Book of the City* 1961. The volumes of *Pen and Pencil* are in a private collection in Oxfordshire. Edmund Gosse lived where he did, because one of the three principal meeting places in London of the Plymouth Brethren, was at 198 Upper Street, Islington. For Gosse, see A. Thwaite *Edmund Gosse* 1984.

*Chapter 6: The two forgers meet*
On the Browning Society, see Peterson, *Interrogating the Oracle*, 1969. The Forman letter to Furnivall is in the Ashley Library (A4152) but now separated from the book as it is a manuscript. All the letters we could trace between Wise and Forman were published as an appendix to Barker and Collins. Several which have surfaced since are printed as an appendix to this book. Furnivall's account of the founding of the Shelley Society, comes from *Frederick James Furnivall A Volume of personal record* 1911. Shaw's note on the Shelley Society is printed in W. Partington *Thomas J. Wise in the original cloth* 1946. Sir Percy Shelley's letter is in the Symington collection at Rutgers University. This source will recur; I must admit I used four aged reels of microfilm supplied many years ago to Sir Maurice Pariser. For the general history of Clays, see J. Moran *Clays of Bungay* 1978. The second Shaw quote is from *Collected Letters 1898–1910* 1972, p.487.

*Chapter 7: The forgeries begin*

The presentation *Poems and Sonnets* is Sotheby sale 4/5 December 1967 (the Pariser sale) lot 291. The 7 July 1888 Wise letter is now in the collection of F.W. Tober of America who has a very fine Wise collection. Forman's copy of the 1870 proof is now in the British Library.

*Chapter 8: Literary and commercial life*

The information about Wise and the Baptist youth group comes from F.B. Maggs *The Delinquent Bibliophile*, duplicated 1965, and personal information from John Maggs. The Garnett letter is at Rutgers. The quotation on 59 Mark Lane, is from G. Stamp and C. Amery *Victorian Buildings of London* 1980. Almost all of Gosse's correspondence with Wise is, like the example quoted, in the Brotherton Library in Leeds; Christopher Sheppard was exceptionally helpful and accommodating during my visit there.

*Chapter 9: The Reading Sonnets*

The correctional note about Miss Mitford is in the introduction to Wise's *A Browning Library* 1929. On Richard Herne Shepherd, see W.D. Paden's two articles in *Studies in Bibliography* 1965 and 1981, the latter solving the problem of the overprinted poems. Miss Ratchford's account comes from her introduction to the invaluable *Letters of Thomas J. Wise to John Henry Wrenn*. For details of Holland, Aldwinckle & Slater, see J. Culme *The Directory of Gold & Silversmiths*, Vol. I, 1987. When W.B. Slater's library was sold in 1944, it contained not only an exceptional number of forgeries, but inserted in one volume, three unused examples of a faked title page for Tennyson's *Idylls of the Hearth*. W. Courthorpe Forman's account of his brother's purchase of Harriet Shelley's last letter is printed in K.N. Cameron *Shelley and his Circle*, Vol. IV, 1970, pp.806–7. Wise's description of Shorter lunches comes from Partington. They seem usually to have taken place on Thursdays, the day of the weekly drug sale in the London Commercial Sale Rooms. Meredith's view of Shorter is also in Partington, as is the account of the divorce (although the name of the co-respondent is given only in the first edition *Forging ahead* 1939).

*Chapter 10: Suspicion aroused*
The quote from William Harris Arnold is from his *Ventures in Bookcollecting* 1923. Swinburne can be followed in Lang's marvellous edition of his letters and Graham Pollard made a particular study of *The Devil's Due* printed in *Thomas J. Wise Centenary Studies* 1960. The Morris letter of 23 July 1894 is in the Ashley Library. The G.D. Smith magazine is *The Literary Collector*, Vol. I, No. 6, March 1901.

*Chapter 11: Ill-gotten gains*
There is a second edition of Miles in twelve volumes. The W.H. Arnold letter is quoted by Ratchford. The letter to Chew is quoted in R.G. Landon (ed.) *Book Selling and Book Buying* 1978. The letter is actually dated 15 February 1908. I am much obliged to the late Robert Nikirk for sending me a copy. The check on twelve plays comes from David Foxon's piece *Thomas J. Wise and the Pre-Restoration Drama* 1959. W.T. Spencer had an autobiography ghosted for him, *Forty Years in my Bookshop* 1923 but it is naturally an innocuous piece of work. Most of the disreputable side comes from book trade gossip though a little may be gleaned from W. Lewis *Collector's Progress* 1952 in which Spencer is called Mr X. It is not absolutely certain that Spencer forged the forgery of *Dead Love*, but it seems probable. On Alexander Turnbull, see E.H. McCormick *Alexander Turnbull* 1974.

*Chapter 12: Wise on the commodity market*
The poetical fragment is from T.S. Eliot's *The Waste Land*. The standard account of the commodity markets is G.L. Rees *Britain's Commodity Markets* 1972; however, it is an economic history and does not give a very vivid picture of what it was like to work in the market. I am very much indebted to Terence Figgis who joined the family firm of S. Figgis & Co. Ltd in 1922 and to his son D.S.J. Figgis, who lent me the short company history *Seventy five years in Mincing Lane* 1965 and their one early sale catalogue, and talked to me a great deal. Terence Figgis said that when he started, his father told him that the firm was very go ahead. 'We do allow our staff to go down Mincing Lane without a hat if they wish to.' Another firm as old as Figgis, is R.C. Treatt & Co. Ltd, essential oil merchants, now of Bury St Edmunds. Their technical director, I.A. Jameson, was extremely

helpful in suggesting possible sources of information. The British Library run of the *Mincing Lane Year Book* is only from 1944 onwards. I must also thank Mr Ferdinand Gutkind for talking to me about his father Felix's foray into Spanish lavender oils which took place at the same time as Wise's; they must have been business rivals. Colonel H.L. Warner in Portugal was kind enough to send me a photostat of The General Produce Brokers' Association of London *The Customary trade allowances and conditions of payment of various East India and Colonial produce*, 3rd edn, 1893 (there seems to be no copy of any edition in the British Library). Rubeck senior died in 1908 and his entire estate descended to his widow who was, like her husband, German born. The commodity trade in London was dominated by Germans and advertisements for vacancies often specify fluency in German. Otto Portman Rubeck took on the running of the firm which went through various vicissitudes after he died in 1953. None of the remaining documentation at Companies House throws any light on the firm during Wise's time. The Company's name took various forms including Sertum (London) Ltd, Felton, Rubeck and finally Felton Worldwide Ltd. The suggestion in Barker and Collins that artificial oils greatly altered the market soon after the First World War, is not correct.

*Chapter 13: Buying up 'The Pines'*
For Craik's position *vis à vis* Tennyson, see Sir Charles Tennyson *Alfred Tennyson* 1949. A.W. Pollard was writing in *Books in the House* 1907. The Shaw quote comes from Partington, as does Amelia Groseman at the end of the chapter. As mentioned before, the Wise/Gosse correspondence is in the Brotherton Library. I must admit, however, I have mostly worked from two volumes of typed transcripts prepared under the aegis of Symington.

*Chapter 14: Forman and his family*
I confess that I have lost the reference to the Forman letter to W.M. Rossetti, though I think it was among the manuscripts at Keats House. The Vanuxern keepsake is in a private collection. It is notable that in the last line of the second verse, Forman spells Widdicombe as a surname and not as the place name (Wide-

combe); is this a clue? The Soord joke was detected by Newman Ivey White in her great biography of Shelley.

### Chapter 15: Forman's death

The Cockerell letters to Gosse are in the Brotherton Library. Forman's funeral instructions in verse, are printed in *St Martin's-le-Grand*, the Post Office magazine. The story about Mr Mudie of Quaritch was told me by Pip Newton of the same firm.

### Chapter 16: Wise carries on

W.A. Smith & Co. was a partnership between Wise and Otto Portman Rubeck and although Rubecks handled their oils extensively, they were separate concerns. The vanillin story came from Graham Pollard in conversation but I could find no evidence for it in the trade papers. The correspondence with Mr Taylor is at Rutgers. The review of the Wrenn catalogue is in *Modern Language Notes*, April 1922. The recent survey and the quotation, are from W.B. Todd, 'Some Wiseian ascriptions in the Wrenn catalogue', *The Library* 1968. The account of Cottonian bindings is partly verbatim from H.M. Nixon *Five centuries of English bookbinding* 1978. For Max Harzof and the Vizetelly *Extracts* see W.E. Colburn in *The Princeton University Library Chronicle*, Vol. 23, 1962. The final paragraph is from the description of lot 423 in Sotheby sale 4/5 December 1967 (the Pariser sale).

### Chapter 17: Wise in retirement

The quotation from Dorothea Braby is from a letter she wrote to me before her death. A formal account of the early history of the Brotherton Library is given by D. Cox, 'The Brotherton Collection – its beginning and development', *The University of Leeds Review*, Vol. 28, 1985/6; as is clear, I was also given a less formal account verbally. The account of the Gosse papers, Symington's thefts and Wise's numerous correspondents all come from Rutgers. Baillie's private diary is MS.691 in the Brotherton Library (John Smurthwaite gave me transcripts). The quotations from the Roxburghe Club archives come from a photostat of the letters supplied many years ago to John Carter. Wise's letters to W.A. Clark are in the William Andrews Clark Jr Library of the University of California, Los Angeles. The Curle letter is printed in J.S. Cox (ed.) *T.J. Wise, Mrs. Hardy & Hardy's Manuscripts* 1969. The final financial point comes from F.B. Maggs *The Delinquent Bibliophile*, duplicated 1965.


*Chapter 18: The exposure*
For biographical details of Graham Pollard see the Festschrift for him, published by the Oxford Bibliographical Society in 1975 and *The Book Collector*, Winter 1977, and for John Carter, the obituaries published in March 1975. I have followed Percy Muir's *An Autobiography*, 1956 for the meeting between Carter and Pollard, but have altered the date. The most lively account of the enquirers' work is given in Dwight Macdonald's article in *The New Yorker*, 10 November 1962. Wise's first reactions to the exposure are from Partington, and Gorfin's accounts from the statements he later swore before a solicitor. The account of Wise and Maurice Buxton Forman is guesswork, but I think a likely guess. I also had the opportunity of discussing the story of the exposure with both Carter and Pollard and some unpublished details come from this source. Of the various published accounts, the most misleading is that published by Sothebys viz. D. Battie and L. Weller *Fakes and Forgeries* 1990.


*Chapter 19: Wise at bay*
The Newton letter is partly quoted in Sotheby sale 4/5 December 1967 (the Pariser sale) lot 370. The Jennings parodies were privately printed as *The Gullible papers* 1934. W.B. Todd *Suppressed commentaries on the Wiseian forgeries* 1969 accounts for the penultimate paragraph of this chapter.


*Chapter 20: Wise's death*
The Roxburghe Club correspondence comes from the same source as quoted for Chapter 17. The late Howard Nixon described to me the British Museum's uplifting of the Ashley Library. Simon Nowell-Smith was kind enough to give me his reminiscences of Maurice. Carter's revenge on Mr Pforzheimer's tardiness was first printed in Dwight Macdonald's *New Yorker* article cited in Chapter 18.

*Epilogue: The forgeries in context*
The forgery stories are taken from obvious secondary sources and book trade gossip. For a much more rigorous and professional account of the philosophy of forgery, with many detailed examples, see M. Jones (ed.) *Fake? The Art of Deception* 1990. Bernard Shaw's view of the case is in Partington.

# APPENDIX

## THE CORRESPONDENCE OF
## FORMAN AND WISE

These letters are supplementary to those published in Appendix 4 of Barker and Collins 1983 and the same conventions apply, viz Forman to Wise: 46 Marlborough Hill (46 M.H.) and the Post Office (G.P.O.). Wise to Forman: 127 Devonshire Road (127 D.R.). Postcards (P.C.) usually carry no address.

127 D. R. F. W. Tober; unpublished

Dear Mr. Forman                                                 Aug. 2 1886
   I am having 3 or 4 copies of "Hellas" pulled on large paper (Post Quarto): may I have copies of S[helley]'s Tomb worked from your plate to insert in them? Of course a copy of the book shall be sent you.
   Trusting you will enjoy your stay at Ilfracombe.

                                                                I remain
                                                        Sincerely yours
                                                          Thos. J. Wise

46 M. H. Rutgers University; unpublished

Dear Wise,                                                    10 Dec. 1886
   If I can find any Whatman copies of "Rosalind & Helen" of course you are welcome to one; but I much doubt whether there are any. I have my suspicion, that that was one of the books of which the Whatman copies were burnt; but [erasure] I will have a hunt at the Office tomorrow or Sunday, & let you know: there is a lot of debris there.

                                                        Yours sincerely
                                                               H.B.F.

G.P.O. Rutgers University; unpublished

Dear Wise, 14 Feb. 1890

All right about Bucke; & I will write to Mrs Neate[?]. The £6
I did not want to pay just at present, for I have a lot of
payments to make – I meant it as a promise for some time this
year. Sorry you can't come to jubilee as of old. Should like to see
your MSS; but next Sunday I am not "at home". All free from
influenza, thanks; & thanks also re quin. sulph.

Yrs. ever
H.B.F.

46 M. H. Rutgers University; unpublished

Dear Wise, 3 March 1890

Do you chance to know any one who reads as well as collects
the latter-day lucubrations of Swinburne. If so, can you get me a
reference to the recent article in which he said something about
the fatuity of divorcing morals from art?

I really do not care one straw whether you mention that item
of Ruskin or not. I thought you wanted me to note any imper-
fection that struck me – for your sake, not mine – & that was
why I noted this one. Sorry I did not observe it on slip proof; but
one cannot be always equally on the alert. There is no difficulty
about inserting the reference if you want it; & I have marked the
page accordingly. For "signed" you can quite well say "subscribed," if I rightly recall the context.

Thanks for enclosures.
Yours very truly
H. Buxton Forman

G.P.O. Rutgers University; unpublished. The letter is not in H.B.F.'s
hand, except for the last four words of the postscript, but it is signed
by him.

Dear Wise, 11 January 1894

Yes, I do know the pamphlet that you mention, and have a
very fine copy of it; which I think you have seen. Further than
that, what is it you want to know about it?

As regards the proposed slaughter at Potts's house, I must say Friday is the least convenient day in the week for me and that Monday the 22nd. instant would suit me better than the 19th. Whatever day is finally fixed, I shall want to know the hour as well. I reciprocate your good wishes, and am

Yours very truly<br>H. Buxton Forman

P.S. This was one of a lot of letters dictated yesterday afternoon before I left for home, and, therefore, before I got yours of the 10th., in which I find the hour mentioned as 8 o'clock. (Friday still <u>not</u> convenient)

G.P.O. Rutgers University; unpublished

Dear Wise,                                        27 March 1894

As to Browning letters, – I also have a good number – about 40, & these to F.J.F.[urnivall] are not of the finest by any means, either for substance or state. They seem to me to be dear, especially if copies of them are to be taken (or have been taken): don't you think so yourself? I will have another look at them tonight, at home, & then return them if I decide "no". Thanks for a Burns fac-simile I have received from Clay's with your Compliments – Reference Catalogue, Part II. It contains an announcement that arrangements have been made (inter alia) for a number about Shelley by H.B.F. Which be they?

As to the account, it seems all right: I agree to it.

Yours ever<br>H.B.F.

G.P.O. Rutgers University; unpublished

Dear Wise,                                        28 Mch. 1894

Like yourself I am rather "full up" with Browning letters – having some 40. I do not much covet these, & am sorry F.J.F. has to part with them. Eight guineas would to my thinking be a liberal price for them & more than I am at all anxious to secure them at. Still, they are of considerable interest; & if it will really facilitate Society affairs, consider me at [sic] buyer at that price.

Yours ever<br>H. Buxton Forman

Shelley Society notepaper. F. W. Tober; unpublished

My Dear Forman                July 18th 1894

Some week or so ago I asked you to give me another "object lesson" in regard to my preface to Ruskin's "Harbours of England" – & you kindly promised to do so.

Tonight's post has brought me the proof of this Preface. I will call at G.P.O. with it tomorrow afternoon – can you then spare me five minutes?

May I ask you to add to your kindness by letting me have it back <u>promptly</u> – as I have to pass the complete book for press next week?

I <u>bring</u> the proof rather then <u>send</u> it because there are one or two points I wish to direct your attention to, which I can shew you in a dozen words, but wh. would occupy a couple of pages to write.

In looking over it pray remember that I have no toes for you to tread upon, & no feelings for you to hurt – in regard to it: & that the more you criticise or condemn or alter the more grateful I shall be!

The following two bits of information may interest you:

(1) Pickering paid £7. 5. 0. for Coleridge's "Ode".

(2) I bought at Puttick's today a d--d bad copy of St. Irvyne, with 18<u>11</u> title; ½ bound, been in a circulating library, very dirty, but <u>quite uncut.</u> Will clean & make a first rate bound copy. I paid £8. 5. 0. for it.

I have put amongst my Notes for August "Bookman" a couple of pars. regarding the 3 copies of "Ode on Departing Year". If Dr. Nicoll don't cut them out (wh. is <u>very</u> unlikely, as he's the best of editors and never takes liberties with what he knows nothing at all about!) I'll send you a copy of the Bookman.

Yrs alys<br>Tom Wise

Have you a copy of "Harbours of England"? If so, would you like me to look over it, & say in a footnote that "I have consulted Mr. Forman's fine copy" – or something of that sort? If so, say so please.

Add to enclosed proof what footnote you like re, your Browning MS.

Shelley Society notepaper. F.W. Tober; unpublished

My Dear Forman                          July 25th 1894
   I'm afraid I'm a nuisance with my <u>Harbours</u> : but your aid has
been so readily & so kindly given that I don't hesitate to appeal
to you again.
   P.<u>X</u>. of this Preface. Your correction causes tautology: i.e.
<u>Public</u> --- <u>public</u>. I've tried to get rid of this, & enclosed is the
best I can do. Will it serve? [erasure] <u>or</u>, am I perhaps being too
critical, & will the par. as you've fixed it do?

                                          Alys Yrs
                                          Thos Wise


Shelley Society notepaper. F. W. Tober; unpublished

My Dear Forman                          July 26th 1894
   Very many thanks for your note, & the returned proof. You've
done in a moment what I've worried over at odd moments all the
day without fixing. You're a brick! –
   I've sent a note to my friend that: "My friend who possess
[sic] a duplicate of <u>Amelia</u> will part with it for 3/3/-," & asked
him if he'll have it. As I leave town now, & as <u>you'll</u> be gone
before I get back, I fear the matter will have to stand open until
your return – so far as actual delivery of the book goes, that is. A
reply to my note will no doubt reach me at Hastings, when I will
communicate with you.

                                          Faith Yrs
                                          Thos Wise


46 M.H. Rutgers University; unpublished

Dear Wise                               14 Feb. 1895
   I could not advise you to give a very long price for 50 or 60
letters of Fitzgerald. There are so many extant and so few
collectors who would care for them that I should think £15
quite an outside price. Indeed I would not myself give more than
£10, & that hesitatingly. However, if you want to be liberal you
might give £15 to secure what attracts you.

                                          Yours very sincerely
                                          H. Buxton Forman

No address. Rutgers University; unpublished

Dear Wise                                    Sunday 25 June 97
   I think the little book you sent me is very well done.
   My private Shelley prints I looked up the Sunday after I saw
you, & they are at the Office. One wants boarding. It is a
Whatman <u>set.</u> I have also the proofs of prints at the Office –
waiting an opportunity to go round to Guildhall.
   I ought to talk this matter of exhibits over with Mr. Welch if
possible.

                                                    Yrs truly
                                                    H.B.F.


G.P.O. Rutgers University; unpublished. The letter is not in H.B.F.'s
hand, but is signed by him.


Dear Wise                                       15 May 1903
   I cannot say for certain what I paid for the "Passion of Dido",
my copy being at present at the bottom of a box remaining at
my brother's house since it and others w[ere] catalogued; but I
am quite sure that I did not pay more than two or three pounds.
   If Lot 864 (misnumbered 834) in Sotheby's next week's sale is
a good copy, you ought to have it at any reasonable price. I have
not known of another copy for sale since I bought mine; and it is
certainly a much rarer book than the 1645 Poems which now so
frequently turn up. If I wanted it myself, I should not think
that I could very well afford to pay £10 for it; but in view of your
aims and your scale of disbursements for items of this class, I
think you will be unwise to drop it at less than £15.

                                             Yours very sincerely
                                             H. Buxton Forman


G.P.O. Rutgers University

Dear Wise                                       1 Dec. 1903
   I'm glad to hear the 4th V. & C. [Victor and Cazire] isn't one.
The thing was getting too pestilently mechanical. Thanks for
the Tales of Terror & Wonder: I will put it in the Shelley Heap

as you suggest. But what a funny book! I'm better now, thanks, & about again; but it's trying weather.

Yours very sincerely
H. Buxton Forman


46 M.H. Rutgers University

My dear Wise, 5 Dec. 1903
I do not think I ever possessed the "thick fcap. 8vo." Idylls of 1869. At all events I dragged out all the front-row Tennysons today to search the back row & make sure; and I regret that I have no copy. You would have received it instead of this letter if I had one – & welcome.

Do you know anything about the Robert Hoe (American) Library – & especially whether yet distributed?

Yours sincerely
H. Buxton Forman


46 M.H. Rutgers University; unpublished

Dear Wise 9 Feb. 1904
On my return to the book-room I find that my account of the 4to Panegyrick in the MS. Bibliography is from an uncut copy I saw many years ago in pamphlet form with blank leaf at each end: so there is no doubt the missing Sig. A1 is a blank. I call this a very good copy & should think it cannot be dear at Magg's price.

My "cold" is persistent – especially nasal catarrh, for which I frequently use the pocket menthol inhaler you gave me when you were so bad. It is as good as ever, & an excellent thing for temporary alleviation: I wonder how it manages to retain its virtue all these years.

Of course I have been using stronger remedies too – salicylate of soda, menthol snuff, a wash-out affair for nose & pharynx, a benzoin. comp. inhalation, & the Lord knows what. Thanks to you & Mrs. Wise for kind sympathy.

I hope to go back to St. Martins the first fine day; & then I'll try to remember the Idylls.

Yours sincerely
H. Buxton Forman

46 M.H. Rutgers University; unpublished

My dear Wise,                                Christmas Day 1908

First of all hearty thanks to you and to Mrs. Wise for Christmas & new Year greetings cordially reciprocated. May your "Booke of Memorie" note in 1909 rows & rows of first editions, folio, quarto, 8vo. uncut; & may Mrs Wise continue to gather a wifely joy in the contemplation of yours, even if not quite so keenly bitten as yourself with the book-gatherer's lust of perfection.

As far as I can trace I do not possess "Evening Love" at all. But I have not found in my protracted domestic researches all of my Dryden things yet; & cannot say what the next parcel dug out may bring forth.

The most interesting thing in the enclosed little book seems to me to be the sketch for "Catarina to the Camoens". But it is an interesting enough book – of transcripts, I presume. Do you know whose hand they are in?

Yours ever
H. Buxton Forman

P.C. Rutgers University; unpublished

23 Jan. 11

7 July 1844 is a mistake for 7 July 18<u>2</u>4, when L.B.'s [Lord Byron's] Exors. got an injunction to restrain Dallas from publishing a vol. of L.B.'s Letters which "had nearly gone through the press". It was to have been a 4to.; & I have seen (but do not own) a copy of the portion that was printed – with, I believe, no title. Dallas afterwards (or rather his son) issued the work with additional material at Paris, thro Galignani★. Sets of the quarto must be very rare. My suppressed Byron book is 8vo. & much later: its genuine leading feature some letters to a woman – not to Dallas. pp. 17–168

H.B.F.

★in 3 vol. 12mo. 1825

46 M.H. Rutgers University; unpublished

My dear Wise                                    1 Oct. 1911

It will be pain & grief to me if you & Mrs. Wise want to come & can't get in! The tickets, I am told, have all been seized upon, & many more applied for. The doors open at 7.50; & if all the ticket holders are not in their places by 7.58, non holders will be admitted to them. If I can get tickets for you & Mrs. Wise tomorrow morning I will send them on to your house. In case I fail, you might present the enclosed note to the Librarian, at, say, fifteen or twenty minutes to 8. I feel sure he would do what he could.

My wife & I certainly got _some_ good at T.W. [Tunbridge Wells?] but we are not either of us feeling very brilliant after our difficult home-coming.

Ever yours sincerely
H. Buxton Forman


46 M.H. Rutgers University; unpublished

My dear Wise                                    24 Dec. 1912

Many thanks to you & Mrs. Wise for the good wishes conveyed in your tasteful Christmas card. May the first year of your retirement (almost) from business prove as great a success as your comparatively short career in the City. And in especial may your Coleridge prosper & soon materialize.

Yours ever faithfully
H. Buxton Forman

P.S.

I wonder whether you got old Bramhall's awful copy of the Byron 1806 4to., & if so whether any one will be able to make it splendid for you.

No address. University of Kentucky Libraries; unpublished

My dear Harry Buxton F.!                                                   [c. 1913]
    Here's the bit of Borrow's first as promised. As soon as you are
well enough come round & bring some more of the <u>E.B.B.</u> or <u>Mary
to Claire</u> letters, & we'll have a "deal". I have a full set of the
pamphlets & a nice representative series of the MSS. & letters
put aside for you.

Ever yours
Tom Wise

If you want a <u>real fine</u> Borrow MS. or two, as you say, you had
better bring a <u>real fine</u> Shelley Letter with you!!!!!! One of the
"good 'uns"! – Now don't tell me I'm never greedy!

# STOP PRESS

A new chimera, Tennyson's *To the queen*, 1873 has just been
discovered by Mark Samuel Lasner of Washington. There is a
legitimate separate printing on two leaves and an illegitimate
one on four leaves (described in Ashley Library, VII, 137). This
latter comprises the appropriate leaves ripped from an 1873
edition of Tennyson's Works, with a new title added. Mr Lasner
will be publishing a full account in *The Book Collector*.

June 1991

# INDEX

References to illustrations are in italics. Books are indexed under authors; periodicals and composite works under title. Lists of books are in chronological order for Forman and Wise, and alphabetical order for everyone else.